Daughters
of Rahab

Series Editors for This Volume

....

Bernadette J. Brooten &

Francis Schüssler Fiorenza

Daughters *of* Rahab

PROSTITUTION AND
THE CHURCH OF LIBERATION
IN BRAZIL

Margaret Eletta Guider

Fortress Press
Minneapolis

Daughters of Rahab
Prostitution and the Church of Liberation in Brazil

Harvard Theological Studies 40

This volume was prepared for publication by the staff of the *Harvard
Theological Review* and appears in substantially the same form in which it
was approved as a doctoral dissertation by the Committee on the Study of
Religion, Harvard University.

Book design and typesetting at the *Harvard Theological Review*
Managing Editor: Tamar Duke-Cohan
Editorial Assistants: Ellen B. Aitken, Greg Schmidt Goering, Laura Nasrallah,
Anthony Rivera, and Naomi Shulman
Cover Design: Evans McCormick Creative
Author photo: Daniel Alex, Boston, Massachusetts

Library of Congress Cataloging-in-Publication Data

Guider, Margaret Eletta, 1951–
    Daughters of Rahab : prostitution and the church of liberation in
Brazil / Margaret Eletta Guider.
        p.   cm. — (Harvard theological studies)
    Includes bibliographical references and index.
    ISBN 0-8006-7093-0 (alk. paper)
        1. Church work with prostitutes—Brazil—History—20th century.
2. Church work with prostitutes—Catholic Church—History—20th
century.   3. Prostitution—Religious aspects—Catholic Church.
4. Catholic Church—Brazil—History—20th century.   5. Brazil—
Church history—20th century.   6. Brazil—Social conditions.
7. Liberation theology.   8. Catholic Church—Doctrines—
History—20th century.   I. Title.   II. Series: Harvard
theological studies
    BX2347.8.P75G85   1995
    261.8'35742'0981—dc20   95-5122
                                                             CIP

The paper used in this publication meets the minimum requirements of
American National Standard for Information Sciences—Permanence of
Paper for Printed Library Materials, ANSI Z329.48-1984. ∞™

Manufactured in the U.S.A.   AF 1-7093

99   98   97   96   95   1   2   3   4   5   6   7   8   9   10

CONTENTS

Acknowledgments

This book could not have been realized without the support and encouragement of numerous individuals, groups, and institutions. Among those who are closest to my heart, I am especially grateful to my cherished family, to my Franciscan sisters and brothers, and to the Religious of the Sacred Heart. Their constant expressions of love and ongoing concern have meant more to me than they will ever know.

Throughout the course of my research and writing, my efforts were enhanced by the assistance given to me by many friends, colleagues, professors, and students. I am particularly grateful to Susan Regan, Iain Maclean, and Maria Aparecida Teles Proto for their generosity of spirit, the timeliness of their countless favors, and the gift of their many years of friendship. Words cannot express my deep gratitude to Harvey Cox, Clarissa Atkinson, Sharon Parks, and Olwen Hufton for their guidance, confidence, and conviction about the importance of this project.

I would like to express my thanks to Harvard Divinity School, the staff of the Harvard Theological Review, Weston Jesuit School of Theology, and the Tinker Foundation for providing me with the necessary resources to complete this book. Likewise, I would like to acknowledge my indebtedness to the many groups and individuals in Brazil who provided me with information, contacts, and access to archival materials, including Dagoberto Boím and Elias Della Giustina of the C.N.B.B., Gabriela Silva Leite of I.S.E.R., Maria José Jaime of I.N.E.S.C., Tereza Cavalcanti, and Zilda Fernandes Ribeiro. I am deeply indebted to Hugues D'Ans, Monique Laroche, and to various members of the Secretariado Nacional da Pastoral da Mulher

Marginalizada for their generosity in allowing me to make their respective writings and documents available in English. I am grateful to Avelino Grassi and Editora Vozes for permission to use as the basis for some my translations the Portuguese publication of selected writings and documents of the P.M.M. as they appeared in *O Grito de milhoes de escravas: a cumplicidade do silêncio* (Petrópolis: Editora Vozes, 1986) and *Serviço de Documentação* [SEDOC] 17/179 (1985).

I am appreciative to the Division of Christian Education of the National Council of the Churches of Christ in the USA for permission to quote passages from the Revised Standard Version of the Bible (copyright 1946, 1952, 1971) as well as to Pantheon Books for permission to include an excerpt from the writings of Sor Juana Inés de la Cruz as translated in *A Book of Women Poets from Antiquity to Now* (ed. Willis and Aliki Barnstone; New York: Schocken, 1980).

Ultimately, my deepest expression of gratitude is extended to the Brazilian women who were both the reason and the inspiration for *Daughters of Rahab*.

In conclusion, I dedicate this work to the memory of Maria Gabriel and to all those who continue to bear witness to the God of Life through ministries of presence in the underworld of the world church.

É muito simples: só se vê bem com o coração.
O essencial é invisível para os olhos.

O Segredo da Raposa[1]

---

[1] Antoine de Saint-Exupéry, *O Pequeno Príncipe* (trans. Dom Marcos Barbosa; Rio de Janeiro: AGIR, 1977) 74.

Preface

In 1975, I made my way to Brazil as a North American Roman Catholic lay missionary. At the age of twenty-three, I was unaware of the ramifications that such an experience would have on my life. Only in subsequent years did I come to realize the ways in which my notions of history, culture, politics, economics, and religion were dramatically changed as a result of the questions that emerged within me and around me during the course of my years in the rural interior of Brazil.

My participation in *comunidades de base* ("base communities") enabled me to do "theology from below" as a precursor, rather than as a corrective, to doing "theology from above." Prior to my arrival in Brazil, I worked as an urban educator in the inner city of Chicago. It was there that my vocational imagination was first engaged as I attempted to grasp the implications of education as a subversive activity. I moved from teaching in a burned-out mobile unit to learning in thatch-roofed huts that served as make-shift schools. In adherence to the advice given to me by one of my Brazilian friends, I submitted myself to the rigors of Paulo Freire's method.[1]

In Brazil, one of the first words to become part of my consciousness-raising vocabulary was *puta*—a Portuguese word for prostitute. For some reason, the word captured my imagination as I struggled to comprehend its meaning and significance in the largest Roman Catholic country in the world.

---

1. According to Freire's method, cointentional education and conciousness raising (*conscientização*) are combined efforts that lead to socially transformative action. See Paulo Freire, *Pedagogy of the Oppressed* (trans. Myra Bergman Ramos; New York: Seabury, 1970) 56.

After living some months in a small municipality, a priest with whom I worked asked if I would accompany him to a wake. The evening was cold and dusty. As we drove out of town on the road leading to the cemetery, I realized that we were making our way into an area that was unfamiliar to me. A few of the shacks alongside the road had electricity, but the vast majority of dwellings did not. We parked the car and a group of women met us. There was little conversation.

After walking a considerable distance, we came to a shack; inside lay the decomposing body of a twenty-six year old woman, aged and worn beyond her years. Candles were burning. There were no men other than the priest. A few women wept, but the majority were stoic. The deceased woman was the mother of four young children. Outside, a conversation ensued regarding who would care for them in the days ahead. Intuitively, I knew that this obscure area was in fact a *zona*— the district of prostitution.

One of the women asked the priest if he would begin the prayers. After the customary funeral oration, he began to speak about Jesus and the women who were his companions. Ordinarily a man of few words, he spoke at length with great conviction and compassion. Although struck by my companion's eloquence, I was distracted from his reflection as my attention became focused on the smell that filled the room—a mixture of the odor of decaying flesh and the smell of jasmine flowers. The woman's body was laid out on a board and wrapped. From all indications, it appeared as though she had hemorrhaged to death. The cause was open to speculation; perhaps a brutal customer, a miscarriage, a self-induced abortion, an attempted suicide, or the rupture of an internal organ. As the priest concluded his reflection, he asked the women if there was anything they would like to share. In their silence, volumes were spoken. In conclusion, he asked them to join him in offering the final blessing and commendation. Then we left, surrounded by the same silence that accompanied our arrival.

On the way home, the priest thanked me for joining him. He confirmed my intuition that we were returning from the town's *zona*. During our conversation, he explained how cautious many priests were about pastoral outreach to prostitutes. Nevertheless, it was obvious that he had little concern about his own reputation and no second thoughts about the appropriateness of his pastoral practice. The fact remained, however, that in many parishes prevailing ecclesial custom and longstanding social prejudice contributed to the rationalization for limiting or avoiding ministerial involvement in potentially compromising moral circumstances.

As I continued to ponder the relationship between the church and prostitutes, I began to raise new questions about who was to be included in the "church of the poor," or rather, who was to be excluded—and why.

When my lay missionary commitment in Brazil came to an end some years later, I made an effort to visit individuals and groups that had been significant to me during four of the most important years of my life. Five days before leaving Brazil, I took a back road bus trip to say good-bye to a group of Brazilian sisters who lived three hours away. It was the rainy season, and a recent storm had turned the soft dirt roads into mud. As we approached a treacherous section of the road, bordering on a ravine, the bus driver refused to drive any further until daybreak. It was a little after ten at night.

Given the circumstances, the passengers descended from the bus amiably, and I happened to find myself in the company of three women who engaged me in a conversation about my purpose in making this journey. I explained to them my reasons and my anxiety about arriving too late the next morning to encounter my friends. From the corner of my eye, I observed that our fellow passengers, most of whom were men, found the dialogue between three *putas* and one *missionária* to be an interesting diversion on a rainy evening—almost as entertaining as a television soap opera.

As the four of us continued our conversation, a station wagon made its way down the muddy road. The three women seemed to recognize the driver and his companions. The car stopped and after a few minutes of negotiation, the three crawled into the rear of the wagon. The car started up again and proceeded about four hundred feet. Then the brake lights went on. The driver shifted into reverse and backed up the car. One of the women called out to me and invited me to join them, assuring me that I would arrive safely at the convent by midnight. Given the alternative of being left alone all night with a busload of men, I expressed my gratitude for the women's consideration and jumped into the back of the car with them.

As we approached our destination, the driver pulled into a motel on the outskirts of the town.[2] We all got out of the car. Two of the women walked with me into town as the third assured the three men that they would return within a half hour. My companions and I arrived at the residence of the sisters in about fifteen minutes. As we approached the convent gate, I thanked them for their kindness to me. They waited for me to get inside the doorway before taking their leave. "Now don't forget to pray for us!" they chuckled. "I won't," I said. "Is that a promise?" one inquired. "To be sure!" I promised. "And when you get back to America, you'll remember the story of this trip, yes?" "I'll always remember the story of this trip!" I replied. "And us? Will you remember us?"

This book is my remembrance.

---

2. Motels are frequently centers for prostitution in the interior of Brazil. They are differentiated from hotels and *pensões* ("rooming houses") which provide lodging for travellers.

Introduction

Christianity and Prostitution: Methods, Resources, and Principles for Inquiry and Interpretation

At all times the Church carries the responsibility of reading the signs of the times and of interpreting them in the light of the Gospel, if it is to carry out its task.[1]

Gaudium et spes, 4

Unfortunately the Christian message about the dignity of women is contradicted by that persistent mentality which considers the human being not as a person but as a thing, as an object of trade, at the service of selfish interest and mere pleasure: the first victims of this mentality are women. This mentality produces very bitter fruits, such as contempt. . . for women. . . slavery. . . [and] prostitution.[2]

John Paul II

Prostitution is very much a matter of definition. Certain factors, nonetheless, appear essential to the existence of prostitution, specifically a moral code that frowns on certain promiscuous practices by females yet tolerates a different standard for males.[3]

Vern Bullough

1. *Gaudium et spes* 4, in Austin Flannery, ed., *Documents of Vatican II: The Conciliar and Post-conciliar Documents* (rev. ed.; 2 vols.; Northport, NY: Costello, 1987) 1. 905.

2. John Paul II, *Apostolic Exhortation on the Family, Origins* 11 (1981) 24.

3. Vern Bullough and Bonnie Bullough, *Women and Prostitution: A Social History* (Buffalo, NY: Prometheus, 1987) 14.

Prostitution is not a new problem for Christianity;[4] rather, it is a recurring problem which ebbs and flows throughout the course of human history.[5] As such, the contemporary challenges that the phenomenon of prostitution presents to Christian mission and ministry are far from being unique to this age. Some of these challenges, it could be argued, were taken up in first-century Palestine by Jesus himself. Other challenges have their precedents in later historical periods and different cultural contexts. In any case, to this day some form of prostitution continues to find a market in most regions of the world. Of particular interest to this study, however, is the extent to which various forms of prostitution prevail in so-called Christian cultures, particularly those, such as that of Brazil, in which the majority of the population is nominally identified as Roman Catholic. The harvest of "bitter fruits" is plentiful and its dependence on the complicity of the church to ensure its bounty is longstanding. For as long as the church, as a human institution,[6] persists in its own duplicity, hypocrisy, and ambivalence with regard to the second sex,[7] it

4. The term "problem" is defined as "a putative condition or situation that is labeled a problem in arenas of public discourse and action" (Stephen Hilgartner and Charles L. Bosk, "The Rise and Fall of Social Problems: A Public Arenas Model," *American Journal of Sociology* 94 [1988] 55). This definition is derived from the thought of Herbert Blumer and others who rejected "the theory that social problems are objective and identifiable societal conditions that have intrinsically harmful effects," arguing instead that "a social problem exists primarily in terms of how it is defined and conceived in society" (Herbert Blumer, "Social Problems as Collective Behavior," *Social Problems* 18 [1971] 300). The research of Hilgartner and Bosk (pp. 53–54) advances the latter position by demonstrating the ways in which "social problems are projections of collective sentiments rather than simple mirrors of objective conditions in society."

5. For historical overviews on this topic, see Bullough and Bullough, *Women and Prostitution*; Charles Chauvin, *Les chrétiens et la prostitution* (Paris: Cerf, 1983); and Jean-Guy Nadeau, *La prostitution, une affaire de sens: études de pratiques sociales et pastorales* (Montreal: Fides, 1987).

6. For a discussion of the distinguishing characteristics of the church as a divinely instituted sign and sacrament of salvation and the church as a human institution, see Leonardo Boff, *Igreja: carisma e poder* (Petrópolis: Vozes, 1981) 110–44.

7. See Simone de Beauvoir, *The Second Sex* (trans. H. M. Parshley; New York: Knopf, 1953) 216, 271; and Mary Daly, *The Church and the Second Sex* (Boston: Beacon, 1968) 53–73.

serves to reinforce the cultural conditions in which prostitution flourishes.

Although it is not within the scope of this book to review in exhaustive detail the historical patterns of relationship between the Christian churches and persons involved in prostitution, it is important to note that there is limited research available on the interactive processes by which social attitudes about prostitution inform and are informed by Christian moral teachings, ecclesial constructions of reality,[8] and pastoral practices. There are very few comprehensive historical analyses devoted explicitly to the study of Christianity and prostitution.[9] As a result, information dealing with the response of Christian churches to the phenomenon of prostitution must be gleaned from a variety of sources, including social histories of prostitution, theological treatises, canonical documents, penitential guides, spiritual exhortations, and ecclesiastical histories.[10] Additional—and frequently overlooked—information may be found in the autobiographies and biographies of individuals whose lives were marked in some way by their experiences in situations where prostitution and Christianity engaged one another for better or for worse. Although such resources can be highly subjective and sometimes questionable in terms of their authenticity, they nonetheless provide important perspectives on the attitudes and actions ascribed to all those concerned.[11] In a similar

8. The notion of an ecclesial construction of reality is derived from Peter L. Berger and Thomas Luckmann, *The Social Construction of Reality: A Treatise in the Sociology of Knowledge* (Garden City, NY: Doubleday, 1966). Of primary importance in my use and development of this notion is the way in which the church, like society, can be understood in terms of its objective reality and its subjective reality.

9. See Charles Chauvin, *Église et prostitution: enquête historique et perspectives pastorales* (3d ed.; Strasburg: Faculté de Strasbourg, 1973).

10. For example, see Marcel Bernos, *Le fruit défendu: les chrétiens et la sexualité de l'antiquité à nos jours* (Paris: Centurion, 1985); James A. Brundage, *Law, Sex and Christian Society in Medieval Europe* (Chicago: University of Chicago Press, 1987); and idem; "Prostitution in Medieval Canon Law," *Signs* 1 (1976) 8:25–45; Vern L. Bullough and James A. Brundage, *Sexual Practices and the Medieval Church* (Buffalo: Prometheus, 1982); and Pierre J. Payer, *Sex and the Penitentials: The Development of a Sexual Code* (Toronto: University of Toronto Press, 1984).

11. It should be noted that questions frequently arise regarding the credibility of many works dealing with the lives of prostitutes. Often, these biog-

fashion, it is important to note the degree to which works of literature, art, and music also provide society with numerous perspectives
on the relationship between Christianity and prostitution.[12]

My task as a practical theologian, however, unlike that of a social
historian, does not conclude with the acquisition and analysis of such
data. Rather, practical theology begins where the social sciences conclude. Understood as "that theological discipline which is concerned
with the church's self-actualization here and now—both that which *is*
and that which *ought to be*," practical theology seeks to use theology
to illumine a "particular situation in which the church must realize
itself in all of its dimensions."[13] At the juncture where social historical data and theological interpretation meet, the contemporary
ecclesiological relevance of an inquiry such as this is disclosed both
in terms of its means and its ends.

The Method

The theological method selected for this study may best be described as one that entails a reconstructive interpretation of the inter-

raphies were based on interviews and surveys conducted by clergy, rescue
workers, and police eager to confirm their own assumptions. See George
Riley Scott, *A History of Prostitution* (1936; reprinted New York: AMS, 1976)
25–27. In other instances, these works formed part of a lurid genre of literature that appealed to a pornographic market. Although one could argue that
exaggeration, misrepresentation, and imagination served to distort the biographies of individuals, it could be argued as well that despite the alleged
distortions, some measure of truth and insight about the world of prostitution
was disclosed nonetheless.

12. For example, see Harold Greenwald and Aron Krich, eds., *The Prostitute in Literature* (New York: Ballantine, 1960); Cecily Miller, *Infidelity,
The Ruin of Representation: The Theme of the Prostitute in Manet's Art* (Cambridge, MA: Harvard University Archives, 1983). In dealing with such categories, however, it is particularly important to take into account the cautions
and concerns that have been raised in recent years by historians and literary
critics influenced by feminist theory. See Joan Kelly, *Women, History and
Theory: The Essays of Joan Kelly* (Chicago: University of Chicago, 1984);
and idem, "Did Women Have a Renaissance?" in Renate Bridenthal and Claudia
Koonz, eds., *Becoming Visible: Women in European History* (Boston: Houghton
Mifflin, 1977) 140.

13. Karl Rahner, "Practical Theology within the Totality of Theological
Disciplines," in *Theological Investigations* (22 vols.; trans. Graham Harrison;
New York: Seabury, 1968) 9. 102.

twining of Christian vision and social praxis.[14] More precisely, it is a method that employs a "reconstructive hermeneutic that entails three distinct elements: hermeneutical reconstruction, retroductive warrants, and background theories."[15] According to Francis Schüssler Fiorenza, hermeneutical reconstruction within the Christian context presupposes the existence of a plurality of diverse beliefs, claims, convictions, and practices in need of interpretation. Its task is "to interpret Christian identity: what it means to be a Christian; in what does the Christian vision consist; and what is Christian praxis."[16] A retroductive warrant is neither deductive nor inductive. Rather, it

> argues from the variety and diversity of inferences that can be drawn from a hypothesis. The argument is not accepted because of logical cogency as in deduction or because of generalizations of data as in induction. Instead, the argument is accepted because the hypothesis generates illuminative inferences.[17]

Background theories guide the application and assessment of theories. They mediate between a theory and an experimental situation.[18] Fiorenza notes that when a coherence between theory and phenomenon is not attained, a revision of theory often results. He goes on to illustrate how "the application of ethical theories involves not only considered moral judgments and moral principles but also relevant background notions about human nature or human society."[19] Fiorenza explains that "the relation between religious faith and contemporary experience entails not simply coherence with experience or correspondence to data, but instead, involves the analysis of background theories by which data and experience are interpreted and interrelated with creedal statements."[20]

Although described as foundational, this theological method does not make its primary appeal to either experience or tradition. Rather,

14. This methodological approach is derived from the work of Francis Schüssler Fiorenza, *Foundational Theology: Jesus and the Church* (New York: Crossroad, 1985) xvi; see esp. "From Fundamental to Foundational Theology," 249–321.

15. Ibid., xvi.

16. Ibid.

17. Ibid.

18. Ibid.

19. Ibid.

20. Ibid.

in seeking a "reflective equilibrium between hermeneutical reconstruction, retroductive warrants, and relevant background theories,"[21] it moves in a circular fashion from the particular to the general and back from the general to the particular. In this spiraling process, mutual critique, justification, and adjustment lead to the ongoing refinement of the reconstructive hermeneutic.[22] It is through the "back and forth movement," identified theoretically as reflective equilibrium, that principles reconstructed from practice are brought into balance with the practice itself.[23] As such, this theory "takes into account diverse elements as foundational" without reducing tradition to experience or vice versa.[24] It seeks to demonstrate the "interaction between initial judgments or practices, principles and background theory;" as Francis Schüssler Fiorenza notes:

> Each not only provides a support to the other two elements but also may challenge and correct them. There is not one single element of foundation; rather, the foundation consists in the constant interchange among the diverse sources and principles.[25]

The merit of this foundational theological method is found in the fact that it is not a static approach to theology. Inasmuch as it advances and values the process of reflective equilibrium, it "realizes not only the diversity of its various elements, but also the need for constant revision and adjustment."[26]

To a large extent, this method is selected because of its intrinsically heuristic character.[27] By this I mean that the method facilitates an interdisciplinary inquiry into the relationship between the church of liberation and the phenomenon of prostitution in Brazilian soci-

---

21. Ibid.
22. Ibid., 301.
23. Ibid., 302.
24. Ibid., 303.
25. Ibid.
26. Ibid., 323.
27. I am grateful to the work of Sally McFague for the notion of a heuristic device, although my application of the term differs in a significant way from hers. See Sally McFague, *Models of God: Theology for an Ecological, Nuclear Age* (Philadelphia: Fortress, 1987) 32–33.

ety.[28] Like all other methods in Christian theology, it is employed by a researcher who chooses a method not in spite of her biases and assumptions, but precisely because of them.

Genealogical Premises and Presuppositions[29]

Convinced of the "particularity and relatedness of all human knowing,"[30] I must anchor the discussion of method in a brief reflection on some underlying principles and experiences that inform my own approach to theological inquiry and investigation.[31] Generally speaking, I am not disposed toward a dualistic fundamentalism, nor am I convinced that pluralistic relativism is a preferred alternative. Rather, I

28. Throughout this book the term *igreja de libertação* ("church of liberation") refers to those members of the Roman Catholic hierarchy, clergy, religious, and laity who put into practice the values expressed in documents and social commitments of the Latin American Episcopal Conference, the Conference of Latin American Religious, and ecclesial base communities. The work of Latin American liberation theologians served to inform and reflect this movement which began to take form in the wake of Vatican II. Essentially, the term is interchangeable with *igreja do povo* ("people's church"), *igreja popular* ("popular church"), and *igreja dos pobres* ("church of the poor"). For a more detailed explanation, see Ralph Della Cava, "The 'People's Church,' the Vatican, and Abertura," in Alfred Stepan, ed., *Democratizing Brazil: Problems of Transition and Consolidation* (New York: Oxford University Press, 1989) 143–67.

29. The notion of genealogy is taken from Michel Foucault. He describes it (*Power/Knowledge: Selected Interviews and Other Writings, 1972–1977* [ed. Colin Gordon; trans. idem et al.; New York: Pantheon, 1980] 83) as the "union of erudite knowledge and local memories which allows us to establish a historical knowledge of struggles and to make use of this knowledge tactically today."

30. See Roger Haight, "Critical Witness: The Question of Method," in Leo J. O'Donovan and T. Howland Sanks, eds., *Faithful Witness: Foundations of Theology for Today's Church* (New York: Crossroad, 1989) 186–87.

31. The critical reader may question the inner coherency of a project that advances a foundational method while appealing to genealogical premises. I would argue in response, following the insights of Jeffrey Stout, that my reliance on a multiplicity of standpoints need not threaten the overall coherency of this study. Rather, it elects to find value in the search for a "middle way between false unity and sheer chaos" (Jeffrey Stout, *Ethics After Babel: The Languages of Morals and Their Discontents* [Boston: Beacon, 1988] 21).

see the need for envisioning a method in theology that affirms and takes seriously the engendering of commitment within a world of relativity.[32] My premises and presuppositions, perhaps more adequately described as my biases and assumptions, are numerous. I have no doubt that they will disclose themselves throughout the course of this book. In the interest of responsible scholarship, however, I would like to identify those which are critical not only to the integrity of my work as a practical theologian, but also to my commitment to seek and practice truth in the service of faith and justice.

First, with regard to the use of the Bible, I am persuaded by a "feminist hermeneutic that shares in the critical methods and impulses of historical scholarship on the one hand and the theological goals of liberation theologies on the other hand."[33] Second, with regard to the history of Christianity, I am influenced by the work of church historians who have taken seriously the retrieval and historical reconstruction of "subjugated knowledges."[34] Third, with regard to systematic theology, I believe that all theology is essentially contextual theology. I do not dispute the fact, however, that some theologies have a relevance for peoples, times, and contexts other than the ones from which they originally emerged. Although grounded primarily in the Franciscan theological tradition, I am influenced as well by European

32. This notion is derived from the work of William J. Perry, *Forms of Intellectual and Ethical Development in the College Years* (New York: Holt, Rinehart, Winston, 1970) 134ff. For further information on its application to theories of faith development and moral imagination, see Sharon Parks, *The Critical Years* (San Francisco: Harper & Row, 1986) 49–53.

33. See Elisabeth Schüssler Fiorenza, *In Memory of Her: A Feminist Theological Reconstruction of Christian Origins* (New York: Crossroad, 1985) 29.

34. The notion of subjugated knowledge is derived from the work of Michel Foucault. According to Foucault, (*Power/Knowledge*, 81–82) subjugated knowledge refers to two things: first, the "historical contents that have been buried and disguised in a functionalist coherence or formal systemisation"; and, second, a "whole set of knowledges that have been disqualified as inadequate to their task or insufficiently elaborated: naive knowledges, located down on the hierarchy, beneath the required level of cognition or scientificity." Examples of historians who take into account "subjugated knowledges" include Margaret R. Miles, Clarissa W. Atkinson, Caroline W. Bynum, John Boswell, Margaret Carney, Janice Farnham, Michael Moffatt, Fredrica Harris Thompsett, Albert Raboteau, Gerta Lerner, Rosemary Keller, Mary Ewens, and others.

existential theology, Latin American liberation theology, and North American feminist theology. Fourth, with regard to moral theology, I would identify myself as a voluntarist, albeit one who is informed by a diversity of approaches and trends in contemporary Christian ethics. Fifth, as a practical theologian, I am convinced of the necessity and wisdom of appealing simultaneously to two hermeneutical approaches—that of suspicion and that of generosity.[35] Informed by the political, economic, and cultural analyses of critical theorists, I am acutely attuned to the challenges that issues of race, culture, gender, and class bring to bear on the relationship between religion and society. Finally, my overarching interest in the study of Christian mission in the postmodern world is born out of the conviction that the *missio Dei* is at once confirmed and confounded by the *missio ecclesiae*.[36]

Social Scientific Resources

The works of selected social historians and social psychologists provide a conceptual framework for gathering and assessing the subject matter of this book. In the course of my own comparative reading and analysis of studies on the social history of prostitution,[37] I have focused my attention on the ways in which the multiple manifesta-

35. See Margaret R. Miles, "Hermeneutics of Generosity and Suspicion: Pluralism and Theological Education," *Theological Education* 23 supp. 34–52 (1987) 34–52.

36. See David J. Bosch, *Transforming Mission: Paradigm Shifts in Theology of Mission* (Maryknoll: Orbis, 1991) 389–93. Bosch discusses the distinguishing characteristics of God's mission in the world as differentiated from the mission of the Church. In describing the notion of the *missio Dei*, Bosch observes that it has "helped to articulate the conviction that neither the Church nor any other human agent can ever be considered the author or bearer of mission. Mission is, primarily and ultimately, the work of the Triune God" (p. 392).

37. See Bullough and Bullough, *Women and Prostitution*; Iwan Bloch, *Die Prostitution* (2 vols.; Berlin: Louis Marcus, 1912–25); P. L. Jacob, [Pierre Dufour], *History of Prostitution, Among All the Peoples of the World, from the Most Remote Antiquity to the Present Day* (trans. Samuel Putnam; 3 vols.; New York: Covici Friede, 1932); Hilary Evans, *Harlots, Whores and Hookers: History of Prostitution* (New York: Taplinger, 1979); Lucia Ferrante, "La sexualité en tant ressource: Des femmes devant le for archiepiscopal de Bologne

tions of religious belief and practice weave their way in and out of these social histories. Through my ongoing study of selected theories and processes associated with symbolic interaction,[38] particularly those related to attribution theory and problem definition,[39] I have adapted

[XVIIième siècle]," *Déviance et Societé* 11 (1987) 41–66; Mary Gibson, *Prostitution in the State of Italy: 1860–1915* (New Brunswick: Rutgers University Press, 1986); Fernando Henriques, *Prostitution and Society* (3 vols.; London: MacGibbon & Kee, 1962–68); Claude Jaget, ed., *Prostitutes, Our Life* (trans. Anna Furse et al.; Bristol: Falling Wall, 1980); Rina Macrelli, *L'indegna schiatitu: Anna Maria Mozzoni e la lotta contra la prostituzione di Stato* (Roma: Reuniti, 1981); Paul McHugh, *Prostitution and Victorian Social Reform* (London: Croom Hel, 1980); Leah Lydia Otis, *Prostitution in Medieval Society: The History of an Urban Institution in Languedoc* (Chicago: University of Chicago Press, 1985); Alexandre-Jean-Baptiste Parent-Duchâtelet, *De la prostitution dans la ville de Paris: La prostitution à Paris au XIXe siècle* (1836; ed. Alain Corbin; reprinted Paris: Seuil, 1981); Mary Elizabeth Perry, "Lost Women in Early Modern Seville: Politics of Prostitution," *Feminist Studies* 4 (1978) 195–214; Lyndal Roper, "Discipline and Respectability: Prostitution and the Reformation in Augsburg," *History Workshop Journal* 19 (1985) 3–28; William W. Sanger, *History of Prostitution: Its Extent, Causes, and Effects throughout the World* (1939; reprinted New York: AMS, 1974); and Scott, *A History of Prostitution*.

38. For a more complete introduction to the theoretical foundations and historical development of symbolic interaction, see Herbert Blumer, *Symbolic Interaction: Perspective and Method* (Englewood Cliffs, NJ: Prentice-Hall, 1969); Robert H. Lauer and Warren H. Handel, *Social Psychology: The Theory and Application of Symbolic Interactionism* (Englewood Cliffs, NJ: Prentice-Hall, 1983); William James, "The Social Self," in Gregory P. Stone and Harvey A. Farberman, eds., *Social Psychology through Symbolic Interaction* (Waltham, MA: Ginn-Blaisdell, 1970); and George Herbert Mead, *Mind, Self and Society* (Chicago: University of Chicago Press, 1934).

39. For a more detailed explanation of attribution theory and its application to studies of human behavior and social interaction, see Fritz Heider, "Social Perception and Phenomenal Causality," *Psychological Review* 21 (1944); Harold Kelley, *Attribution in Social Interaction* (Morristown, NJ: General Learning Press, 1972); and Dietmar Gorlitz, ed., *Perspectives on Attribution Research and Theory* (Cambridge, MA: Ballinger, 1980). Regarding problem definition, see Blumer, "Social Problems" 298–306; Malcolm Spector and John I. Kituse, "Social Problems: A Re-formulation," *Social Problems* 21 (1973) 145–59; idem, *Constructing Social Problems* (2d ed.; New York: de Gruyter, 1987); Armand I. Mauss, *Social Problems as Social Movements* (New York: Lippencott, 1975).

and applied the work of Stephen Hilgartner and Charles Bosk[40] as a schema for examining how interest in the phenomenon of prostitution increases and decreases within the ecclesial arena. In this regard, I believe it is important to understand how prostitution comes to be recognized not only as a social problem with implications for the Christian community, but more specifically as an ecclesial problem with a life of its own.

Attending to the Insurrection of Subjugated Knowledge[41]

As previously noted, comparative analyses of studies in the social history of prostitution provide numerous insights into how the roles, functions, and statuses of prostitutes are constructed and defined in different contexts. To the extent that the phenomenon of prostitution is regarded by many to be universal, persons who engage in prostitution—those identified as prostitutes—oftentimes are not understood on their own terms, but rather on those of physicians, police, rescue workers, or playwrights. In recent years, however, the research efforts of numerous social historians have provided the academy with new ideas about the lives of prostitutes and alternative views on the phenomenon of prostitution in various cultural contexts and historical periods. Such scholarship often illustrates how the content of research findings does not always fit or conform to the paradigmatic understandings of institutions and authorities.

As subjugated knowledges surface, theories of multiple causality begin to eclipse single factor attributions. For example, poverty is frequently given as a single cause. Such a theory of attribution, however, has its limitations inasmuch as it cannot account for why all

40. See Hilgartner and Bosk, "The Rise and Fall of Social Problems," 53–78.

41. Informed by the work of Michel Foucault, feminist liberation theologian Sharon D. Welch (*Communities of Resistance and Solidarity: A Feminist Theology of Liberation* [Maryknoll: Orbis, 1985] 19–20) uses this term to refer to the "the history of subjugation, conflict, and domination, [that is] lost in an all-encompassing theoretical framework or erased in a triumphal history of ideas." The insurrection of such knowledge calls attention to the relation between power and knowledge by questioning "whose knowledge is taken as real and whose is rejected as inadequate."

poor women do not become prostitutes. As alternative theories of attribution emerge, they call into question the adequacy of traditional categories of inquiry that take as their primary focus promiscuity or poverty. In their stead, new categories of inquiry give rise to another line of questioning which deals with issues and concerns that have been largely unexplored. For example, in focusing on sexual exploitation and abuse as a category of inquiry, the question arises: Do women engaged in prostitution have an early history of being sexually exploited or abused as children, as slaves, as employees, as lovers or spouses? In examining recidivism, it is important to explore the extent to which women "rescued" from lives of prostitution are "rehabilitated" for employment in the very trades in which they were engaged before becoming prostitutes. In coming to terms with the life histories, it is necessary to determine in what ways the lives of prostitutes are different from the lives of other women sharing similar ethnic origins and economic backgrounds—and in what ways they are the same. Inasmuch as Christianity prescribes chastity, obedience, and often times poverty as hallmarks of female virtue, to be preserved and preferred even when a woman is threatened with the diminishment or loss of her life, the apparent failure of any woman to adhere to these moral expectations could result in her being characterized as less than virtuous. Despite the scrutiny and condemnation of church authorities, however, the religious imagination of prostitutes, as with other women, is beyond the control of any institution. For this reason, speculations about the religious imagination of women elicit scholarly interest in the images, attitudes, and activities that are central to the religious and spiritual lives of the prostitutes. Careful analysis of demographic patterns requires that attention be given to the significance of charting the incidence of women engaged in casual and short-term prostitution. This serves to highlight the importance of understanding their particular conditions and individual purposes. Regard for the issue of social control of prostitution raises questions about the attitudes of prostitutes toward regulation, abolition, and prohibition, along with the long-term and short-term effects of these. Finally, interest in the social representation of prostitutes engages the minds of researchers concerned about how artistic and literary depictions of prostitutes compare with reality.

In addition to disclosing new insights into the lives of prostitutes themselves, the retrieval of subjugated knowledges also discloses information about the relationship of the church to both prostitutes and the phenomenon of prostitution. Beyond those traditional theories of attribution used to account for the teachings and ministries of the church with regard to prostitutes—such as the salvation of souls, care for the poor, and the defense of Christian female virtue—additional theories of attribution require researchers to attend to a wider range of issues and concerns.

For example, motivations for ministry come under scrutiny as we question not only the religious motivations that lead ecclesial leaders or representatives of Christian churches to take an interest in the pastoral and/or temporal care of women engaged in prostitution, but also those motivations that arise from social concerns, political realities, or personal responsibility. For what duration of time do such ministries prevail and who supplies the financial resources to sustain them? Further inquiries take as their focus the circumstances under which ecclesial leaders or representatives of Christian churches distinguish prostitutes as sinners, as victims, or as entrepreneurs. Inevitably, related questions surface in terms of the public and private interests that are served by such characterizations. In a similar fashion, the contextual nature of ecclesial politics comes under examination as prostitution is found to be tolerated by some ecclesial leaders and condemned by others. Ecclesial leaders and representatives of Christian churches modify or negotiate their *public* positions with regard to the controversies surrounding the regulation, abolition, and prohibition of prostitution; inquiry into the conditions under which this occurs logically takes its place alongside ongoing interest in the conditions under which ecclesial authorities censure, control, or disclose information regarding human sexuality or sexually transmitted diseases.

Frequently, researchers who attend to subjugated knowledges provide substantial evidence of the ongoing glossing and modification of the teachings and practices of Christian churches by their leaders.[42]

42. The Roman Catholic church is one among many Christian churches to come under the scrutiny of social historians. For this reason it is important to note that the Roman Catholic church is marked not only by its size and influ-

Insights from the social history of prostitution disclose a generalized—rather than incidental—incongruity between beliefs and behaviors, not only on the part of Christians but on the part of ecclesial
authorities as well. As such, these leaders, in emphasizing the un-
changing principles and fixed moral claims said to govern human
sexuality, succeed in withholding from the faithful the rendering of a
more accurate account of the contingencies and dispensations of
Christian casuistry as it has been practiced contextually throughout
the history of the church.

Unquestionably, new categories of inquiry emerge as attention is
given to subjugated knowledges. In light of this fact, it is important
to note that in the overall investigative process, particular attention
must be given not only to the questions, but also to the criteria used
for gauging the relative repression or expansion of the power and
knowledge of women as well as for determining the quality of their
historical experience.[43] In this regard, it is essential that we appropriate the following criteria as we inquire into the different historical
and cultural contexts. The criteria include:

> 1) The regulation of *female sexuality* as compared with male
> sexuality;
>
> 2) Women's *economic* and *political roles*, e.g., the kind of work
> they performed as compared with men, and their access to prop-
> erty, political power and the education or training necessary for
> work, property and power;
>
> 3) The *cultural roles* of women in shaping the outlook of their
> society, and access to the education and/or institutions necessary
> for this; and
>
> 4) The *ideology* about women, in particular the sex-role system
> displayed or advocated in the symbolic products of the society,
> its art, literature, and philosophy.[44]

ence, but also by broad cultural and regional diversities. Although the church
is characterized as universal, the particularities of local churches remain a
constant throughout ecclesiastical history. Although local churches are part of
the larger whole as well as representative of it, it is necessary to exercise
caution in efforts to generalize from the particular to the universal or to generalize from one particular church to another. See Robert J. Schreiter, *Constructing* 1–21.

43. Kelly-Gadol, "Did Women Have a Renaissance?" 139.

44. Ibid., 139–40.

To the extent that this study takes as its broad focus the relationship between the church and prostitution, it addresses itself in a particular way to the role, status, and function of the prostitute, but in a more general way, to the role, status, and function of all women. In this regard, it is important to discern the ways in which the collective definition of prostitution as an ecclesial problem discloses not only dominant attitudes about prostitutes but about women, in general.

In short, are the conceptions about women identified as prostitutes radically different from the conceptions held about all women? To the extent that categories of inquiry and criteria for inquiry make it possible to recognize and distinguish patterns of interaction between the church and the phenomenon of prostitution, they contribute as well to a heightened understanding of the church and its relationship to women.

Historical Patterns of Interaction

In considering the history of interaction between the church and the phenomenon of prostitution, we discover three patterns.[45] The first is that of *toleration* which in general is marked by the regulation of prostitution by ecclesial and/or civil authorities. The church thus accommodates itself to what it judges to be a given condition within human society. Its moral rationalization is predicated on the characterization of prostitution as a necessary or lesser evil.[46] A second pattern is that of *prohibition*. In general, this is marked by the repression of prostitution by ecclesial and/or civil authorities. In this situation, the church takes a stand of resistance against all forms of sexual immorality; at times, this stance is accompanied or superseded by overarching negative attitudes toward all expressions of human sexuality. Dualistic attitudes about human sexuality serve to reinforce the representation of the body as evil and sexual activity as sinful. The condemnation, punishment, and marginalization of transgressors is decidedly directed toward women, as Christian leaders entrusted with

45. For further information on this point see the appendix, p. 179.

46. This position would be in accord with the thought of Augustine (*De ordine* 2.4.12) and Aquinas (*Summa Theologiae* 2–2.10.11 and *De regimine principium* 1.14), the former asserting that prostitution was a "necessary" evil given man's concupiscent nature, the latter suggesting that it was a "lesser" evil given greater evils such as sodomy. For further discussion of this point, see Nadeau, *La prostitution*, 257–65.

the responsibility for safeguarding the purity and righteousness of the community endeavor to ensure moral integrity by force. The third pattern is that of *abolition*. In general, it is marked by ecclesial and/ or civil efforts to liberate prostitutes from the conditions of poverty and marginalization that confine them to prostitution. It advances the decriminalization of prostitution and promotes the prosecution of those who derive financial profit from prostitutes through abuse, exploitation, and extortion.

These three patterns of interaction rarely occur independently of each other. Rather, they exist on a continuum and in some circumstances they exist simultaneously. Moral theology, canon law, and pastoral practice tend to set the ecclesial agenda for interaction, but not necessarily in a fashion that is in direct correspondence to the civil agenda. In an effort to achieve, maintain, or preserve its moral equilibrium, the church is found to accommodate, resist, or assimilate the challenges that prostitution poses to the larger society. Different choices are made in different contexts and different historical periods. Although the challenges that prostitution poses do not present a constant threat to the church's moral equilibrium, the church is required, nonetheless, to deal with the potentially destabilizing effects of these challenges on its own sense of balance and security. In order to do this, the church must ascribe to prostitution—or to some aspect of prostitution—a collective definition that identifies the precise threat, thereby identifying the nature and scope of the ecclesial problem.

In accord with insights derived from the theory of symbolic interaction,[47] which views social problems as products of a process of collective definition, it becomes important to attend not only to the historical patterns of social interaction but likewise to the symbolic interactions that inform the ways in which these historical patterns are determined. I propose that as the church comes to recognize pros-

47. The theory of symbolic interaction calls into question the supposition that social problems are objective and identifiable societal conditions that have intrinsically harmful effects. Likewise, it seeks to disclose the biases and assumptions (for example, racial, ethnic, economic, geopolitical, religious, and gender-based) that are inherent in the recording and interpretation of historical data. See Hilgartner and Bosk, "The Rise and Fall of Social Problems," 53–54.

titution as an ecclesial problem, comprised of many components, it is called to assess its attitudes and practices in six areas. These include:

1) the church's operative images of the prostitute; examples of such images include the characterization of the prostitute as harlot, whore, victim, slave, seductress, sinner, entrepreneur, survivor, and heroine.

2) the social realities contributing to the church's interest in or concern with prostitution, for example, rapid social change, wars, pilgrimages, migrations, shifts in labor and economy, epidemics, expeditions, colonization, foundlings and orphans, venereal diseases, and demographic shifts.

3) the church's attribution theories for explaining why individuals become prostitutes; these might include poverty, unemployment, idleness, vagrancy, coercion, harassment, abuse, lust, ambition, ineligibility for marriage, sexual slavery, abandonment, self-deprecation, and despair.

4) the church's preferred mode of dealing with prostitutes, such as moral exhortation, confinement to centers for rehabilitation, spiritual encouragement, opportunities for reparation, public interrogation, and punishment.

5) the church's provisions for viable alternatives; these might include a life of penance in a convent or enclosure, a dowry for marriage, training and rehabilitation, and refuge in an asylum.

6) the church's understanding of the life trajectory of those who persist in prostitution; these might include exclusion from the sacramental life of the church, social marginalization, separation from offspring, exclusion from family, imprisonment, infirmity, and early death.

As data from selected social histories contribute to a more complete understanding of the multiple and differentiated world views held by clerics, physicians, police, and prostitutes, it is important to be attentive to the ways in which false causality[48] often contributes to the formulation of the collective definition. In short, the reasons given for the problem are not necessarily the only reasons, the most significant reasons—or the real reasons.

48. This is a notion derived from the world of magic, in which the attention of people is purposely misdirected so as to give the observer a believable, yet false, impression of what has taken place.

Conclusion

The methods, resources, and principles discussed in this introductory chapter guide a theological inquiry that takes as its subject a study of the church of liberation and the problem of prostitution. In the process of such inquiry, it is important to recognize the patterns of insight that emerge as the subjugated knowledge of Christian history is set in correspondence with the subjugated knowledge of the biblical tradition as well as the subjugated knowledge of present-day realities. Attentive to these patterns of insight, I begin my inquiry with an examination of the Rahab narrative, an assessment of its theological and ecclesiological implications, and a proposition about its significance for the promotion of faith and justice in the Brazilian context.

1

The Ecclesiological Challenge of Rahab the Harlot
The Prostitute as an Exemplar of Faith and Justice

> By faith Rahab the harlot did not perish with those who were disobedient, because she had given friendly welcome to the spies.
> *Heb 11:31*

> Was not Rahab the harlot justified by works when she received the messengers and sent them out another way?
> *Jas 2:25*

> Rahab, the prostitute justified [by faith], saves us.[1]

Those who have followed the evolution of Latin American liberation theology during the course of the past twenty-five years know the extent to which the Exodus narrative has been foundational to its origins and development both in terms of theological speculation and pastoral practice.[2] Gustavo Gutierrez was among the first of

1. Jerome *Epistolae* 22 (PL 22. 123).
2. See Paul VI, *Populorum Progressio* (New York: Paulist, 1967) nos. 20–21; Second General Conference of Latin American Bishops, "Introduction to the Final Documents," no. 6, in *The Church in the Present-Day Transformation of Latin America in the Light of the Council: II Conclusions* (Washington, DC: United States Catholic Conference—Latin American Division, 1973); Gustavo Gutierrez, *A Theology of Liberation* (trans. Caridad Inda and John Eagleson; Maryknoll: Orbis, 1973) 155–60, 295–96; Congregation for the Doctrine of the Faith, "Instruction on Certain Aspects of the 'Theology of Liberation'," *Origins* 14 (1984) §4.1–6; idem, "Instruction on Christian Freedom and Liberation," *Origins* 15 (1986) §3.43–47; Ignacio Ellacuria, *Free-*

the Latin American liberation theologians to assert that "the Exodus experience is paradigmatic" for the poor and oppressed inasmuch as it provides the model for "breaking away from a situation of despoliation and misery and the beginning of the construction of a just and fraternal society."[3] Within this hermeneutical framework the liberation of Israel is understood to be a "political action."[4] God intervenes in human history and liberates the Israelites from their slavery in Egypt. In short, God takes sides. Although this interpretation is criticized and disputed both within the Roman Catholic church and outside of it,[5] it nonetheless continues to prevail and to inspire.[6]

---

dom Made Flesh (trans. John Drury; Maryknoll: Orbis, 1976) 15–18; Oscar Cullmann, *Salvation in History* (trans. Sidney G. Sowers; New York: Harper & Row, 1967); José Severino Croatto, *Exodus: A Hermeneutics of Freedom* (trans. Salvator Attanasio; Maryknoll: Orbis, 1981); George V. Pixley, *On Exodus: A Liberation Perspective* (Maryknoll: Orbis, 1987); Robert McAfee Brown, *Theology in a New Key: Responding to Liberation Themes* (Philadelphia: Westminster, 1978) 88–90; and Carlos Mesters, *Palavra de Deus, história dos homens* (Petrópolis: Vozes, 1971) 11–15.

3. Gutierrez, *A Theology of Liberation*, 155.

4. Ibid., 155, 159.

5. See Alfred T. Hennelly, ed., *Liberation Theology: A Documentary History* (Maryknoll: Orbis, 1990) for English translations of the following documents: International Theological Commission, *Declaration on Human Development and Christian Salvation* (September 1977) 209; Congregation for the Doctrine of the Faith, "Ten Observations on the Theology of Gustavo Gutierrez" (March 1983) 349; and Joseph Cardinal Ratzinger, "Liberation Theology" (March 1984) 374. Also see Congregation for the Doctrine of the Faith, "Instruction on Certain Aspects," §10.5; Carl F. Henry, "Liberation Theology and the Scriptures: Five Objections to Liberation Theology," in Ronald H. Nash, ed., *Liberation Theology* (Milford, MI: Mott Media, 1984) 191–202; and Jon Levenson, "Exodus and Liberation," *Horizons in Biblical Theology* 13 (1991) 134–74.

6. A comprehensive examination of the polemics that shape ongoing debates about the correct understanding and appropriate application of the biblical narrative to the concrete economic, cultural, political, and religious realities of Latin America is beyond the scope of this study. Suffice it to say that I shall make use of the perspective advanced by Elisabeth Schüssler Fiorenza as "critical feminist hermeneutics"; see *In Memory of Her*, 3–40. I would like to highlight Schüssler Fiorenza's critique of the "hermeneutic circle" as proposed and explained by Juan Luis Segundo. See Elisabeth Schüssler Fiorenza, *Bread Not Stone: The Challenge of Feminist Biblical Interpretation* (Boston:

As with all paradigms, however, the Exodus paradigm not only has limits, but it also sets limits. Essentially, the narrative discloses a divine plan for human liberation. It defines and determines the types of experiences considered to be most significant for the realization of this process.[7] Those committed to such a process find themselves advancing the paradigm with undaunted courage and tenacity. At issue in this process, however, is the fact that where dependency on a given paradigm is high, self-critical reflection regarding the adequacy of the paradigm often tends to be limited or restrained.[8]

It comes as no surprise, therefore, that efforts to identify and critique the problematic elements of the Exodus narrative, along with the theoretical incoherencies and practical inconsistencies inherent in its paradigmatic usage, would tend to be viewed by proponents of liberation theology with some measure of suspicion, disdain, and contempt.[9] Negative responses to such criticisms are not without warrant. The criticisms themselves are not as much a cause for concern as the potential power of the critics to undermine not only the liberation

---

Beacon, 1984) 43–63; and Juan Luis Segundo, *The Liberation of Theology* (Maryknoll: Orbis, 1976) 7–38. Segundo describes the hermeneutic circle as "the continuing change in our interpretation of the Bible which is dictated by the continuing changes in our present-day reality, both individual and societal" (p. 8). According to Schüssler Fiorenza, the method, while employing the hermeneutics of suspicion, fails to extend its application to the Bible itself. The critique is extremely important given the fact that Segundo's method, coupled with that of the biblical theologian Carlos Mesters, informs and influences much of Latin American liberation theology. Mesters's method provides a model for exploring in community the relationship of biblical texts to the realities of life. This method examines the dynamic relationship of pretext, text, and context. See Carlos Mesters, "The Use of the Bible in Christian Communities of the Common People," in Sergio Torres and John Eagleson, eds., *The Challenge of Basic Christian Communities* (Maryknoll: Orbis, 1981) 197–210.

7. See Ian G. Barbour, *Myths, Models and Paradigms: A Comparative Study in Science and Religion* (San Francisco: Harper & Row, 1974) 149.

8. Ibid., 179–81.

9. Examples of such critiques focus on concerns related to distributive justice, nonviolence, and proportionalism. The justification of divine actions taken against the Egyptians, the dispossession of the Moabites and Canaanites, widespread human carnage, and infidelity to the covenant are but a few of the disconcerting components of the narrative.

process, but the very structures and support systems that the paradigm inspires and sustains.[10] From the perspective of its proponents, concerted actions must be taken to ensure that the integrity of the Exodus paradigm is not put at risk. Offering resistance to criticism is not an exercise in academic freedom. It is a strategy for survival.

In spite of this reality, however, the fact remains, whether acknowledged or not, that over the course of nearly three decades, the very process of liberation has disclosed certain paradigmatic inadequacies and limitations. Within the Brazilian context, an illustration of this fact can be found in ongoing ecclesial efforts to respond to the manifold challenges presented to the church by marginalized women.

As the historical project evolves, it becomes necessary within particular situations to adjust—and in some cases to reconceive—the relationship between the Exodus paradigm and the liberation struggle. For example, as the church in Brazil made efforts to respond to the problem of prostitution, the very efforts gave rise to questions and concerns that required a particular kind of paradigmatic adjustment and reconceptualization to take place.[11] Such a movement could be understood as a shift from one paradigm to another. It could also be argued, however, that the shift did not take place *between* paradigms, but rather, *within* the paradigm itself.

For nearly three decades, the Exodus paradigm has contributed to the emergence of a transformative ecclesial vision in Latin America. This vision has been exemplified in episcopal conferences, basic Christian communities, schools of theology, training centers for ministry, and countless pastoral and political initiatives. Over the years, the church of liberation has faced many obstacles, such as military regimes, multinational corporations, the mass media, the International Monetary Fund, the Vatican, the Congregation for the Doctrine of the

10. See E. Schüssler Fiorenza, *In Memory of Her*, xxi–xxii.

11. The themes of captivity and slavery are central to the Exodus narrative. Reflections on these themes by ostracized unwed mothers, sexually exploited domestics, and actual prostitutes provide very different interpretive correlations with reality from those of landless farm laborers or underpaid factory workers. Given the particular circumstances of each group, the category of the oppressor shifts from the beneficiaries of imperialism and classism to the beneficiaries of machismo and racism.

Faith, and natural disasters. Given these realities, it is no wonder that self-critical reflection on the theoretical and practical limitations of the Exodus paradigm was not undertaken as prescribed.[12] Likewise, it is important to note that such reflection would have been precipitous and premature. The very life of the project could have been jeopardized and ultimately rendered inviable just as unearthing a seedling to assess its growth and development carries with it the danger of killing the plant altogether. At what point, however, does such reflection become necessary and inevitable? At what point is it appropriate to require those of us who advance the paradigmatic use of the Exodus narrative to respond to the challenges posed by hundreds of thousands of Brazilian prostitutes in the largest Roman Catholic country of the world? At what point does a commitment to faith and justice require us to consider what liberation looks like not only from the shores of the Red Sea but from the banks of the Jordan river as well?

In this study, I propose that the challenge to take the *end* of the Exodus narrative as seriously as the *beginning* is an effort to underscore the centrality of women as agents of resistance and solidarity in the life project called survival.[13] The survival saga of the tribes of Israel is laden with intrigue and irony. It opens with the strategies and actions of Hebrew midwives (Exod 1:15–22)[14] and concludes with the strategies and actions of a Canaanite prostitute (Joshua 2). The tribes of Israel survive because, in cooperation with the divine plan, women possess the courage to make moral decisions that subordinate the

12. See Francis Schüssler Fiorenza on "Hermeneutical Reconstruction and Reflective Equilibrium" in his *Foundational Theology*, 301–311.

13. For a more complete discussion of resistance and solidarity in the struggle for human liberation, see Sharon D. Welch, *Communities of Resistance and Solidarity: A Feminist Theology of Liberation* (Maryknoll: Orbis, 1985) 32–54.

14. This interpretation was highlighted by Dom Luciano Mendes de Almeida, S.J., president of the National Conference of Brazilian Bishops (C.N.B.B.), in an address he gave promoting the theme for the bishops' 1991 Campanha da Fraternidade entitled "Solidários na Dignidade do Trabalho," focusing on the rights of workers and the dignity of work, *Veja*, 20 February 1991, 24. Also, Phyllis Trible elaborated on this perspective during a lecture entitled "Miriam, Moses, and a Mess," paper presented at the Annual Meeting of the Society of Biblical Literature, Boston, MA, November 1987.

primacy of law to the primacy of relationship.[15] In the judgment of men, these women break the law through their lies, concealments, and deceptions. The problem, however, is that they seem to do so under divine inspiration and for reasons of faith and justice.[16]

In light of this assessment, it is worth noting that in terms of contemporary parallels, many women committed to the struggle for human liberation might be more inclined to identify themselves as

15. It is interesting to note how these actions on the part of women are consistent with the contemporary psychological theory of Carol Gilligan regarding the moral development of women. See Carol Gilligan, *In a Different Voice: Psychological Theory and Women's Development* (Cambridge, MA: Harvard University Press, 1982) 24–63.

16. Augustine went to great lengths to sort out the morality of these women's actions. He argued that they are not rewarded by God for their deceit, but rather for their benevolence and their benignity of mind. He reached the conclusion that God honors the good that was done while overlooking the evil; see Augustine "To Consentius: Against Lying" 32-34 (translated in Philip Schaff, ed., *The Nicene and Post-Nicene Fathers* [14 vols.; trans. H. Browne; Grand Rapids, MI: Eerdmans, 1956] 3. 495–97). See also Bonaventure, *Commentaria in quatour libros sententiarum magistri Petri Lombardi* 3, dist. 38, q. 2; and John Duns Scotus, *Ordinatio* 3, dist. 38. Martin Luther treated the example of Rahab and also tried to resolve it by distinguishing three types of lies: the harmful lie, the obliging lie (of compassion), and the playful lie (of jest); see Martin Luther, *Lectures on Genesis* (translated in Jaroslav Pelikan, ed., *Luther's Works* [55 vols.; St. Louis: Concordia, 1968] 5. 40–41; see also *LW* 43. 456–57) on Gen 26:9. John Calvin, although scrupulous with regard to excusing sin in any of its manifestations, also expressed some uneasiness with regard to the Rahab dilemma, in terms of both her lying and her disloyalty to the nation. He concluded, however, that it was therefore "only the knowledge communicated to her by the mind of God which exempted her from fault, as having been set free from the common rule"; see John Calvin, *Commentaries on the Book of Joshua* 2.4 (trans. Henry Beveridge; Grand Rapids, MI: Eerdmans, 1949) 46. The moral dilemma posed by these examples of Luther and Calvin engages the moral arguments of John Duns Scotus regarding the contingent element governing the natural law on the last seven precepts of the Decalogue; see John Duns Scotus, *Opus Oxoniense* 3, dist. 37, q. un. According to Robert Prentice ("The Contingent Element Governing the Natural Law on the Last Seven Precepts of the Decalogue, According to Duns Scotus," *Antonianum* 42 [1967] 261–92), Scotus's reasoning can be summarized as follows: "God cannot dispense from the law of nature. But he seems to have dispensed from certain of the ten commandments. Therefore it would seem that not all precepts of the decalogue are strictly of the law of nature."

midwives of the future rather than as prostitutes of the Promised Land. Nevertheless, as the claims and clamors of ever growing numbers of prostitutes throughout Brazil receive a wider hearing, the latter narrative may provide a more adequate grounding than the former for foundational theological thinking about the relationship between women engaged in prostitution and those who profess a preferential option for the poor.

In accord with the methodological insights of feminist liberation hermeneutics and the practical grass roots approach of "see, judge, and act," I propose this biblical trajectory as a starting point for theological reflection on the church of liberation and the problem of prostitution. Prior to considering the contemporary significance of the Rahab narrative, however, a review of the interpretations it has received from Jewish and Christian commentators throughout the centuries is in order.

Liberation Hermeneutics, the Bible, and Women

During the past decade, the influence of North Atlantic feminist biblical scholarship on the reflection of Latin American liberation theologians is evidenced in numerous publications.[17] Likewise, insights from liberation theologies from around the world tend to be an ongoing point of reference for many feminist theologians. For those who, like myself, adhere with some qualifications to the method of Latin American liberation theologians, the foundational usage of the biblical text continues to prevail as a starting point for most theological reflection.

Within the Brazilian context the paradigmatic use of preferred biblical texts is quite common. Rarely, however, is the selection and use of the texts themselves brought under the scrutiny of the hermeneutic of suspicion. Although biblical resources for examining prostitution from a liberation perspective are admittedly limited, efforts to retrieve biblical texts about women in the interest of human liberation are not

17. A review of the citations and references used by Brazilian women theologians reflects the influence of North Atlantic feminist biblical scholars more so than feminist theologians and church historians. It is important to note that such influence tends to manifest itself through the reception and application of insights that resonate with the Brazilian reality.

free of problems. For example, in focusing on the Hebrew Scriptures, many interpreters attend to stories of matriarchs, queens, prophetesses, and benefactresses who are upheld within the tradition as exemplars. Overall, they depict women who possess a good measure of personal power, privilege, and prestige. These stories may speak to the lives of some women, but how do they speak to those whose lives are characterized by powerlessness or marginalization?

Although the stories of Hagar, Jael, and Gomer may be reflected upon in a few settings, the stories of Sarah, Miriam, Ruth, Deborah, Judith, and the mother of the Maccabees tend to predominate. Although in recent years considerable attention has been given to the study of sacred prostitution in the ancient Near Eastern context, the application of insights from such scholarship to the lives of common prostitutes of the twentieth century is limited.[18] For the most part, the study of temple prostitutes was—and continues to serve as—a means to specific end. One end is the substantiation of how women's loss of religious power and authority coincided with the replacement of goddesses with gods. The study of temple prostitutes also pursues another end, namely, an explanation of how women, in an effort to fulfill devotional vows, resorted to prostitution in order to finance their payments to temple officials.[19] With a few exceptions, biblical prostitutes of a more common sort tend not to attract the interest of biblical scholars or pastoral theologians.[20]

In drawing upon resources from the New Testament, a wide variety of women are a part of the life of Jesus and the early Christian communities. Attention, once again, tends to focus on women worthy of emulation, such as Mary, the mother of Jesus, Elizabeth, Mary and Martha, and other women disciples. Although Mary Magdalene is an

---

18. See Airton José da Silva, "De Canaã à Corinto: o sexo explorado," in Faculdade de Teologia Nossa Senhora da Assunção, eds., *A Prostituição em debate* (São Paulo: Paulinas, 1986) 42–58.

19. See Karel van der Toorn, "Female Prostitution in Payment of Vows in Ancient Israel," *JBL* 108 (1989) 193–205.

20. See Phyllis Bird, "The Harlot as Heroine: Narrative Art and Social Presupposition in Three Old Testament Texts," *Semeia* 46 (1989) 119–40. See also Josephine Ford, "*Pornē* or *Hetaira* or Adultress: The Social and Sociological Background of Rev 17–18" (unpublished working paper, 1990).

important character, her longstanding reputation in the Christian tradition as a repentant prostitute has been undone, at least in the minds
of biblical scholars.[21] The woman at the well (John 4:7–30) and the
woman caught in adultery (John 8:2–11), while considered disrepu-
table, are not prostitutes. The unnamed woman of the city (Luke 7:36–
50; Mark 14:3–9; Matt 26:6–13) might be a prostitute, but an effort
is made to deconstruct her identity as prostitute-disciple by subsum-
ing it into the broader category of a marginalized woman-disciple.[22]

Left to their own imaginative resources, there is little doubt that
grass roots audiences will persist in their adherence to traditional—
albeit inaccurate—images. In the world of feminist biblical scholarship, however, one of the few remaining prostitute stories approved
for retrieval is that of Rahab. Thus I retrieve her narrative in order to
draw attention to her as a biblical exemplar for attesting to the faith
and justice of the prostitute as prostitute. Keeping in mind the thinking of St. Jerome, who acclaimed Rahab's house as a model for the
church itself, the significance of her life merits consideration and
reflection.[23]

21. In recent years, some feminist biblical scholars and theologians have
devoted themselves to correcting the errors of hagiography that have no biblical foundations. Deconstructing the mythology of Mary Magdalene the repentant prostitute has been regarded as necessary to the process of recovering
the true Mary Magdalene. As disciple and leader, she represents a model for
women in the church. It is important that she be taken on her own terms and
that biblical texts are understood accurately. Although the significance of
such scholarship is evident, it does tend to reinforce the attitude that the
prostitute is somehow very different from other women. Considering Mary
Magdalene's seven demons, one may conclude that her background might not
have been all that different from the prostitute, even though she was exorcised
before becoming a prostitute and thus spared from the fate of women forced
into lives of prostitution as a consequence of social marginalization.

22. See E. Schüssler Fiorenza, *In Memory of Her*, 127–29. See also Kathleen
E. Corley, "Were Women Around Jesus Really Prostitutes? Women in the
Context of Greco-Roman Meals," in the *Society of Biblical Literature Annual
Seminar Papers* (Atlanta: Scholars Press, 1989) 487–521.

23. Jerome, "Homily 91: On the Exodus" (translated in *Homilies 60–96* [2
vols.; trans. Marie Liguori Ewald, I.H.M.; Fathers of the Church 57; Washington, DC: Catholic University of America, 1964] 2. 237).

The Rahab Narrative and Commentaries

After journeying for forty years, the Israelites were brought to the borders of the promised land (Deuteronomy 29–33). With the death of Moses and the raising up of Joshua, the process of the Exodus was brought to a climax (Deuteronomy 34; Joshua 1). As the tribes of Israel prepared to cross the river Jordan, they were unaware of the fact that their entrance into the promised land was contingent on the faith and deeds of the prostitute Rahab (Joshua 2). After the conquest of Jericho, the first action taken by the Israelites was the safeguarding of Rahab, her father's household, and all who belonged to her (Josh 6:25).[24] The texts read:

Chapter 2:[1]And Joshua the son of Nun sent two men secretly from Shittim as spies, saying, "Go, view the land, especially Jericho." And they went, and came into the house of the harlot whose name was Rahab, and lodged there. [2]And it was told the king of Jericho, "Behold, certain men of Israel have come here tonight to search out the land." [3]Then the king of Jericho sent to Rahab, saying, "Bring forth the men that have come to you, who entered your house; for they have come to search out all the land." [4]But the woman had taken the two men and hidden them; and she said, "True, men came to me, but I did not know where they came from; [5]and when the gate was to be closed, at dark, the men went out; where the men went I do not know; pursue them quickly for you will overtake them." [6]But she had brought them up to the roof, and hid them with the stalks of flax which she had laid in order on the roof. [7]So the men pursued after them on the way to the Jordan as far as the fords; and as soon as the pursuers had gone out the gate was shut.

[8]Before they lay down, she came to them on the roof, [9]and said to the men, "I know that the Lord has given you the land, and that the fear of you has fallen upon us, and that all the inhabitants of the earth melt away before you. [10]For we have heard how the Lord dried up the Red Sea before you when you came out of Egypt, and what you did to the two kings of the Ammorites that were beyond the Jordan, to Sihon and Og, whom you utterly destroyed. [11]And as soon as we heard it, our hearts melted, and there was no courage left in any man, because of

24. For a summary of the biblical data and rabbibical literature, *The Jewish Encyclopedia*, 10 (1905), "Rahab."

you; for the Lord your God is he who is God in heaven above and on earth beneath. [12]Now then, swear to me by the Lord that as I have dealt kindly with you, you also will deal kindly with my father's house, and give me a sure sign, [13]and save alive my father and mother, my brothers and sisters, and all who belong to them, and deliver our lives from death." [14]And the men said to her, "Our life for yours! If you do not tell this business of ours, then we will deal kindly and faithfully with you when the Lord gives us the land."

[15]Then she let them down by a rope through the window, for her house was built into the city wall, so that she dwelt in the wall. [16]And she said to them, "Go into the hills, lest the pursuers meet you; and hide yourselves there three days, until the pursuers have returned; then afterward you may go your way." [17]The men said to her, "We will be guiltless with respect to this oath of yours which you have made us swear. [18]Behold, when we come into the land, you shall bind this scarlet cord in the window through which you let us down; and you shall gather into your house your father and mother, your brothers and all your father's household. [19]If any one goes out of the doors of your house onto the street, his blood shall be upon his head, and we shall be guiltless; but if a hand is laid upon any one who is with you in the house, his blood shall be on our head. [20]But if you tell this business of ours, then we shall be guiltless with respect to the oath which you have made us swear." [21]And she said, "According to your words, so be it." Then she sent them away, and they departed; and she bound the scarlet cord in the window.

Chapter 6:[22]And Joshua said to the two men who had spied out the land, "Go into the harlot's house, and bring out from it the woman, and all who belong to her, as you swore to her." [23]So the young men who had been spies went in, and brought out Rahab, and her father and mother and all who belonged to her; and they brought out all her kindred, and set them outside the camp of Israel. [24]And they burned the city with fire, and all within it; only the silver and gold, and the vessels of bronze and of iron, they put into the treasury of the house of the Lord. [25]But Rahab the harlot, and her father's household, and all who belonged to her, Joshua saved alive; and she dwelt in Israel to this day, because she hid the messengers whom Joshua sent to spy out Jericho.

In order to explore how this narrative might be interpreted at the close of the twentieth century, we must review how it has been understood by Jewish and Christian interpreters in past centuries.[25] The rabbinic tradition provides insights into the identity of Rahab. According to Rabbi Eleazar, Rahab was ten years old when she left Egypt. For forty years she was a harlot in the desert and at the age of fifty, she became a proselyte.[26] In different periods, efforts were made to identify Rahab as an innkeeper rather than a harlot; these interpretations, however, were unpersuasive.[27] According to tradition, Rahab's beauty was unsurpassed, and the mention of her name gave rise to sexual desire.[28] It is said that, as a result of her numerous liaisons, Rahab heard about the drying up of the Red Sea and about the escapades of the Israelites. Since there was "no prince or ruler that had not possessed Rahab the harlot," she knew from her own experience of the sexual impotence of those who had lost their virility as a consequence of their encounters with the Israelites.[29] She is included along with Noah's wife, Sarah, Rebekah, Leah, Rachel, Miriam, Hannah, Naomi, Ruth, and Esther as a woman of valor.[30] In defense of the integrity of her faith and the bestowal of God's favor, it is noted that the "Divine Spirit rested upon her, before Israel entered the land. For how did she know that the pursuers would return in three days? Hence we must say that the Divine Spirit of prophecy rested upon her."[31] Among her descendants were seven kings, along with numerous priests and prophets, including Jeremiah, Baruch, Ezekiel, and Huldah.[32] According to Jewish tradition she married Joshua.[33]

25. See James L. Kugel and Rowan A. Greer, *Early Biblical Interpretation* (Philadelphia: Westminster, 1986).

26. *b. Zebaḥim*, 116a–b.

27. See Josephus *Ant.* 5.1.2; *The Jewish Encyclopedia*, s.v. "Rahab."

28. *b. Meg.* 15a.

29. *b. Zebaḥim*, 116a–b (translated in Isidore Epstein, ed., *Babylonian Talmud* (34 vols.; trans. H. Freedman; London: Soncino, 1948) 27. 575.

30. See Louis Ginzberg, *The Legends of the Jews*, vol. 5: *From the Creation to Exodus* (Philadelphia: Jewish Publication Society, 1913) 258.

31. *Midrash Rabbah*, vol. 8: *Ruth* 2.1 (eds. H. Freeman and Maurice Simon; trans. L. Rabinowitz; 3d ed.; New York: Soncino, 1983) 24–25.

32. Ibid., 25. See also Louis Ginzberg, *The Legend of the Jews*, vol. 4: *From Joshua to Esther* (Philadelphia: Jewish Publication Society, 1913) 171 n. 12.

33. See *The Jewish Encyclopedia*, s.v. "Rahab"; and Ginzberg, *From Joshua to Esther*, 5.

Rahab is mentioned three times in the New Testament: in the genealogy of Jesus (Matt 1:4),[34] the Letter to the Hebrews (Heb 11:31),
and the Letter of James (Jas 2:25). The first citation in Matthew is a
source of contention, for the Rachab of whom the author spoke, if the
mother of Boaz, could not be the Rahab of the conquest.[35] Scholarly
opinion, however, favors the view that the Rachab mentioned in Matthew is indeed the Rahab of Jericho. In effect, her theological significance takes precedence over historical accuracy. The two passages
from Hebrews and James highlight the faith and deeds of Rahab.
Inasmuch as her actions are paralleled with those of patriarchs and
matriarchs—and most pointedly, with Abraham—she should hardly
be considered incidental to the tradition.

Among the church fathers, Clement of Rome noted Rahab's faith
and hospitality as the reason for her salvation. It is Clement who
made the claim that Rahab possessed not only the gift of faith, but
also that of prophecy, inasmuch as the scarlet cloth hung from her
window makes "clear to all that through the Blood of the Lord all
those that believe and hope in God will be redeemed."[36] In Jerome's
thinking, Rahab, who saves her household, prefigures the church.[37] In
disclosing his mystical understanding of the passage, Jerome identified the two Hebrew spies as Peter and Paul. He explained,

34. For a thoughtful analysis of Rahab's inclusion in the genealogy of
Jesus, see Jane Schaberg, *The Illegitimacy of Jesus: A Feminist Theological
Interpretation of the Infancy Narratives* (New York: Crossroad, 1990) 20–22,
25.

35. See J. D. Quinn, "Is Rachab in Mt 1,5 Rahab of Jericho?" *Biblica* 62
(1982) 225–228; R. E. Brown, "Rachab in Mt 1,5 Is Rahab of Jericho," *Biblica*
63 (1982) 79–80; Yair Zakowitch, "Rahab als Mutter des Boas in der Jesus-
Genealogie (Matth.I.5)," *NovT* 17 (1975) 1–5; A. T. Hanson, "Rahab the Harlot
in Early Christian Tradition," *JSNT* 1 (1978) 54; and Esther Fuchs, "Who Is
Hiding The Truth?" in Adela Yarbro Collins, ed., *Feminist Perspectives on
Biblical Scholarship* (Chico, CA: Scholars Press, 1985) 137–44; cited in
Schaberg, *The Illegitimacy of Jesus*, 208–9 nn. 27, 28, 32, 38.

36. See Clement of Rome *Epistle to the Corinthians* 12 (translated in *The
Epistles of St. Clement of Rome and St. Ignatius of Antioch* [trans. James A.
Kleist; Westminster, MD: Newman Bookshop, 1946] 18).

37. See Jerome "Letter 22," 38.6 (translated in *The Letters of St. Jerome*,
book 1: *Letters 1–22* [trans. Charles C. Mierow; Ancient Christian Writers 33;
New York: Newman, 1963] 175); and "Homily 91: On the Exodus," 237.

> Jericho seeks to kill them; the harlot takes them in, meaning of
> course, the Church gathered together of the Gentiles. She be-
> lieves in Jesus; and those whom Jericho is determined to de-
> stroy, she protects in safety on her own roof. She harbors them
> on the roof—in the loftiness of her faith.[38]

Examining the anagogic significance of Rahab's name, Jerome prof-
fered two interpretations: "broad space" or "pride." He saw in Rahab
an example of those who were "at one time on the broad road to
perdition" but who now have "mounted upward into the memory of
God." Because they turn to him in hope, God is mindful of those who
know him.[39] Recalling how the church—like Rahab, if she wills it—
becomes a virgin, Jerome goes on to say, "Understand, therefore, that
she who was a prostitute conceives of God and is in labor and brings
forth the Savior. . . and he who has established her is the Most High
Lord."[40]

In Augustine's reflections on Psalm 87, a psalm that he believed to
be composed out of love for the City of God, Rahab is understood to
represent the church of the Gentiles. Recalling the passage from
Matthew, "Truly, I say to you, the tax collectors and the harlots go
into the kingdom of God before you" (Matt 21:31), Augustine emphasized that "they go before because they do violence: they push their
way by faith, and to faith a way is made, nor can any resist, since
they who are violent take it by force" (Matt 11:12).[41] Once again, the
faith of Rahab is emphasized and the memory of the harlot of Jericho
prevails not only as a model for Christians, but for the church itself.[42]

---

38. Jerome, "Homily 18: On Psalm 86 (87)" (translated in *The Homilies
Saint Jerome*: vol. 1: *Homilies 1–59* [trans. Marie Liguori Ewald; Fathers of
the Church 48; Washington, DC: Catholic University of America Press, 1964]
138).

39. Ibid., 140.

40. Ibid., 144–45.

41. See Augustine "Psalm 87" 6 (translated in C. Marriot, ed., *Expositions
on the Book of Psalms*, vol. 4: *Psalm 76–110* [Library of the Fathers II; London: Rivington, 1850] 219–20).

42. Since the time of the Reformation, identification of the church as harlot
has taken on a pejorative connotation, since the sins—rather than the faith—
of the church of Rome distinguished her from the church of Christ. See Martin
Luther, "Psalm 87" 4 (translated by Herbert J. A. Bouman in Hilton C. Oswald,

In addition to religious and theological interpretations, modern interpreters provide contemporary readers with a wide range of historical and literary insights which broaden the understanding of the narrative.[43] As Windisch notes, examples of other stories attesting to the actions of heroic prostitutes can be found in Greek and Roman classical literature.[44] This could—but need not—mean that etiological material is without historical foundation.[45] Considering the location of the narrative in the book of Joshua, how should we interpret the description of a pagan prostitute as among the first to articulate the themes that were a preamble to the constitution of the ancient Israel?[46] How should we understand the text's description of a harlot as

---

ed., *First Psalm Lectures*, vol. 11: *Luther's Works* [St. Louis: Concordia, 1976] 177; see also *LW* 4. 25, 26).

43. See Michael David Coogan, "Joshua," in Raymond E. Brown et al., eds., *The New Jerome Biblical Commentary* (Englewood Cliffs, NJ: Prentice Hall, 1990) 110–20. See also, Robert G. Boling, *Joshua* (Anchor Bible 6; Garden City, NY: Doubleday, 1982); John Bright, *Joshua* (The Interpreter's Bible 2; New York: Abingdon, 1953); G. A. Cooke, *The Book of Joshua* (Cambridge Bible for Schools and Colleges; Cambridge: Cambridge University Press, 1918); Ronald E. Clements and Matthew Black, eds., *Joshua, Judges and Ruth, The New Century Bible Commentary* (Grand Rapids, MI: Eerdmans, 1986); J. Maxwell Miller and Gene M. Tucker, *The Book of Joshua* (Cambridge Biblical Commentary; New York: Cambridge University Press, 1974); J. Moran, "The Repose of Rahab's Israelite Guests," in Giorgio Buccellati, ed., *Studi sull' Oriénte e la Bibbia* (Genoa: Studio e Vita, 1967) 272–84; Murray L. Newman, "Rahab and the Conquest," in James T. Butler et al., eds., *Understanding the Word: Essays in Honor of Bernard W. Anderson* (JSOTSup 32; Sheffield: JSOT Press, 1985) 167–85; Martin Noth, *Das Buch Josua* (2d ed.; Tübingen: Mohr, 1953); J. Alberto Soggin, *Joshua: A Commentary, Old Testament Library* (Philadelphia: Westminster, 1972); and Manfred Weippert, *The Settlement of the Israelite Tribes in Palestine: A Critical Survey of Recent Scholarly Debate* (Naperville, IL: Allenson, 1971).

44. See Hans Windisch, "Zur Rahabgeschichte (Zwei Parallelen aus der klassichn Literatur)," *ZAW* 37 (1917–18) 188–98; as cited by Phyllis A. Bird, "The Harlot as Heroine: Narrative Art and Social Presupposition in Three Old Testament Texts," *Semeia* 46 (1989) 136 n. 36.

45. See Boling and Wright, *Joshua*, 152. For further discussion of this debate, see Weippert, *The Settlement of the Israelite Tribes*; and Burke O. Long, *The Problem of Etiological Narrative in the Old Testament* (Berlin: Topelmann, 1968).

46. Ibid., 146.

the first to use the word *ḥesed*, with its multiple English meanings, which include covenant, loyalty, mercy, justice, loving kindness, and responsible caring?[47]

The issues of covenant making and the fulfillment of promises are central to the narrative. They are further highlighted in Rahab's concern for the welfare of her family, despite her identity as a prostitute.[48] For Rahab, obedience to God became the highest loyalty and "contravene[d] all other attachments."[49] As Bright notes, "in the long run the highest loyalty includes all other loyalties and does not contradict them."[50] Rahab's designation as *ʾisha zonah* ("harlot" or "secular prostitute"), rather than *qedeshah* ("sacred prostitute," devotee of a fertility cult) is important to note.[51] Rahab was astute. As she found her own countrymen to be without spirit and lacking in courage (Josh 2:11), she recognized in her contacts with them the absence of *ruaḥ*, the loss of the invasive divine influence.[52] Without a doubt, her story engages not only literary and historical imaginations,[53] but moral imaginations as well.

Recovering the Memory of Rahab

The incorporation of Rahab into the Christian tradition as an exemplar of faith (Heb 11:31) and justice (Jas 2:25) is straightforward. It

47. Ibid., 147. See also Katherine Dobb Sakenfeld, *The Meaning of Ḥesed in the Hebrew Bible* (Harvard Semitic Monographs 17; Missoula, MT: Scholars Press for the Harvard Semitic Museum, 1978); and Dennis J. McCarthy, "The Theology of Leadership in Joshua 1–9," *Biblica* 52 (1971) 165–75.

48. See Bright, *Joshua*, 562, 563.

49. Ibid.

50. Ibid.

51. For a brief discussion on the distinction between these terms, see Gray, *Joshua, Judges and Ruth*, 64. Although some scholars, such as Hölscher and Mowinckel, would question whether a clear differentiation between the two types of prostitutes can be made, others, such as Noth and Gray, assert that in the case of Rahab, sufficient evidence exists to support the claim.

52. Ibid., 65.

53. Gene M. Tucker, "The Rahab Saga (Joshua 2): Some Form-Critical and Traditio-Historical Observations," in James M. Efird, ed., *The Use of the Old Testament in the New and Other Essays: Studies in Honor of William Franklin Stinespring* (Durham, NC: Duke University Press, 1972) 76.

remains puzzling, however, why so few individuals or communities concerned about issues of faith and justice have retrieved her story. Efforts to whitewash her character and preserve ecclesial amnesia do provide a few clues. At no point in the Roman Catholic liturgical year does the lectionary of readings contain the passages from Joshua, Hebrews, or James concerning Rahab. Except for the reading of Matthew's genealogy (Matt 1:5), the memory of Rahab is relegated to the realm of subjugated knowledge.

Nonetheless according to the biblical tradition, unappealed to as it may be, it is apparent that what Rahab did by faith, she also did for faith.[54] Her ethics, although scrutinized by many, appeal to a higher law than those to which men and women conform themselves. Her conscience and sense of personal agency are informed by experience and the exercise of inner authority. She calls into question static notions about righteousness[55] and, ironically, is raised up alongside Abraham as a model of justification by faith *and* by works. Still, Rahab's identity as a harlot seems to be an obstacle for those who control knowledge and who, in this current age, find it to be in the best interest of the church *not* to include her as an exemplar of faith and justice.

Why, we may ask, is it so important that knowledge about Rahab be subjugated, suppressed, and erased? Perhaps it is because a prostitute, rather than a penitent, upholds faith and justice. Rahab was a harlot when she made her declaration of faith, and she was a harlot when she took action on behalf of the Israelites. Her harlotry does not seem to be an issue for the God who includes her as a partner in bringing about the divine plan. No amount of nuancing or glossing can change that fact.

Conclusion

In Brazil today, countless daughters of Rahab are committed in faith to the works of justice, not as penitents, but as prostitutes. To

54. James Moffat, *The International Critical Commentary*, vol. 40: *Epistle to the Hebrews* (Edinburgh: T. & T. Clark, 1957) 184.

55. See Joseph A. Fitzmyer, "Responses," in John Henry Paul Reumann, *Righteousness in the New Testament: Justification in the United States Lutheran-Roman Catholic Dialogue* (Philadelphia: Fortress, 1982) 222–23.

draw parallels between their lives and the harlot of Jericho is not my task, however, but theirs. My task as I see it is to recall Rahab and to remember her story as a means for engaging and stretching the moral imaginations of theologians and ministers who have yet to take seriously the ecclesial and pastoral challenges that prostitutes, be they baptized or not, present to the world church of the twenty-first century.

Guided by the insights of the Rahab narrative, I have chosen to provide some perspectives on the social history of prostitution in Brazil as a backdrop to my study of the evolution of the Pastoral da Mulher Marginalizada ("Pastoral Project for Marginalized Women"). Through this study, I intend to examine the challenges that the church of liberation faces as it comes to terms with its own limitations for including in the preferential option for the poor and the oppressed an ongoing pastoral commitment to women engaged in prostitution. On the basis of my research, I identify the need for a theology of incarnate presence. I conclude with a brief reflection on the significance of this study for understanding challenges that women in prostitution currently present to the church and its commitment to promote the New Evangelization.[56]

56. The term "New Evangelization" has its origins in Vatican and Latin American documents dating from the late 1980s when the Latin American Episcopal Conference, the Conference of Latin American Religious, and Pope John Paul II began to anticipate the five hundreth anniversary of evangelization in the Americas. Although the term has been defined and discussed in diverse ways and in a variety of circumstances, it is best known in Latin America and the Caribbean for its use as the designated theme for the Latin American Episcopal Conference held in Santo Domingo, Dominican Republic, in October 1992. Further information on this topic is provided in chapter 6 (p. 170 n. 4).

2

Prostitution in Brazil
Historical Perspectives

Foolish men who accuse
women unreasonably,
you blame yet never see
you cause what you abuse.

You crawl before her, sad,
begging for a quick cure;
why ask her to be pure
when you have made her bad?

You combat her resistance
and then with gravity,
you call frivolity
the fruit of your intent. . . .

Who is at fault in all
this errant passion? She
who falls for his pleas, or he
who pleads for her to fall?

Whose guilt is greater in
this raw erotic play?
The girl who sins for pay
or man who pays for sin?[1]
Sor Juana Inés de la Cruz

---

1. Sor Juana Inés de la Cruz, "She Proves the Inconsistency of the Desires and Criticisms of Men Who Accuse Women of What They Themselves Cause," in Willis and Aliki Barnstone, trans., and eds., *A Book of Women Poets from Antiquity to Now* (New York: Schocken, 1980) 264–66. As a young girl, Inés Ramirez de Asbaje y Santillana (1651–1695) was raised in the Mexican town of Panoayan. In her youth, she entered the convent of San Jerónimo in Mexico City. The creative genius and intellectual power of her plays and poetry were renowned in Spanish and Portuguese regions. As a consequence of ecclesiastical politics and intrigue, she and her works were forgotten for more than two hundred years following her death. Given her knowledge and writings in the disciplines of philosophy and theology, she is noted today as the first woman theologian of the Americas. See Octavio Paz, *Sor Juana or, The Traps of Faith* (trans. Margaret Sayers Peden; Cambridge, MA: Harvard University Press, 1988).

Inasmuch as this study was undertaken during the year of the quincentenary of the voyage of Columbus, its findings serve to illustrate how the so-called discovery of the Americas was not only a turning point in the general history of the world, but also in the history of Christianity, the history of women, and, most particularly, the history of prostitution.

In this chapter the social history of prostitution in Brazil will be examined in light of the country's political and ecclesiastical history. The analysis will also take into account relevant facts pertaining to the history of women within Brazilian society. The aim of the chapter is to provide some perspective on the complex historical factors that have influenced the contemporary reality of female prostitution in Brazilian society.

There are certain limitations inherent in an overview that spans five centuries. Nevertheless, for a reader unfamiliar with the history of Brazil, the following survey provides some essential historical background. It helps to create a better understanding of both the contemporary Brazilian reality and the historical factors that contribute to the fact that growing numbers of women and girls in the largest Roman Catholic country are or have been involved in some form of female prostitution.[2] Furthermore, this chapter will elucidate why the church is constrained in its efforts to promote faith, justice, and human liberation among marginalized women.

Prostitution in modern Brazil traces its social origins to the early modern period, shortly after the arrival of the first Iberian explorers in 1500. It is difficult to ascertain the existence, form, or degree of prostitution that existed prior to this time among the indigenous peoples of the region.[3]

2. This estimate is based on composite figures derived from various reports of the World Health Organization, UNICEF, and the Centro de Estatística Religiosa e Investigações Sociais ("Center for Religious Statistics and Social Studies") issued during the 1970s and 1980s.

3. To the extent that European understandings of prostitution are informed by the assumptions and biases of Western culture, it is difficult to establish in any conclusive manner evidence of the presence or absence of prostitution among various Amerindian civilizations. If, however, one is persuaded by global theories of prostitution, it is not unreasonable to assume that some

The history of prostitution in Brazil is enmeshed in a larger historical network of relationships among peoples, powers, and principalities. Essentially, it is a history within a history, or rather, within numerous histories. Without attempting to be comprehensive, the following overview highlights certain political, social, cultural, economic, and religious points of reference that provide a contextual and theoretical framework for understanding the evolution of prostitution in Brazil.

In this chapter the evolution and diversification of female prostitution will be studied in conjunction with the major periods of Brazilian political history from 1500 to the present. I shall describe some of the major characters, events, and movements of these periods in order to demonstrate their relevance for the study of prostitution in Brazilian society.

The Settlement and the Early Colony (1500–1580)

History credits a Spanish explorer and companion to Columbus, Vicente Yanez Pinsón, as being the first European to come upon the eastern coast of South America on 26 January 1500.[4] Pedro Alvares de Cabral, however, is recorded as claiming the land for the cross of Christ and the crown of Portugal on Easter Sunday, 26 April 1500, two days after his arrival.[5] Assisted by the Franciscan friar Henrique

---

forms of prostitution undoubtedly existed among certain tribes. It is also within the bounds of reason to conclude that these forms underwent some measure of change and modification as a result of European invasions and the subsequent colonization of South America. See Havelock Ellis, "Sex in Relation to Society," in idem, *The Psychology of Sex* (4 vols.: New York: Random House, 1936) 2. 224–28; and J. D. Unwin, *Sex and Culture* (London: Oxford University Press, 1934).

4. On 4 May 1493, a bull of Pope Alexander VI established a dividing line between Portuguese and Spanish possessions. In 1494, this line was renegotiated. As a result of the Treaty of Tordesillas, Spain was denied any claims to the eastern portion of South America.

5. For further information on the church and the history of Brazil in the colonial period, see Riolando Azzi, *A Cristandade colonial: um projeto autoritário* (São Paulo: Paulinas, 1987); *The Catholic Encyclopedia*, s.v. "Brazil"; Eduardo Hoornaert, *Formação do Catolicismo brasileiro 1550–1800: ensaio de interpretação a partir dos oprimidos* (Petrópolis: Vozes, 1974); Boaventura

de Coimbra, Cabral saw to the christening of the *Terra da Vera Cruz* ("land of the true cross").[6] Portugal's claim to territories in the so-called New World held great promise for the future of the empire. In an era of exploration and expansion, the prospects of colonial ventures in lands across the sea engaged the royal imagination. The decision to extend Portuguese interests beyond maritime commerce and trade gave rise to new hopes and aspirations.

This age, however, was marked not only by a promising dream, but by a terrifying nightmare as well. The appearance and spread of a virulent and seemingly new form of venereal disease sent waves of fear and panic throughout Europe.[7]

As syphilis ravaged various regions of the European continent, the restriction of prostitution and the prosecution of prostitutes increased exponentially. In 1521, Dom Manuel I, the king of Portugal (1495–1521), banished prostitutes from the city of Lisbon and its confines.[8] Although many factors contributed to the action taken by the king, preoccupation with the dread disease and its consequences was promi-

---

Kloppenburg, "Brazil," in William J. McDonald et al., eds., *The New Catholic Encyclopedia* (New York: McGraw-Hill, 1967); Oscar de Figueiredo Lustosa, *A presença da Igreja no Brasil* (São Paulo: Giro, 1977); J. Lloyd Mecham, *Church and State in Latin America* (rev. ed.; Chapel Hill, NC: University of North Carolina Press, 1966); and Sônia A. Siqueira, *A Inquisição portuguesa e a sociedade colonial* (São Paulo: Ática, 1978).

6. In subsequent years, the title was changed from *Vera Cruz* to *Santa Cruz* ("Holy Cross").

7. To this day, longstanding debates about the origin of syphilis, which is dated to 1493, have resulted in controversy concerning whether it was imported to Europe, thereby attributing its source to the Americas. An alternative theory suggests that it was introduced into Spain and Portugal by slaves brought back from Africa during the expeditions of Prince Henry of Portugal. According to this theory, the disease was then brought to the New World by the Portuguese explorers themselves and/or by the African slaves they transported. See Alfred W. Crosby, Jr., *The Columbia Exchange: Biological and Cultural Consequences of 1492* (Westport, CT: Greenwood, 1972).

8. According to Guido Fonseca (*História da prostituição em São Paulo* [São Paulo: Editora Resenha Universitária, 1982] 25) the decree is dated 8 July 1521. For further information regarding the influence of such action on the colony, Fonseca makes reference to the work of Fernando Mendes de Almeida, "O folclore nas ordenações do Reino," *Revista do Arquivo Municipal de São Paulo*, 56, n.d., 101.

nent among these.[9] If prostitutes were not the cause of the epidemic, they were certainly to be counted among its carriers;[10] as such, they were subjected to harassment and marginalization. They were scapegoated, ostracized, and punished. Not only were Portuguese brothels closed, but financial penalties were leveled against men caught with women of ill repute.[11] Historically, the mandatory closing of brothels has failed to suppress prostitution. In fact, it often has resulted in the exacerbation of more precarious and clandestine forms of prostitution. Such was the case in Portugal. Despite sanctions, the practice of prostitution continued, as did the spread of venereal disease. As prostitutes bore the blame, Portuguese sailors and settlers continued to spread the disease at home and abroad.[12]

Portugal's quests for wealth and land extended from the Far East to the coast of Africa and South America. Brazil held a particular attraction for the Crown. As a Portuguese settlement, it promised to be a land of abundant resources. The establishment of the settlement, however, was dependent upon the ability of the Portuguese to secure and develop the region. Dom Manuel's heir to the throne, Dom João III (1521–1557), proved to be as fascinated by the lucrative prospects of colonization as his father. To ensure the success of the Brazilian settlement effort, Dom João provided prominent Portuguese men with incentives to take part in the establishment of the colony. At his discretion, selected individuals were apportioned large tracts of land,

9. For a more complete discussion of the contributing factors, see Leah L. Otis, *Prostitution in Medieval Society: The History of an Urban Institution in Languedoc* (Chicago: University of Chicago Press, 1985) 40–50.

10. For example, in 1536 the Imperial Diet of the Holy Roman Empire prohibited prostitution. See Bullough and Bullough, *Women and Prostitution*, 152–53; and Richard Waldegg and Werner Heinz, *Geschichte und Wesen der Prostitution* (Stuttgart: Welspiegel, 1956) 95–97.

11. See Bullough and Bullough, *Women and Prostitution*, 153–56.

12. The spread of syphilis to various regions of the world has been attributed by some historians to Portuguese sailors, settlers, and merchants. Medical accounts of syphilis appear in countries such as China, Japan, and India only after the arrival of the Portuguese. The Japanese term for syphilis, *mambakassam*, literally means "disease of the Portuguese." For a detailed description of the effects of syphilis in Brazil, see Gilberto Freyre, *The Masters and the Slaves* (trans. Samuel Putnam; 2d ed.; New York: Knopf, 1956) 71–75.

given feudal power over their assigned holdings, and encouraged to expand their appropriation of territory as far inland from the sea coast as they desired.[13]

Over time, the coastal settlements of Brazil gradually increased in number and size. The Portuguese population was comprised largely of men, many of whom were unmarried. The scarcity of Portuguese women had numerous implications for life in the early years of the colony.[14] The absence of Portuguese wives, concubines, mistresses, and common prostitutes added to the rigor of settlement existence. Under such conditions, the settlers were left to their own designs; unfettered as they were from the legal, medical, and religious preoccupations of Portugal, the early settlers had few inhibitions about engaging in sexual relations with indigenous women.[15] As far as venereal pleasures were concerned, Brazil became renowned throughout the world of Portuguese seafarers as a land without obstacles or restraints.[16]

Although little is known about prostitution during the settlement of Brazil, the absence of direct references to prostitution in documents dating from the early colonial period must be viewed with some measure of circumspection. In an atmosphere of generally licentious behavior, it seems reasonable to assume that European chroniclers, particularly those obsessed with the sin of fornication, found no reason to distinguish the differences between rape, free love, and the exchange of material goods for sexual favors. Descriptions provided

13. *The Catholic Encyclopedia*, s.v. "Brazil."

14. See Capistrano de Abreu, *Capítulos de história colonial (1500–1800)* (6th ed.; Rio de Janeiro: Civilização Brasileira, 1976) 28–29.

15. See Ronaldo Vainfas, *Trópico dos pecados: moral, sexualidade e Inquisição no Brasil* (Rio de Janeiro: Campus, 1989) 49–51. Descriptions of such behaviors can be found in letters written by the Jesuit missionary José de Anchieta, who blamed Indian women for contributing to the promiscuous behaviors of the settlers inasmuch as the women were naked, encouraged the advances of the foreigners, freely gave themselves over to them, and apparently derived great pleasure from attracting the attention of Christian men. See José de Anchieta to Ignatius of Loyola, July 1554, in Serafim Leite, ed., *Monumenta Brasiliae* (5 vols.; Rome: Monumenta Historica Societatis Iesu, 1957) 2. 77.

16. Fonseca, *História da prostituição*, 15.

by their European critics and observers indicate that the sexual activities of the early colonists ranged from sordid to torrid.[17] Over time,
the forebears' legacy became the norm against which the virility and
temerity of subsequent generations of Brazilian men were measured.
As noted in the classic work of Gilberto Freyre, *Casa Grande e
Senzala*, Brazil was literally "syphilized before it was civilized."[18]

In the late 1540s, the Portuguese captains endeavored to maintain
and defend their territorial holdings against Indian resistance and the
calculated advances of Spain and France. They decided to consolidate
their forces by giving all authority over to a governor general appointed by the king. Indigenous tribes continued their struggle to
oppose the invasion of their lands and the decimation of their peoples
by Portuguese disease and self-interest.[19] The Spanish had little regard for Portugal's colonial territorial claims and much less for the
papal authority invoked to guarantee those claims. The French were
simply intent on gaining a foothold in the region by any means possible.

In 1549, the king appointed Thomé de Sousa as governor of the
colony. When Bahia was established as the capital, the first foundation of Jesuits arrived in Brazil, headed by Manuel da Nóbrega (1517–
1570). With the arrival of the Jesuits, the governor general formally
confirmed the Crown's commitment to evangelization in the colony[20]
and reaffirmed the significance of the *patronato real* ("royal patronage").[21] Under the system of royal patronage, the church and its min-

17. Ibid., 12. The observations include those of priests, sailors, travellers,
and chroniclers.

18. See Freyre, *The Masters and the Slaves*, 71.

19. At the time of colonization, estimates on the numbers of indigenous
peoples living within the confines of the region known as Brazil range between three and five million. The population in the 1990s is estimated to be
approximately two hundred thousand.

20. Franciscan friars from Portugal had been present in some of the early
fort settlements. Spanish friars were actively engaged in missionary activity
among Indians in the territory bordering on Paraguay. In the absence of a
centralized colonial government, however, the endeavors of the Franciscans
were scattered and uncoordinated.

21. *Patronato real* referred to the right of temporal lords to exercise power
in the naming of ecclesiastical authorities. In a broader sense, this also in-

isters, in exchange for privileged status and protection, became subject to the Crown in all things. In effect, the king of Portugal exercised ecclesiastical power as well as civil authority.[22]

In the effort to ensure absolute control over the expansion and
development of the territory, colonial authorities representing the interests of the king elaborated various strategies for increasing produc-
tivity and populating the region. As the colony grew, so did the need
for a larger labor force. Over the years, three strategies for addressing
this need were proposed and implemented. These included the enslavement of indigenous peoples, the large scale transport of African
slaves,[23] and the forced relocation from Portugal to Brazil of various
sorts of criminals, vagrants, and undesirables. These strategies had
serious implications for everyone concerned, perhaps especially for
women, whether captive Indians, enslaved Africans, or exiled Portuguese. Like their male counterparts, these women were forced to work
as servants and laborers, some in colonial settlements and others on
colonial plantations. Unlike most of their male counterparts, however,
they also were expected to supply the venereal demands of their cap-
tors, their masters, their employers, and the men with whom they
shared their lot in life. As sexual captives, sexual slaves, sexual

---

cluded ecclesiastical honors, responsibilities, and duties. Knowledge of this
system is essential for understanding the ways in which the role and function
of the church were prescribed in accord with the vested interests of the Crown
and the colony. For further information on the origins and evolution of patronage, see Mecham, *Church and State*, 1–44.

22. Over the course of many years, popes conferred upon the kings of
Portugal the right of administrative authority over ecclesiastical affairs. In
part, this was to ensure that the faith would be defended and promoted throughout
the Portuguese domain. Like his father, Dom João III was named by the pope
to be the high master of the Order of Christ, the successor of the Order of
Templars. He and those who would follow him were entrusted by the Roman
pontiff not only with the establishment of the church in the colony, but with
its financial support and governance as well. See Azzi, *A Cristandade colonial*, 15–24.

23. Between 1538 and 1840, it is estimated that more than five million
Africans were brought to Brazil as slaves. See Robert Edgar Conrad, *World
of Sorrow: The African Slave Trade to Brazil* (Baton Rouge: Louisiana State
University Press, 1986) 34.

workers, and sexual companions, they were pressed into rendering further service to the colony as the designated labor force for increasing its population.

In a world of conquest marked by the unrestrained pursuit of wealth and power, the end justified every means. Violence and brutality went unquestioned, as did the idea that captives, slaves, and exiles were expendable. Within this context, the early Jesuits assumed responsibility for the evangelization and moral reform of the colony as well as the alleviation of the enslavement and exploitation of the Indians. The goal they set for themselves, however, was difficult to achieve. For the most part, their only recourse was not the advancement of *alternatives to slavery*, but rather the use of *alternative slaves*. In large measure, their efforts to defend and protect indigenous peoples from the abuse and exploitation of Portuguese colonists were contingent upon two major substitutions for Indian captives: African slaves and Portuguese women, whether exiles or emigrants.

In the case of the first group, the toleration of African slavery was rationalized as the only means by which the Jesuits could safeguard the lives of the Indians as well as the Jesuit mission in the colony.[24] To protest all forms of enslavement would not only call into question the teachings of the church,[25] but would also incur the wrath of the Crown and provoke certain expulsion from the colony. This scenario would leave the Indians without defense and the Africans subject to even more brutality at the hands of slave holders. In the minds of the Jesuits, such an option was unacceptable. Concerted efforts to console and minister to African slaves in the midst of their captivity were

24. In this period, it is difficult to ascertain the extent to which the enslavement of Africans was a question of conscience. See the correspondence from Manuel da Nóbrega to Miguel Torres, 2 September 1557, in Leite, *Monumenta Brasiliae*, 2. 411; see also Manuel da Nóbrega to Diego Laynes, 12 June 1561, in Leite, *Monumenta Brasiliae*, 3. 360–61.

25. Debates about the distinctions between the licit and illicit nature of slavery were continuations of patristic and scholastic arguments. One line of reasoning proposed that unlike the Indians, Africans were descendants of Ham and as such were destined to be slaves as a punishment for sin and judged to be inferior. For further information, see José Geraldo Vidigal de Carvalho, *A Igreja e a escravidão: uma análise documental* (Rio de Janeiro: Presença, 1985) 17–52.

deemed to be the only feasible alternatives available to the members of the Society of Jesus.[26]

In the case of the second substitution, Jesuits recommended the importation of marginalized women from Portugal for a number of reasons.[27] For Portuguese prostitutes and their daughters, the colony provided a second chance in life[28] and the possibility of securing a Christian marriage.[29] For the colonists, the presence of Portuguese women insured access to a more familiar female population. With regard to Indian women and girls, the importation of prostitutes from Portugal was advanced as one means for alleviating indigenous sexual slavery, exploitation, and violation.[30] In effect, the Jesuit recommen-

26. For further discussion of the complexities of the slavery question and the position of the Jesuits, see Ronaldo Vainfas, *Ideologia e escravidão: os letrados da sociedade escravista no Brasil colonial* (Petrópolis: Vozes, 1986) 65–83; and Carvalho, *A Igreja e a escravidão*, 53–58.

27. The Jesuit Manuel da Nóbrega requested that the Crown send orphans and even women of questionable reputation to the colony in order to curtail the capture and abuse of Indian women. For further information, see Manuel da Nóbrega to Simão Rodrigues, 9 August 1549, in Leite, *Monumenta Brasiliae*, 1. 119–21.

28. See Manuel da Nóbrega to Simão Rodrigues, 6 January 1550, in Leite, *Monumenta Brasiliae*, 1. 165–66. The *Recolhimento da Encarnação* ("house of correction/refuge/recollection") functioned as a supply source, sending so-called Portuguese orphans to the colony. For a more complete discussion of the exportation of women and girls from Portugal, see Afonso Costa, "As órfãs da Rainha," *Revista do Instituto Histórico e Geographico Brasileiro* 190 (1946); and Rodolfo Garcia, *As órfãs* (Rio de Janeiro: S.D. do M.E.S., 1946).

29. In accord with the traditions of medieval Europe, a man who married a prostitute, thereby contributing to the woman's reform, was given papal assurance that such action would count for the remission of the man's own sins. See reference to *Decretalis D. Gregorii papae IX suae integrati una cum glossi*, liber 4, titulus I, canon 20, in Emil Friedberg, ed., *Corpus Juris Canonici* (2 vols.; Leipzig: Tauschnitz, 1879; reprinted Graz: Akademische Druck- und Verlag-anstalt, 1959) as cited in Bullough and Bullough, *Women and Prostitution*, 130.

30. In an effort to address the problems experienced by Indian women and girls, Manuel da Nóbrega saw to the construction of houses for their education and protection. It is unclear from the Portuguese whether these women and girls were prostitutes, concubines, or simply involved in amorous affairs. In any case, an effort was made to receive them, train them, and prepare them

dation carried with it the two prospects. Not only did it safeguard Indian women, but it ensured the viability of a colonial population that was Portuguese and Christian.

Thus, in the early years of the colony, marginalized women were exported and exiled from Portugal for reasons of order as well as reasons of faith. They made their way to the colony not only in order to curtail the abuse of Indian women and serve the sexual needs of their countrymen, but more precisely in order to work out their own salvation through the production of Christian offspring for the greater honor and glory of God and the Portuguese Crown.

In 1557, the death of Dom João resulted in a woman's rise to power. His widow, Dona Catarina, became regent for their grandson, Dom Sebastião (1557–1577), the heir to the Portuguese crown. During the reign of Dona Catarina, the commercial expansion of Portugal in the Indies and the coast of Africa resulted in economic gain. Such power contributed to the church's ongoing renegotiation of patronage privileges, rendering it completely dependent on the royal treasury and for the most part under the control of the Crown.

As mentioned earlier, the missionary initiatives of the Jesuits continued to inform the moral conscience of the colonists with regard to the religious questions raised by sexual immorality and the enslavement of indigenous peoples. During the second half of the sixteenth century, growing numbers of Jesuits proved to be successful in their pastoral and catechetical efforts among the indigenous peoples. They worked to defend and safeguard them from unscrupulous traders and mercenaries. In addition, the Jesuits established numerous educational

---

for Christian marriage. See Manuel da Nóbrega to the Jesuits in Coimbra, 13 September 1551, in Leite, *Monumenta Brasiliae*, 1. 286. Ten years later, in a letter from Manuel da Nóbrega to Diego Laynes (12 June 1561, in Leite, *Monumenta Brasiliae*, 3. 365–66), Nóbrega discussed his concern about poverty and misery driving young Indian girls to extremes and his desire to acquire a house where they could be taken care of and educated. It would be interesting to know to what extent Nóbrega was familiar with the activities of Ignatius and his early companions regarding the establishment of a house for prostitutes and their children known as the Casa Santa Marta. For further information on the pastoral outreach of the Jesuits to prostitutes and their children in Rome a decade earlier, see John O'Malley, *The First Jesuits* (Cambridge, MA: Harvard University Press, 1993) 178–85.

centers on behalf of the Indians along the coast as well as in the highlands of São Paulo.

As the colony developed, predictable conflicts arose between the Jesuits and the colonists. This was due in part to the Jesuit defense of the Indians and, in particular, of Indian women and girls. Of equal importance was the fact that bold and charismatic individuals, such as Manuel da Nóbrega, arose from among the Jesuits. These individuals were intent on preserving the integrity of the church's mission and were courageous enough to stand against those who would undermine that integrity.

It is important to note how Jesuit efforts to protect and defend indigenous women in particular proved to be of broader significance in later years. Although the reasoning and consciousness that undergirded the convictions and actions of the Jesuits with regard to Indian women did not necessarily extend to all women, the profound effect of their advocacy upon the life of one woman proved to have far-reaching consequences as she took upon herself the protection and defense of other women and girls.

In 1551, one of Nóbrega's letters highlighted the name of a free Indian woman named Meirinha, who had done a great deal to assist him in the religious formation of other Indians, both women and men.[31] Evidence suggests that around the same period, Nóbrega officiated at the marriage of Meirinha to Captain Pedro Leitão.[32] Twenty-five years later, in 1576, this same Meirinha—then a widow and known as Maria da Rosa—became the foundress of a *recolhimento* in Olinda.[33]

---

31. See Manuel da Nóbrega's letter of 13 September 1551, in Leite, *Monumenta Brasiliae*, 1. 286.

32. See António Pires to the Priests and Brothers of Coimbra, 2 August, 1551 and Nóbrega's letter of 13 September 1551 in Leite, *Monumenta Brasiliae*, 1. 263 n. 44 and 1. 286 nn. 8, 10, respectively.

33. The *recolhimentos* had several functions and often served more than one end. According to Riolando Azzi and Maria Valéria V. Rezende ("A vida religiosa feminina no Brasil colonial," in Riolando Azzi, ed., *A vida religiosa no Brasil: enfoques históricos* [São Paulo: Paulinas, 1983] 30–31) its principal objective was to offer refuge to four groups. First, the *recolhimento*—similar to the initial Jesuit project that educated young Indian girls with the help of virtuous matrons—served young girls; later they served Portuguese girls in particular, whether orphans or separated from family members, until

As a Franciscan tertiary, she set up a house for women and girls, which was similar to the one that Nóbrega founded two decades earlier.[34]

At issue in the historical identification of this woman are two related discoveries. The first is that a *recolhimento* was set up by a woman for women.[35] The second is that such an institution is the first evidence of an unofficial form of religious life in Brazil.[36] In both instances, Maria da Rosa defied—or at least avoided—colonial custom and colonial rule. She was successful in her efforts to resist the customs that promoted the enslavement and exploitation of vulnerable women and girls. Furthermore, she was able to circumvent a rule that prohibited religious life for women.[37]

Although noteworthy, the case of Maria da Rosa, along with her efforts on behalf of women, is far from representative of the larger reality. The fact remains that the use and abuse of women for material gain was an essential feature of life in the early colony. As we see in chronicles from the late 1560s, the strength and consolidation

---

the time of marriage. Second, they provided refuge for "fallen" girls and women (often called "Magdelenes"), who were rejected by society, but desired rehabilitation. Third, they protected women desiring a life of prayer and penance, many of whom were widows or abandoned by their husbands; and fourth, they sheltered women desiring to live a vowed monastic life despite the Crown's refusal to permit the establishment of convents.

34. Ibid., 30.

35. For further information regarding this point, see Riolando Azzi, "Beatas e penitentes: uma forma de vida religiosa do Brasil antigo," *Grande Sinal* 30 (1976); Eduardo Hoornaert, "De beatas a freiras: evolução histórica do Recolhimento da Glória no Recife," in Azzi, *A vida religiosa*, 61–73; and Susan Soeiro, "The Feminine Orders in Colonial Brazil," in Asunción Lavrin, ed., *Latin American Women: Historical Perspectives* (Westport, CT: Greenwood, 1978) 173–97.

36. Unlike the Spanish colonies, where convents flourished, it is important to note that until 1677 the Portuguese enforced a prohibition against the establishment of religious orders of women. See Márcio Moreira Alves, *A Igreja e a política no Brasil* (São Paulo: Brasiliense, 1979) 22; and Susan A. Soeiro, "The Social and Economic Role of the Convent in Colonial Bahia, 1677–1800," *The Hispanic Historical Review* 54 (1974) 210.

37. For more information on the prohibition of religious orders of women in the colony, see Azzi and Rezende, "A vida religiosa feminina," 27. This subject is discussed later in this chapter; see pp. 51–52, 58.

of the Portuguese colony was dependent upon the successful employment of various strategies to fill its coffers.[38] An example of this is
found in the attempts of colonial officials to glean for their settlement
a measure of financial gain from sexual liaisons that occurred between Portuguese men and Indian or African women. Records from
1576 provide evidence that in São Paulo men were prohibited from
going into areas where Indian and slave women often gathered, such
as springs, rivers, and wells. If found in these places, men were fined;
whether the women received remuneration for whatever deeds they
performed is uncertain. It is clear, however, that the colonial treasury
managed to ensure its own interests by profiting from any illegal
liaisons between Portuguese men and women of color.[39]

The Colony under Spanish Dominion (1580–1640)

The untimely death of Dom Sebastião in 1577 led to the brief
reign of Dom (Cardinal) Henrique (1578–1580).[40] It also ushered in
a turbulent period for the colony of Brazil as Portugal was forced to
submit to Spanish domination. In 1580, the Portuguese empire came
under the power of King Phillip II of Spain; and, over the course of
the next sixty years, the intrigues of European hostilities against Spain
were transplanted to the soil of several Portuguese colonies, including
Brazil.

38. For more than a decade, colonial forces had struggled against French
Huguenots, who over the course of several years intensified their efforts to
take permanent hold of the bay islands and coastal area of Rio de Janeiro. In
an effort to secure the region, the Portuguese established São Sebastião de
Rio de Janeiro as a major settlement. Ultimately, the French were driven out
of Brazil. The continued strength of the Portuguese, however, was contingent
not only upon the expansion of settlements, but also upon the financial stability of the colonists.

39. Atas da Câmara Municipal de São Paulo (23 vols., São Paulo: Câmara
Municipal, 1562) 1. 95. See Fonseca, *História da prostituição*, 16. See also
Sérgio Milliet, "A prostituição na Colônia," *Investigações* 2 (1950) 8.

40. The young Sebastião had become a knight errant and subsequently lost
his life in a failed attempt on the part of the Portuguese to conquer North
Africa. His death had grave implications for the future of the Portuguese
empire.

Under Spanish rule, the Jesuits ceased to be the dominant religious influence within the colony. In the early 1580s, Benedictines, Franciscans, and Carmelites began to make their way to Brazil in large numbers.[41] Gradually, these three religious orders, like the Jesuits, came to exercise some measure of power and authority in the various regions where they established themselves.[42] They amassed considerable wealth and privilege as they participated in the cultural, economic, and political life of the colony.[43]

Unlike the situation in other colonies in the Americas, the growth of men's religious orders in Brazil was not paralleled by the simultaneous foundation of women's religious orders. The establishment of convents for women religious was not officially authorized in Brazil until 1677, nearly two centuries after the foundation of the colony. Even under Spanish rule, three longstanding conditions continued to militate against the establishment of convents: first, the scarcity of European women; second, the need to foster population growth; and third, relative disinterest on the part of elite benefactors. The absence of convents of women religious has deprived us of a major source of women's history during this particular period of Brazilian history. To the extent that ecclesiastical powers collaborated with colonial powers, religious and regal authorities insured that women would have no alternative but to conform to the demands of the patriarchal social

41. Although Franciscans had ventured in and out of the colony since the arrival of the Portuguese in 1500, they did not formally establish themselves in Recife until 1584, when they rapidly became the largest religious order of men.

42. See Alves, *A Igreja e a politica*, 23. For a more extensive survey of religious orders in Brazil, see Júlio Maria, *O Catolicismo no Brasil* (Rio de Janeiro: Agir, 1950) 82–110.

43. For example, the lifestyle of Franciscan friars reflected a colonial cultural ethos that was marked more by the guile of the rich than the simplicity of their founder. The Franciscan flair for guilded opulence, however, paled in comparison to that of the Carmelites, whose magnificent convents housed the treasures of Olinda, Santos, Rio de Janeiro and the mining cities of Minas Gerais. As for the Benedictines, they not only participated in the privilege and prestige associated with cultural and economic resources, but also in the power associated with their political importance given the fact that their monasteries were used for military purposes in combatting the Dutch and the French.

order—namely, the production of children and the sexual satisfaction of men.[44]

In effect, women remained virtually undifferentiated from each other in terms of roles and functions. Within Brazil, the European distinctions that had long separated virgins from whores and whores from wives and mothers were of little significance. Most women, regardless of their age, race, or social position, were destined to be used and controlled by men for the exclusive purposes of sexual reproduction and sexual pleasure.

Toward the end of the sixteenth century, representatives of the Holy Office of the Inquisition made their way to Brazil, a land regarded as the "tropic of sin," in order to scrutinize the faith and morals of the colony. Among the Inquisition's proceedings, as might be expected, several cases dealt with sexual matters.[45] What is surprising, however, is that these cases focused primarily on sexual activities deemed to be *unnatural* deviations:[46] sodomy, lesbianism, and witchcraft received a great deal of attention.[47] Fornication and prostitution, to the extent that they remained within the realm of natural deviations, were of little interest or concern.

One explanation for this finding may be that the proceedings of the Inquisition were arranged, judged, and recorded by men whose point of reference was a moral construct undergirded by the predominant customs and mores of the late sixteenth century.[48] Portugal and Spain

44. See Alves, *A Igrega e a política*, 22–23; Azzi and Rezende, "A vida religiosa feminina," 25–27; and Soeiro, "The Social and Economic Role of the Convent," 210.

45. For tables and statistics outlining the offenses and occurrences, see Siqueira, *A Inquisição portuguesa*, 227–28, 255, 301, 361–97.

46. Fonseca, *História da prostituição*, 15. See also Vainfas, *Trópico dos pecados*; and Ligia Bellini, *A coisa obscura: mulher, sodomia e Inquisição no Brasil colonial* (São Paulo: Brasiliense, 1987). The first visitations took place between 1591–1595 and the second visitations occurred between 1618–1620 in Bahia and Pernambuco.

47. Various studies note efforts to demonstrate a correspondence between deviant sexual practices and the practice of witchcraft. See Bellini, *A coisa obscura*, 9–10; and Laura de Mello e Souza, *O Diabo e a terra de Santa Cruz* (São Paulo: Companha das Letras, 1986) 227–28, 260.

48. See Milliet, "A prostituição na Colônia," 7–15.

had undergone significant social upheaval and religious change as prevailing attitudes and practices were adapted or modified in accord with the realities of the time. In some regions, particularly those with major cities and ports, prostitution was a problem and a concern.[49] Still, it remained a cultural given, if not a social necessity. There were those who attempted to address the problem of prostitution by devoting energies to its eradication or containment. Moral advocates as well as public defenders, however, were forced to face the reality that many religious and social circles regarded prostitution as one of the lesser sins and evils. Within the context of a patriarchal social order dependent on de facto toleration, even the most rigorous efforts to eliminate or control the world's oldest profession often proved to be of limited consequence.[50]

Under Spanish rule, the social circumstances of the colony began to change. The discovery of gold, the establishment of new settlements along the trails penetrating the frontier, the continued growth of seacoast settlements, the emergence of some semblance of colonial

49. See the chapter "The Pox and Reform" in Bullough and Bullough, *Women and Prostitution*, 139–56. See also Lucia Ferrante, "'Malmaritate' tra assistenza e punizione" [Bologna Sec. 16–17] in *Forma e soggetti dell'intervento assistenziale in una città de antico regime* (Bologna: Instituto pert la storia di Bologna, 1986) 2. 65–109; Salvator di Giacomo, *Prostitution in Naples in the Fifteenth, Sixteenth and Seventeenth Centuries* (Bresden: , 1904); Liliane Motta-Weber, "Les femmes dans la vie économique de Geneve," *Bulletin de la société d'histoire et d'archéologie de Geneve* 16 (1979); Mary Elizabeth Perry, "Lost Women in Early Modern Seville: Politics of Prostitution," *Journal of Feminist Studies* 4 (1978) 195–214; and Lyndal Roper, "Discipline and Respectability: Prostitution and the Reformation in Augsburg," *History Workshop Journal* 19 (1985) 3–28.

50. The studies cited in the previous footnote highlight the fact that although religious and/or civil authorities decried prostitution and legislated against it, historical evidence suggests that for the most part intolerance and prohibition were ineffective strategies. In general, they failed to reduce sex trade, and in some cases such strategies actually exacerbated the incidence of other sorts of vice and crime, such as pimping, kidnapping, blackmail, assault, and rape. Failure to enforce legislation against prostitution was a common means for both curtailing the negative consequences of suppression and maintaining the status quo of de facto toleration.

familial structures, and various efforts to regulate slavery set in place the ideal conditions for the evolution of colonial prostitution.

Reports regarding the sexual enslavement of Indian and African women began to surface.[51] Women "dressed like men" began to accompany *garimpeiros* to mining regions where the women's entrepreneurial aims and activities included sexual favors in exchange for gold.[52] "Undesirables"—the name given to women accused of prostitution—began to make their way into official colonial records.[53]

By the 1630s, women outnumbered men in some regions of the colony. Children of mixed race were in abundance. Misery, hunger, and disease often marked the existence of women and their children; abandonment of women and children was a common practice. In general, ecclesiastical and colonial authorities were slow to respond to the needs of the poor and marginalized.[54] In a number of cases, they failed to do so altogether. Fortunately for the church, the colony, and most especially, for the poor and abandoned, responsibility for the works of mercy was assumed by lay confraternities known as *irmandades*.[55]

51. See references to the case of Pascoal Barrufo as cited in Fonseca, *História da prostituição*, 27–31. Barrufo held one hundred and fifty Indian women in captivity for the expressed purpose of providing sexual favors to visitors passing through Bertioga. For further information, see Edmundo Amaral, *Rótulas e mantilhas* (Rio de Janeiro: Civilização Brasileira, 1932) 140.

52. The term *garimpeiro* refers to a man panning, digging, or mining for precious metals and minerals. In 1622, official records from Vila Rica describe in detail the activities of women accompanying these men. See Fonseca, *História da prostituição*, 22–23.

53. In 1641, in the region of São Paulo, the first two prostitutes to be named in official records and to be punished were Mariana Lopes and Joana Pereira. Both women were married. See ibid., 24.

54. It is important to note that most ecclesiastical activities were subject to the control of colonial authorities and restricted exclusively to clerics and religious orders of men. For the most part, these men were unprepared or unwilling to address the claims and needs of impoverished women and children.

55. The term *irmandade* refers to a lay fraternity or sorority. In some cases, members of the *irmandades* were tertiaries of religious orders such as the Franciscans.

In many ways, the *irmandades* were a dynamic element of colonial Catholicism and were extremely important in the development of Brazil both in terms of their scope and influence.[56] Most *irmandades* directed themselves to some sort of philanthropic or benevolent activity.[57] Although understood ecclesiastically as lay fraternities and sororities, they drew upon diverse religious charisms to inspire and sustain their efforts to provide resources for support and security for others.

The *irmandades* served as a collective force for social and religious cohesion. The degree to which they were independent of the ecclesiastical and colonial authorities of the period remains the subject of ongoing research.[58] What is apparent, however, is that they persisted in their commitments despite efforts on the part of external authorities to compromise or control them.[59]

The Middle Colony (1640–1713)

Under the political influence of the French cardinal Richelieu, Portugal revolted against Spain in 1640. The union with Spain was dissolved and Dom João IV (1640–1656) assumed the Portuguese Crown. As Portugal regained its independence, hostilities with the

56. This is best exemplified in the activities of particular social institutions such as the Santa Casa de Misericordia. See Alves, *A Igrega e a politica*, 22–23. For further information see Caio Prado Junior, *Formação do Brasil contemporâneo* (São Paulo: Brasiliense, 1965) 383; Fritz Texeira Sales, *Associações religiosas do Ciclo do Ouro* (Belo Horizonte: Universidade de Minas Gerais, 1963) 45; and A. J. R. Russell-Wood, *Fidalgos and Philanthropists: The Santa Casa da Misericordia of Bahia, 1550–1755* (London: MacMillan, 1968).

57. For example, fraternities with Afro-Brazilian members often directed their attention to buying the freedom of slaves. Some fraternities constructed churches, orphanages, and hospitals. Others devoted themselves to the creation of religious art. Others focused on religious devotions, festivals, and pilgrimages.

58. See Riolando Azzi, *O Episcopado do Brasil frente ao Catolicismo popular* (Petrópolis: Vozes, 1977) 78.

59. This remained the case even in subsequent periods of Brazilian history. For further details in this regard, see ibid., 79–109.

Dutch in the northeast of Brazil ended; and colonial development efforts increased in the agricultural production of cotton, tobacco, sugarcane, and coffee, along with the mining of gold and diamonds.[60] Portugal became increasingly reliant upon the English, to the point of becoming a protectorate in 1703. Although the colony of Brazil underwent an unprecedented period of growth, its continued development was skewed by certain obstacles, particularly those created by the progressive isolationism of Portugal.

Inasmuch as slavery was foundational to the growth and development of the colony, it remained nonnegotiable.[61] During the second half of the seventeenth century, intense debates and conflicts regarding the slavery of Indians took place between the Society of Jesus and the colonial authorities.[62] In mounting their case against colonial practices, the Jesuits appealed once again to the teachings of Pope Urban VIII.[63] In 1680, their longstanding objective to abolish the enslavement of Indians was recognized by Portugal. By the time of the decision, however, it was clear that the colonial powers had little to lose

60. Portugal broke with all that was culturally hispanic and concerned itself instead with the cultures of France and Italy. It also broke with all that was politically and economically hispanic. In separating from Spain, the Portuguese found themselves in a better position to establish relationships with the English and to negotiate with the Dutch. As a consequence, longstanding European rivalries and hostilities were no longer enacted on Brazilian soil. By the mid-1600s, Holland and England replaced Spain and Portugal as major world powers. According to Maria Luisa Nunes (*Becoming True to Ourselves: Cultural Decolonization and National Identity in the Literature of the Portuguese-Speaking World* [New York: Greenwood, 1987] 4), it was during this period that Portugal "turned its back on the Iberian cultural patrimony which was its own."

61. For more detailed information on the role and function of slavery in the development of the colony, see Perdigão Malheiro, *A escravidão no Brasil: ensaio histórico, jurídico, social* (2 vols. in 1; Petrópolis: Vozes, 1976).

62. Antônio Vieira was among the most renowned Jesuits involved in the defense of the Indians during this period. See Carvalho, *A Igreja e a escravidão*, 60–64. For further information, see Antônio Vieira, *Sermões* (15 vols. in 7; São Paulo: Editora das Américas, 1958) vols. 7, 10, and 14.

63. In 1639, Pope Urban VIII issued the decree *Comissum nobis* prohibiting the enslavement of Indians. At the time of its promulgation, news of the decree set off a wave of persecution against the Jesuits in Brazil. See Carvalho, *A Igreja e a escravidão*, 57.

in granting the Jesuits their claim. In many regions, African slaves already had proven themselves to be a far more efficient labor force than the Indians. Whether abolished in principle or practice, the Indian slave trade was no longer of great consequence in terms of colonial interests. Inasmuch as the Indian slave trade had already been superseded by the enslavement of Africans—a form of slavery for which the church itself had established biblical and theological justifications[64]—the colonists, including some clergy and religious, were easily able to take full advantage of the situation to serve their own ends.

Among the theological reflections addressing the subject of slavery in the late 1600s, the ideas of the Jesuit Jorge Benci are of particular significance for understanding how the notion of the Christian patriarchal family influenced the social consciousness of the colony not only with regard to slaves, but with regard to women as well.[65] By advancing strict Christian morals within a patriarchal social order, Benci believed that both the inhumane treatment of slaves and licentious sexual practices could be effectively redressed and controlled through the authority and example of the truly Christian master.

It was no mere coincidence that the ideological and theological foundations for the patriarchal family emerged in the colony precisely during the period in which the ratio of white men to white women came into balance for the first time. Given the necessary social conditions, European traditions regarding females and families were re-

64. For a detailed presentation of the biblical and theological legitimation of the enslavement of Africans, see Ronaldo Vainfas, "O projeto escravista-cristão," in his *Ideologia e escravidão*, 93–124.

65. The primary work of Jorge Benci was entitled "The Christian Economy of Masters in the Governing of Slaves." Although formally published in 1700, his ideas were well in place during the final decades of the seventeenth century. See Jorge Benci, *Economia cristã dos senhores no governo de escravos* (1700; reprinted São Paulo: Grijalbo, 1977). Benci stressed the need for transforming the world of slavery into the Christian patriarchal family, thereby converting the African slave into a Christian servant and the master into a new man who would assume the values of Christianity as the norm for thinking and acting. In accord with the thought of Benci, the moral crises at work in the life of the colony could be resolved by constructing and reinforcing the notion of family. See Vainfas, *Ideologia e escravidão*, 130.

constituted.[66] After one hundred and seventy-seven years of prohibition, permission for the establishment of convents for women was
finally granted.[67] In contrast to the past, the colony had a great deal
to gain from the establishment of convents and houses of refuge and
retreat. Rather than posing a threat to the patriarchal social order,
these new organizations secured its future. On the one hand, convents
ensured a place of seclusion for upper-class women, especially "those
denied the possibility of marriage."[68] On the other hand, *recolhimentos*
guaranteed housing and rehabilitation for growing numbers of
marginalized women, such as prostitutes.[69] Unquestionably, they also
served the particular interests of those intent on creating and forming
a dominant Lusitanian class.

With the establishment of convents and the development of *recolhimentos*, the roles and functions of women in the colony were rede-
fined. Female sexuality came under the controls, restrictions, and
scrutinies of colonial authorities. Nowhere was this displayed more
clearly than in the lives of prostitutes and nuns. As a result of the
ascendancy of the patriarchal social order, questions of honor took on
new significance within the colony. The contagion of dishonor quickly

66. See A. J. R. Russell-Wood, "Female and Family in the Economy and
Society of Colonial Brazil," in Asunción Lavrin, ed., *Latin American Women:
Historical Perspectives* (Westport, CT: Greenwood, 1978) 60–100.

67. See Carole A. Myscofski, "Women's Religious Role in Brazil: A History of Limitations," *Journal of Feminist Studies* 1 (1985) 47; Eduardo Hoornaert
et al., eds., *História da Igreja no Brasil: primeira época* (Petrópolis: Vozes,
1979) 226–35; and Maria, *O Catolicismo no Brasil*, 82–110. In 1677, Poor
Clares from Évora founded the first convent in the colony, the famous Convent of Santa Clara de Nossa Senhora do Desterro in Salvador, Bahia. For
further information on life in Desterro, see Ana Amélia Vieira Nascimento,
*A postura escravocrata no convento de religiosas: Santa Clara do Desterro
na Bahia, 1680–1850* (Salvador: Centro de Estudos Baianos da Universidade
Federal da Bahia, 1990).

68. See Myscofski, "Women's Religious Role in Brazil," 44–46. Statistics
from the colonial capital of Salvador reveal that during the period between
1680 and 1797, of one hundred and sixty Portuguese-descended women eli-
gible for marriage, fourteen percent were married, eight percent remained
celibate and seventy-seven percent entered a convent. See Soeiro, "The Social
and Economic Role of the Convent," 211.

69. See Myscofski "Women's Religious Role in Brazil," 48–49; and Hoornaert,
História da igreja, 231–33.

made its way into the social consciousness of the colony as women became differentiated from each other by race, class, and sexual status.

At the turn of the eighteenth century, efforts were underway to protect and deter women from lives of prostitution. Although largely unsuccessful in their attempts to enforce legislation regarding prostitution, the colonial authorities endeavored to establish the boundaries and limits of sexual behavior in various regions of Brazil. In São Paulo, for example, responsibility to shelter and protect Indian women subjected to sexual violence by white colonists was taken up by the Regimento para o Procurador Geral dos Indios ("Regiment for the Attorney General of Indians").[70] In this particular case and in other similar cases, culpability for the dehumanizing exploitation of Indian women was not only ascribed to the *bandeirantes* ("explorers and pioneers") but to clerics and members of religious orders as well.[71]

The Late Colony (1713–1822)

In 1713, as a consequence of the Treaty of Utrecht, Portugal and Spain resigned their control of the seas. A steady move toward increased Portuguese isolationism led to political, religious, and economic shifts throughout the colony. During this period, the rule of Dom José (1750–1777) was in effect the rule of the Marquis de Pombal, whose influence in Portugal and Brazil had enormous political and ecclesiastical consequences.[72]

Under Pombal, the power of the church of Rome was fettered. For the most part, the ecclesiastical life of the colony was in disarray. Secular and religious clergy were equally dependent upon the colonial structures of the times. The Jesuits, however, remained an exception to the rule. As a direct consequence of their influence and activities in various regions of the colony, Pombal responded to their challenges and threats by expelling all members of the Society of Jesus from Brazil and Portugal in 1759.

70. Fonseca, *História da prostituição*, 29.
71. Ibid., 30.
72. For further discussion of Pombal's influence on the church in Brazil, see Thomas C. Bruneau, *The Political Transformation of the Brazilian Catholic Church* (New York: Cambridge University Press, 1974) 19–21.

For a church already in decline, it took little to diminish institutional Catholicism in the colony. Vestiges of Roman Catholic culture and tradition appeared to survive, but they did so in a secularized form and fashion.[73] Having taken its cues from the church in Portugal, the church in Brazil had little identity of its own. The church in Brazil mirrored the weaknesses of the church in Portugal. The colony magnified the power of Pombal.[74]

The reign of Maria I (1777–1816) and her husband Pedro III (1777–1786) was marked by efforts to undo the deeds of Pombal. In 1789, rumblings of the French Revolution sent shock waves throughout Portugal, as did news of the first Brazilian rebellion against Portuguese authority led by José Joaquim da Silva Xavier, commonly known as Tiradentes.

With the invasion of Napolean's troops in 1807, the prince regent, Dom João, and the royal family fled Portugal; in the company of numerous sympathizers, the court took up residence in Brazil in 1808. The colony became engaged once again in the world of commerce and trade, particularly with British companies, bringing previous isolationism to an end. With the overthrow of Napoleon, Dom João IV began ruling Portugal from Brazil, which became the seat of the kingdom in 1815.

During the eighteenth and early nineteenth centuries, violence, aggression, and corruption intensified throughout the colony. Upheavals in the social, political, religious, and economic conditions in Brazil lent themselves to the widespread development of houses of prostitution, particularly in the large cities, in established *fazendas* ("plantations"), and at the crossroad settlements leading to the interior regions of the colony.

73. See Alves, *A Igreja e a politica*, 17–18.
74. Ibid., 26. Through the strategic interventions of the Marquis de Pombal, Jansenism, Gallicanism, and liberalism emerged as the primary spiritual, ecclesiastical, and political orientations of powerful and influential clerical elites. This reality, combined with the ignorance, corruption, decadence, and self-interest that marked the lives of other clergy and religious did not bode well for the future of the church in Brazil. Clerics were found in the ranks of businessmen, landlords, usurers and slave owners, soldiers, conspirators, and political leaders. With each new role they assumed, the ecclesiastical identity of priest as pastor was further eroded.

In addition to houses of prostitution, the sexual trafficking of women increased along with the growing demand for prostitutes to accompany men seeking mineral fortunes in the backlands. Women and girls of every sort were included in the enterprise. By law, men suspected of trafficking were to be fined and jailed. Penalties of this nature, however, failed to be a deterrent.

In certain regions, the preoccupation with public morality became an obsession. Suspicions, accusations, and judgments abounded. Women found or presumed to be guilty of prostitution were arrested and sent to remote unpopulated areas. Two objectives were accomplished by such practices. First, the honor and moral order of certain places was restored by the banishment of prostitutes. Second, the population growth of certain regions was engineered through compulsory relocation and the restriction of prostitutes' freedom of movement.

The Monarchy (1822–1889)

As liberal ideas continued to foment revolt against the rule of the Portuguese Crown in various regions of Brazil, active resistance in the state of Pernambuco proved to be a cause for grave concern. By 1820, Portugal itself was plagued by revolution. Convinced that he should return to Portugal, Dom João IV entrusted the governance of Brazil to his son, Dom Pedro. In 1822, however, Brazil declared its independence from Portugal and Dom Pedro was named emperor.[75]

75. After the departure of Dom João IV, Portuguese loyalists began to have doubts about the affinities of his son, Dom Pedro. To some, he seemed to be more Brazilian than Portuguese. Ongoing revolutionary activities in several provinces created a climate of suspicion and fear. To circumvent any movement toward Brazilian independence, the Portuguese court in Brazil attempted to revive colonial conditions through repressive measures. In 1822, they ordered Dom Pedro to return to Portugal. Aware of the support he had from Brazilians, he refused the order. The Portuguese troops could not put up sufficient resistance. On 7 September 1822, Brazil declared its independence from Portugal; and in December, Dom Pedro I was crowned emperor.

Dom Pedro was quick to convene an assembly and proposed the introduction of various liberal ideas into the constitution, his ideas met with considerable opposition. The assembly was dissolved and the leading voices of opposition exiled. A committee wrote and enacted a constitution. In time,

Bound to the customs of a colonial past, the newly declared empire of Brazil carried on the traditions of patronage. It was important to secure the Vatican's recognition of the Brazilian empire, and Dom Pedro I spared nothing to obtain curial endorsement. Unaware or unconcerned that the emperor was hardly moved by zeal, the Vatican gave its approval for a price.[76]

Ecclesiastical recognition of the empire added little stability to Don Pedro's reign. By 1831, discontent and opposition on the part of various constituences contributed to his demise. Hampered by resistance, Don Pedro returned to Europe, leaving the empire to his young son, Don Pedro II. During subsequent years, growing republican sentiment surfaced ever more forcefully and prevailed as a source of constant concern for the government.[77] Politically involved priests such as Deigo Feijó, the minister of justice and regent of the empire, endeavored to put in place a form of religious politics that contributed to the demise of the Roman Catholic church in Brazil.[78] Numerous restrictions were placed on religious orders in the empire. Roman Catholic missionaries from other countries were refused entrance into Brazil, while Protestant missionaries were welcomed. The foundation of new religious congregations was prohibited. Those religious who belonged to congregations under the governance of superiors outside

---

questions began to arise regarding the emperor's real loyalties as Portuguese continued to be appointed as high ranking officials and Brazil's resources were squandered in ongoing meddling in the affairs of Portugal. Dom Pedro's prohibition of the slave trade sealed his fate. Republican sentiments ran deep and Brazilians were led to revolt. Efforts to put down the rebellion failed.

On 7 April 1831, Dom Pedro I returned to Portugal, leaving his young son, Dom Pedro II, as the new emperor. A regency took over the government for nine years. In 1840, those discontent with the policies of the regency demanded that the young emperor take control. On 23 July 1840, Dom Pedro II assumed control of empire and the regency was dissolved. See "Brazil, history of" *The New Encyclopedia Britannica: Macropaedia* 15 (1993) 200–8.

76. For further information see Hélio Vianna, *História do Brasil: período colonial, monarquia e república* (São Paulo: Melhoramentos, 1980) 432–552.

77. Alves, *A Igreja e a política*, 26.

78. Ibid., 26. See Pablo Richard, *Death of Christendoms, Birth of the Church: Historical Analysis and Theological Interpretation of the Church in Latin America* (trans. Phillip Berryman; Maryknoll: Orbis, 1987) 37–60.

of Brazil were expelled from the country.[79] Convents and monasteries were gradually appropriated by the empire as the diminishing numbers of religious aged and died.

Overall, the mid-nineteenth century proved to be a time of great turbulance, not only in terms of religion, but also in terms of numerous socio-political and socio-economic concerns. The Brazilian empire was ravaged by disease and armed conflict. In 1853, yellow fever plagued the country. The origin of the disease was attributed to incoming African slaves. As a consequence, the importation of slaves to Brazil was prohibited. Between 1855 and 1870, a constellation of tensions and armed conflict among the countries of Argentina, Paraguay, Uruguay, and Brazil resulted in grave losses for Brazilians both in terms of human lives and material resources. Demographic changes in the population of Brazil, caused by immigration and efforts to bring about emancipation, revealed new issues and concerns. Growing numbers of immigrants from various European countries settled in the south of Brazil. The efforts of the noted abolitionist Joaquim Nabuco de Araújo gained momentum, and the process of gradual emancipation was undertaken. On 13 May 1888, in the absence of her father, Dom Pedro II, Princess Isabel proclaimed the abolition of slavery. It is estimated that seven hundred thousand slaves were freed by this decree with no compensation given to the owners. Once heralded as progressive, liberal, and enlightened, the emperor began to fall out of favor with groups holding significant economic and sociopolitical power, such as the freemasons and land owners, whose interests were prejudiced by the emancipation of the slaves. On 15 November 1889, after a reign of nearly fifty years, Dom Pedro II was deposed by a bloodless revolution. Brazil joined the growing ranks of new republics.

In the years leading up to the emergence of the new republic of Brazil, the phenomenon of prostitution took on new and more flagrant dimensions, such as that of child prostitution.[80] This sexual exploitation of children was preceded and paralleled by the abandonment of large numbers of foundlings, the majority of whom were the children

79. Alves, *A Igreja e a política*, 28.
80. Fonseca, *História da prostitutição*, 60–61.

of prostitutes.[81] Poverty and misery were rampant in populated areas such as São Paulo. In major cities, it was not uncommon to find orphans and abandoned children past the age of seven begging and prostituting themselves.[82] Unlike slaves, they were free. Their freedom was undermined, however, by the realities of the socioeconomic order in which they found themselves.

All too often, the fate of the children replicated that of their mothers. On the one hand, women slaves were subject not only to the rigors of forced labor, but to the sexual exploits of masters and the sons of masters. On the other hand, free women—particularly those who were single, abandoned, or widowed—also proved to be the victims of a slave economy that provided few alternatives for the gainful employment of unattached women. Relegated to jobs as seamstresses and lace makers—jobs with low wages or none at all—their survival and the survival of their children was often dependent upon various forms of prostitution.[83]

The magnitude of the problem increased, leaving in its wake the long-term consequences of illegitimacy, disease, malnutrition, and misery. While the lives of slaves continued to be marked by oppres-

81. Due to limited resources, efforts to save the lives of these children were often futile. The actions of religious and civil authorities varied from place to place. *Amas de leite*, the wet nurses upon whom the survival of these children depended, took up the task of nursing under a variety of conditions. Some volunteered; others were paid; still others—as in the case of many slave women— were forced. In any event, there were more children than wet nurses, a situation accompanied by a high incidence of infant mortality. Social critics questioned how the wealthy could endow the building of churches (and one might question further how the church could accept money) when the needs of countless children were so evident and so urgent. See ibid., 69–81.

82. Ibid., 66.

83. According to the social historian Olwen Hufton, this phenomenon— namely, the coupling of seamstresses and lace makers with women engaged in prostitution—is not unique to Brazil. Social histories of prostitution in Ireland, England, and France also note this reality. Often, women arrested or censured for being prostitutes were required by civil or ecclesiastical authorities to enter programs designed for their moral and social rehabilitation. Ironically, efforts at social rehabilitation often included job training programs preparing them to be seamstresses, lace makers, and milliners—the very jobs they had before becoming prostitutes.

sion, torture, and humiliation, the lives of growing numbers of sup-
posedly free men, women, and children were marked by crime, des-
titution, and marginalization. In many ways, the confused and
conflictual religious dynamics present in nineteenth-century Brazil
contributed to the unrestricted exacerbation of dehumanization within
the social order.

With the erosion of ecclesiastical authority,[84] the depletion of personnel, and the fragmentation of resources, pastoral activities were
undermined as were the traditional works of mercy. This coincided
with heightened efforts on the part of Protestant missionaries to address themselves to proselytization and moral reform in several regions of Brazil. Single-minded in their theory that the decadence found
within empire could be attributed to the Roman Catholic church, they
maintained that social relief was contingent on a conversion.[85] Conversions, however, were few, and their concomitant social benefits
limited to a small minority.

Toward the end of the nineteenth century, another form of prostitution that had emerged a few decades earlier became increasingly
more attractive to the privileged and powerful, who had cultivated a
certain taste for higher-class prostitutes. Like their European counterparts, Brazilian elites were fascinated by the intrigue and fame of
hetaira ("courtesans").[86] In a similar fashion, artists, poets, musicians,
and intellectuals heralded the women of the *café-concertos* ("salons").
In both cases, prostitution took on a new character, and this character
was often made more exciting and precarious because of its
embeddedness in the underworld network of narcotics.[87]

Another factor contributing to the evolution of high and middle
forms of prostitution was the preoccupation on the part of some privi-

84. See Mecham, *Church and State*, 305–26.
85. See Harlan P. Tucker, "Brazil," in idem et al., *Protestant Missions in
South America* (New York: Student Volunteer Movement for Foreign Mis-
sions, 1907) 59–88; and Webster E. Browning, *Roman Christianity in Latin
America* (New York: Fleming H. Revell, 1924).
86. See José Machado Pais, *A prostituição e a Lisboa boémia do século
XIX aos inícios do século XX* (Lisboa: Querco, 1985); Lúcia Castello Branco,
Eros travestido: um estudo do eroticismo burguês brasileiro (Belo Horizonte:
Editora Universidade Federal de Minas Gerais, 1985).
87. Fonseca, *História da prostitutição*, 191–98.

leged men with the good health of the prostitutes with whom they kept company.[88] Syphilis was once again an object of concern. In the nineteenth century, new evidence regarding the effects of the third and worst stage of syphilis eclipsed the fevers, ulcers, and lesions identified with the disease since the sixteenth century. The threat of paralysis, insanity, and hemorrhage was real. Although the devastating effects of the disease were widespread throughout the general population, cases of congenital syphilis passed on to elite women who were infected by their husbands gave elite men new reason for concern, as they saw their heirs born deaf, blind, crippled, or insane. Controlling the contagion among the elite was both a political and social concern.[89]

The opening of Brazilian ports to commercial traders and tourists from around the world was yet another factor that shaped the course of prostitution during this period. Increased trade and tourism gave rise to a new clientele.[90] In accord with the demand, the supply for "hotel" prostitutes grew, making way for the sexual trafficking of both foreign and Brazilian women.[91]

The sexual exploitation of women from every race and from many nations brought yet another dimension to the legal and political ramifications of prostitution. Restaurants, bars, and other areas of diversion often had a double agenda—one for which they were officially recognized and one which emerged as a matter of course.[92] Gradually, the "policing" of prostitution emerged as a predominant criminal justice concern. The actual imprisonment of Brazilian pimps and the deportation of foreign ones, however, was more an exception than a rule. Investigations and trials that resulted in convictions were few.[93]

88. See Luiz Carlos Soares, *Prostitution in Nineteenth-Century Rio de Janeiro* (Occasional Papers 17; London: University of London Institute of Latin American Studies, 1988) 27–43.

89. For an extended discussion of this point, see Bullough and Bullough, *Women and Prostitution*, 232–58.

90. Fonseca, *História da prostituição*, 116–18.

91. Ibid., 127–49.

92. Ibid., 179–90.

93. Ibid., 148–49.

The Republic (1889 to the Present)

Within a year of the 1889 proclamation of the republic, a constitution modeled on that of the United States of America was set in place. Positivism fueled the spirit of liberty. Actions on the part of the state to legislate its separation from the Roman Catholic church surprised and distressed the social forces of the time. The absolute power and authority of the church was dissolved by civil society. Ironically, however, it was only at this point in time that the direct authority and influence of the Vatican over the actual governance of the Roman Catholic church in Brazil was finally put in place. As a consequence, religious orders and European clergy began to make their way to Brazil in great numbers.[94] Although many devoted their energies to educating the privileged classes and ministering to compatriot immigrants, many also committed themselves to caring for the poor, infirmed, and vulnerable.

Although the principles of freedom and democracy were heralded throughout Brazil, the actual practice of governing was more dictatorial than constitutional.[95] Some perceived the principles of democratic republicanism to be incompatible with the Catholic cultural heritage.[96] Other political forces believed that these principles established a socioeconomic order that guaranteed the rights of those already privileged by virtue of their class, race, and gender. Needless to say, the political, social, and religious restructuring of society had numerous consequences on the lives of women, particularly poor women and women engaged in prostitution.

In the early years of the republic, the presidency was destabilized due to revolution and rebellion. Gradually, the new form of government regulated itself and became more secure. During World War I, Brazil abandoned its position of neutrality and supported the Allied Forces. As a consequence, its ties with the United States of America

94. See José Oscar Beozzo, "Decadência e morte, restauração e multiplicação das Ordens e Congregações religiosas no Brasil 1870–1930," in Azzi, *A vida religiosa*, 118–29.

95. See Vianna, *História do Brasil*, 563–74.

96. See Mecham, *Church and State*, 327–30.

were strengthened. The postwar period was marked by economic
growth and unregulated spending. Within a short period of time, the
country was faced with severe economic problems. Growing discontent, particularly on the part of the military, threatened the security of
the civilian government as political and economic power shifted from
the northeast of the country to other regions of Brazil.

In the 1930s and 1940s, a populist dictatorship contributed to the
unraveling of the democratic political process. Although attempts
toward national social reform were undertaken during this period,
governmental efforts to respond to the demands and needs of the
people were challenged by various constituencies, including the military. In the mid-1950s, Brazil entered a period of national industrial
growth and agricultural development; however, high inflation and an
increased foreign debt led to a steady decline in the standard of living
for many people. In the early 1960s, efforts to bring about agrarian
reform and the nationalization of all industry led conservative forces,
wary of economic and sociopolitical destabilization, to support a
military revolution. A repressive military dictatorship ensued and gave
rise to one of the most torturous and dehumanizing periods of Brazilian history. In the 1980s, efforts toward redemocratization were seriously constrained by hyper-inflation, international debt, corruption and
the socioeconomic marginalization of millions.[97]

During this ninety year period of constant social, political, and
economic upheaval, the phenomenon of prostitution continued to grow
and diversify. For the most part, however, changes in Brazilian civil
society had limited impact on one of the nation's oldest social institutions. Beginning with the early years of the republic until and after
the time of the revolution of 1964, efforts on the part of *policia de
costumes*, or vice squads, to maintain order and vigilance in areas and
districts known for prostitution were often marked by conflict or

97. See Thomas E. Skidmore, *Politics in Brazil, 1930–1964: An Experi-
ment in Democracy* (New York: Oxford University Press, 1967); and
Encyclopaedia Britannica, Macropaedia, 15th ed., s.v. "Brazil, history of."
For further information on the role of the Roman Catholic church throughout
the course of this turbulent history, see Scott Mainwaring, *The Catholic Church
and Politics in Brazil, 1916–1985* (Stanford: Stanford University Press, 1986).

corruption. Disagreement regarding the regulation of prostitution and the confinement of prostitutes to specific locations was not uncommon. Regulations governing the behavior of prostitutes on the streets were difficult to enforce. The prohibition of houses of prostitution near schools, churches, or within family neighborhoods localized prostitutes in the commercial centers of the cities or on the peripheries. Claims of heightened criminal activity in districts of prostitution, however, led to a concern that such locations produced more difficult and dangerous circumstances for civilians and police alike.[98] Nevertheless, "for the sake of public health and safety," efforts to control prostitution through regulation continued, although opposition to such confinement also existed.

In the 1940s social reform efforts in major cities such as Rio de Janeiro and São Paulo led to the breaking up and leveling of *zonas* in accord with abolitionist ideals. In principle, the practice of de facto confinement was labeled "unconstitutional."[99] Although authorities attempted to uphold the conviction that prostitution districts led to greater vice and corruption not only on the part of prostitutes, but also on the part of police and other regulatory agents, such convictions proved to be of little consequence over time.

In the aftermath of such decisions, observers were quick to note that in areas where such policies were actually enforced, the result was a higher incidence of crimes—such as rape—against women in the general population, as well as an inability to control and curtail the spread of venereal disease.[100] Critics of such policies vigorously contended that the eradication of *zonas* did not augur well for the majority of poor women of the *baixo meretrício* ("low-class prostitution") who made up the population of the *zona*. Many of these women were former domestics, factory workers, and vendors. Overall, most

98. Fonseca, *História da prostitutição*, 159–78. See Waldyr de Abreu, *O submundo da prostituição, vadiagem e jogo do bicho* (Rio de Janeiro: Livraria Freitas Bastos, 1984) 115–24.
99. In São Paulo, for example, the issue of regulation was first raised in 1879, but was not well received. Attempts to bring about regulation failed again in 1896 and 1913.
100. Abreu, *O submundo da prostituição*, 146–47.

of these women received more money during one night of prostitution than during one month of so-called honest work.[101]

Needless to say, Brazilian men also had vested interests—such as convenience, anonymity, and wide selection, to name a few—in keeping the *zonas* in place. Although abolitionist policies prevailed juridically, de facto regulation continued to be upheld in many cities and municipalities. Where efforts to eliminate *zonas* proved to be more successful, the displaced workers found employment in massage parlors, roadside solicitation, and drive-in motels.[102]

Although this overview of the social history of prostitution in Brazil has focused primarily on women, and to some extent children, for the sake of interest, some final comments on male prostitution merit inclusion. To begin with it is important to note that occasional and incidental references to male homosexuality are found in chronicles about colonists and Indians in the 1580s, about transvestites in the 1620s and 1640s, about priests and their students in 1700s, and about effeminate soldiers in the 1770s. Preoccupation with male prostitution in particular, however, is a relatively modern phenomenon that emerges in the late nineteenth century.[103] Often associated with transvestites, male prostitutes in Brazil have been generally localized in major cities. As is the case with female prostitutes, they have been differentiated according to their particular attractiveness to various classes and distinct clienteles.

One of the most critical social aspects of male prostitution in the twentieth century is related to its protection under law. Controversies among Brazilian jurists and moralists abound. In brief, one may question to what extent Brazilian legislation regarding female prostitution can serve as a precedent for male prostitution. The Brazilian penal code in effect reflects an abolitionist stance that decriminalizes pros-

101. See Nautilde Batista da Costa Valente, "Serviço de recuperação moral e social da mulher prostituída," *Arquivos da Policia Civil de São Paulo*, 22 (1951) 154; cited in Fonseca, *História da prostitutição*, 213.

102. See Armando Pereira, *Sexo e prostituição* (Rio de Janeiro: Gráfica Record Editora, 1968) 48–49.

103. Fonseca, *História da prostitutição*, 217–37; and Soares, "Prostitution in Nineteenth-Century Rio de Janeiro," 24–27.

titution. De facto *regulation* of female prostitution, however, reveals the enforcement of local control and confinement to be pervasive.

With regard to male prostitution, there is evidence of de facto *prohibition*, marked by the surveillance, arrest, and imprisonment of male prostitutes for vagrancy rather than for prostitution. Although female prostitution is considered immoral, it is nonetheless licit. The same attitude does not consistently apply to male prostitution, which in some quarters is identified as both immoral and illicit.

Conclusion

Although this survey provides some insights into the historical realities that have shaped the evolution of prostitution in Brazil, the topic defies summation. Variances in time, geography, culture, and politics militate against any effort to generalize. Nevertheless, historic impressions, incidental and particular as they may be, provide a historical perspective from which to view the phenomenon of prostitution in contemporary Brazilian society.

If nothing else, this chapter illustrates some of the historical dynamics that condition the perceptions of religious and civil leaders who regard prostitution as a problem. The example of the Jesuits in the early colony demonstrates the limitations of ecclesial consciousness with regard to which persons should be defended and which persons can be expended. The example of the Inquisition highlights the church's preoccupation with certain unnatural sexual activities and its tendency to give little attention to female prostitution. In the era of colonial development, it is important to note how the church began to focus its concern on female virginity and family values around the same period that the social, economic, and racial heirarchy of the colony was established in terms of prestige, power, and privelege. In the nineteenth century, the financial and personal resources of the church were so depleted that even if it were interested in caring for the plight of the many suffering women and children, it was virtually unable to do anything. In the early twentieth century, however, with the restoration of the church, priests, religious, and laity were in a different position. The emergent strength of the church, however, was aligned with the interests of the powerful and privileged. With few exceptions, ecclesiastical attitudes and outreach toward prostitutes remained unchanged. For the most part, the values of neofeudalism, patriarchy, and ecclesiastical ambivalence prevailed despite the passage of time.

In the coming chapter, I endeavor to examine how the church in Brazil broke with its past and began to understand prostitution not only as a cultural given or a social concern, but more precisely as an ecclesial problem in need of an ecclesial solution.

3

The Church of Liberation and the Problem of Prostitution

Why choose to be with the poor? [Because] it is the practice of Jesus and the teaching of Jesus. . . . He listened to the cry of the poor [and] he paid a very high price. This should inspire us.

Among the poor, marginalized women are found and among marginalized women prostitutes are found. Through the teachings of Jesus, we are led to the conclusion that the poor person is Jesus. The prostitute is Jesus. Whoever does not help the prostitute does not help Jesus. Whoever claims to love the God who cannot be seen and does not love the prostitute who can be seen is a liar.

In addressing ourselves to a broad and inclusive pastoral effort, we have no right to create a plan that leaves the marginalized woman and the prostitute off to the side. . . . As such, we cannot take the prostitute from the *zona* in order to liberate her. The journey of prostitutes is part of a collective exodus [and] it is shared with all the poor of the world who journey toward the promised land.[1]

Dom Antônio Batista Fragoso

The Origins and Evolution of the Pastoral da Mulher Marginalizada

For more than two decades, the Pastoral da Mulher Marginalizada (P. M. M.), an ecclesiastical movement oriented toward women in prostitution, was promoted and sustained by the National Conference

1. Dom Antônio Batista Fragoso, "Deepening the Preferential Option for the Poor," in "Pastoral da Mulher Marginalizada," *Serviço de Documentação* 17 (1985) 828–29.

of Brazilian Bishops.[2] The origins of the movement are traced to the 1960s, when a pastoral initiative was launched in the northeast of Brazil with the assistance of a few bishops who recognized the necessity and importance of such a project. It emerged at a time when the Roman Catholic church in Brazil was profoundly influenced by the transformative effects of the Second Vatican Council and the Second General Conference of Latin American Bishops.[3]

During this period the church throughout much of Latin America began to take account of its identity and mission in a world besieged by savage inequalities and brutal repression. With courage and tenacity, episcopal leaders, in the company of clergy, religious, and laity, dared to challenge the idols of death as they proclaimed the God of life. Through their articulation of the church's preferential option for the poor and oppressed, they committed themselves to the promotion of faith and justice and set in place the ecclesial vision of the church of liberation.

2. Familiarity with the documentary history of the Pastoral da Mulher Marginalizada ("Pastoral Project for Marginalized Women") is assumed. Annotated translations of proceedings from national meetings of the P.M.M. from 1974–1990 appear in the appendix. They have been translated from the original Portuguese in order to make them accessible to the English-speaking reader. An effort has been made to present each translation in a format that is consistent with the original document. Occasionally, explanatory footnotes that are not part of the original document accompany its translation for purposes of information or clarification.

3. The Second Vatican Council was a turning point in the history of the Roman Catholic church. For the purposes of this study, it is important to note that the voices of bishops from around the world—especially the voice of Dom Helder Camara of Brazil—impressed upon the Second Vatican Council fathers not only the plight of the poor, but their claim for justice as well. Likewise, at the conference in Medellín, Colombia, the bishops of Brazil exercised significant leadership and influence on the Latin American Episcopal Conference in its prophetic articulation of the church's preferential option for the poor and oppressed. See Austin Flannery, ed., *Documents of Vatican II: The Conciliar and Post Conciliar Documents* (rev. ed.; 2 vols.; Northport, NY: Costello, 1987); and regarding the Second General Conference of Latin American Bishops in Medellín, Colombia, in 1968, see Louis Michael Colonnese, ed., *The Church in the Present-Day Transformation in Latin America in the Light of the Council*, vol. 1: *Position Papers* and vol. 2: *Conclusions* (Washington, DC: Latin American Division of the United States Catholic Conference, 1969).

The Pastoral da Mulher Marginalizada is but one example of numerous ecclesiastical efforts advanced by the church of liberation. The particular importance of this movement, however, rests upon the fact that it is judged by some to be among the most prophetic and unsettling in terms of its claims and consequences, not only for women involved in prostitution, but more precisely for the church itself. Given the fact that the history and significance of the Pastoral da Mulher Marginalizada is largely unknown outside Brazil, the following analysis has been undertaken in order to provide a broader audience with information on the origins and evolution of the movement from 1965 through 1990.

The purpose of this chapter is to use the documentary history of the P.M.M. as a case study for exploring the interactive processes that informed and influenced the ways in which the Roman Catholic church in Brazil came to recognize, define, and address prostitution as an ecclesial problem. As such, the nature of this analysis is investigative and stems from a practical missiological interest in understanding the adaptive challenges that the so-called church of liberation faced in its efforts to minister among prostitutes.

In the previous chapter, an effort was made to demonstrate the fact that while the phenomenon of prostitution prevailed as a social given throughout most of modern Brazilian history, it was only identified as a social problem during certain periods and under certain conditions.[4] Although there is evidence to suggest that during such periods the church, given its role and function as an actor within the social arena, often contributed to the definition of prostitution as a social problem, it had limited institutional awareness of prostitution as an ecclesial problem.

In this chapter, I intend to acknowledge the dramatic changes that took place within the Roman Catholic church in Brazil during the past three decades and account for how these changes gave rise to radical shifts in ecclesial consciousness with regard to the phenom-

---

4. A few specific examples of this would include the late 1600s with the institution of *recolhimentos*; the mid-1700s with the diversification of urban, rural, and migrant prostitution; the mid-1800s with the rampant abandonment of women and children; and, finally, the early 1900s with the immigrant white slave trade.

enon of prostitution. This chapter advances the position that one of
the best illustrations of these shifts in consciousness is found in a
complete analysis of the Pastoral da Mulher Marginalizada. To this
end, the selected method for analysis is based on an approach to
investigation adapted from the field of social psychology.

This method is properly understood as an evolutionary approach to
problem analysis inasmuch as it focuses on identifying the stages of
development involved in the construction of prostitution as an ecclesial
problem.[5] I have chosen this approach in order to describe the progressive stages involved in the process of problem construction and to
demonstrate how this stage theory illuminates our understanding of
the shifts in consciousness and action that led the church in Brazil
into a new awareness of itself and of prostitutes. The analysis of the
origins and evolution of the Pastoral da Mulher Marginalizada is used
to illustrate how prostitution was constructed by the church of liberation as an ecclesial problem.

During the course of the past thirty years, social psychologists
interested in the process of symbolic interaction have devoted a great
deal of attention to the "stages" through which social problems evolve
in the course of their rise and fall.[6] Their research has resulted in the
development of an approach to problem analysis that is evolutionary
and that is characterized as an interactionist perspective. According to
this approach, the progression of a problem can be traced through the
following stages: incipiency, coalescence, institutionalization, fragmentation, and demise.[7] An interpretative adaptation of this developmen-

5. This approach is adapted from the work of Stephen Hilgartner and Charles
L. Bosk as described in "The Rise and Fall of Social Problems" 53–78.

6. The following sources are cited and discussed in ibid., 53–55. See Blumer,
"Social Problems as Collective Behavior," 298–306; Armand I. Mauss, *Social
Problems as Social Movements* (New York: Lippencott, 1975); Malcolm Spector
and John I. Kituse, "Social Problems: A Re-formulation," *Social Problems* 21
(1973) 145–59; and idem, *Constructing Social Problems* (Menlo Park, CA:
Cummings, 1977).

7. These five categories are taken from the analysis of Hilgartner and
Bosk, "The Rise and Fall of Social Problems," 54. For further application and
discussion of stage theories, see Steve Woolgar and Dorothy Pawluch, "On-
tological Gerrymandering: The Anatomy of Social Problems Explanations";
Stephen Pfohl, "Toward a Sociological Deconstruction of Social Problems";
Joseph W. Schneider, "Defining the Definitional Perspective on Social Prob-

tal stage theory to the study of the construction of prostitution as an ecclesial problem results in the following framework.

Evolutionary Stages in the Construction of Prostitution as an Ecclesial Problem[8]

Stage zero, or the *baseline*, is marked by the presence of prostitution in the broader society, but the absence of any explicit concern or preoccupation with prostitution on the part of the church. In effect, the church reflects what it understands to be the *sensus fidelium* ("consensus of the faithful"). Prostitution exists. It always has and it always will. As long as the ecclesial equilibrium is not upset, the church conforms itself to a social reality that is taken to be a fact of life. Prostitutes are rendered invisible and treated with indifference.

Stage one, or the *incipiency*, is marked by the presence of prostitution and a heightened ecclesial awareness of prostitution as a potential threat to the ecclesial equilibrium. Christian communities and their leaders are invited, coerced, or persuaded, by individuals, groups, or institutions from within the church and the broader society to recognize that the church has something to lose if it fails to acknowledge the emergence of an existent social problem that threatens to manifest itself as an ecclesial problem as well. In effect, the church responds to the problem not on the terms set by society, but on the church's own terms. It addresses some aspect of prostitution in a limited and informal way, ordinarily in the private sphere, but occasionally in the public sphere as well.

Stage two, the *coalescence*, is marked by the presence of prostitution and the presence of an organized ecclesiastical effort to contain what is now understood to be a serious problem. It is deemed inevitable that prostitution will upset the ecclesial equilibrium. For this reason, the church both advances the abolition, prohibition, or regulation of prostitution and attempts to influence the actions of those entrusted with making and enforcing laws for the larger society. The

lems;" and Lawrence E. Hazelrigg, "Were It Not for Words"; all in *Social Problems* 32 (1985) 214–37.

8. In the development of the following schema, I rely on the stage descriptions used by Hilgartner and Bosk, "The Rise and Fall of Social Problems," 54.

church publicly admonishes transgressors and calls for reparation or restitution from those acting outside the law.

Stage three, the *institutionalization*, is marked by the presence of prostitution, the actual upset of ecclesial equilibrium, organized ecclesial efforts to address the problem, and the realization on the part of some members that this is not only an ecclesial problem with domestic ramifications, but an ecclesial problem with social implications. Prostitution is not a random phenomenon. Rationalizations for prostitution are grounded not only in the social construction of reality, but in the ecclesial construction of reality as well.

Stage four, or the *fragmentation*, is marked by the presence of prostitution, the accommodation or resistance of the church to the ongoing upsets to its equilibrium, contradictory or disorganized ecclesial efforts to cope with the problem, and the identification of the church as complicit in the exacerbation of prostitution as an ecclesial problem. In this stage, there is recognition of the fact that prostitution is symptomatic of a far larger ecclesial problem. Admission of this awareness causes a shift in consciousness which directs or diverts the attention of the church to a different problem.

Stage five, the *demise*, is marked by the persistence of prostitution, a concentrated ecclesial effort to regain equilibrium, and the collapse of ecclesial efforts to address the problem of prostitution. In effect, the ecclesial problem of prostitution is neither resolved nor remedied. Rather, it falls out of ecclesial consciousness as a problem category, often as the result of displacement by another ecclesial problem. Ultimately, it becomes invisible once again.

In accord with the framework described above, the following periodization is provided as an outline for delineating the evolutionary stages involved in the construction of prostitution as an ecclesial problem by the church in Brazil over a period of three decades.

Stage Zero:	Baseline	1960–1967
Stage One:	Incipiency	1967–1973
Stage Two:	Coalescence	1974–1976
Stage Three:	Institutionalization	1977–1986
Stage Four:	Fragmentation	1986–1990

Before proceeding, it is important to underscore that the application of this evolutionary stage theory to the Brazilian context is performed

in the interest of providing a descriptive analysis that is both historical and interpretative. It is undertaken for the purpose of generating
hypotheses, rather than proving them. As with all stage theories, this
particular approach to analysis is not without inherent limitations.
Despite these limitations, however, the theory offers a formidable
means for gaining insight into the interactive processes that continue
to shape and influence the church's understanding of prostitution as
an ecclesial problem, specifically within the Brazilian context.

The Social Setting of Brazil

Reform, revolution, and resistance distinguished the 1960s as an
era of unprecedented change throughout Brazil. The political climate
of the country was tumultuous. Likewise, the Roman Catholic church
found itself in a state of upheaval, brought about in part by the changes
called for by the Second Vatican Council and in part by the
sociopolitical orientation of the Conferência Nacional dos Bispos do
Brasil ("National Conference of Brazilian Bishops" or the C.N.B.B.).[9]
It was during this same period that significant numbers of priests,
religious, and laity from Europe and North America responded to the
missionary appeals of the Vatican.[10] Included among them were groups
and individuals who came to Brazil with longstanding commitments
to the poor and marginalized of their own countries. Building upon
the traditional work of rehabilitation begun by missionaries decades
before,[11] a few added their efforts to ministries of outreach among

9. Thomas C. Bruneau, *The Church in Brazil: The Politics of Religion*
(Austin: University of Texas Press, 1982); and idem, *The Political Transformation of the Brazilian Catholic Church* (New York: Cambridge University
Press, 1974); Scott Mainwaring, *The Catholic Church and Politics in Brazil,
1916–1985* (Stanford, CA: Stanford University Press, 1986); and Luiz Gonzaga
de Souza Lima, *Evolução política dos católicos e da Igreja no Brasil* (Petrópolis:
Vozes, 1979).

10. For a detailed account of the initiatives taken by the Vatican, and in
particular Pope John XXIII's and Pope Paul VI's appeals for missionaries to
go to Latin America, see Gerald M. Costello, *Mission to Latin America: The
Successes and Failures of a Twentieth Century Crusade* (Maryknoll: Orbis,
1979).

11. The first group was founded by a retired Spanish Benedictine, José
Maria Benito Serra (b. 1810) and a Swiss educator in the Spanish court, Antonia

women in prostitution. Joining forces with their Brazilian counterparts, the actions of foreign missionaries contributed decisively to the
ecclesiastical conditions that gradually gave rise to a heightened consciousness about the problem of prostitution in Brazilian society in
the late 1960s.

Stage Zero: Baseline (1960–1967)

Although much of Brazilian life and culture was unsettled by the
turbulent spirit of the decade, attitudes about the lives of prostitutes
and the enterprise of prostitution remained relatively intact. As a social
problem, prostitution was of little concern to the dominant forces at
work within Brazilian society and culture. While it undoubtedly served
as an occasional point of reference for those intent on establishing a
new social order[12] as well as those determined to defend the old,[13] it

---

Maria de Oviedo Schoental (b. 1822). Serra was the first missionary bishop
of Port Victoria, Australia. Upon his return to Spain, the two joined forces to
establish the first house of rehabilitation in Madrid in 1864. They became
affiliated with the Redemptorist Missionaries of Alphonse Ligouri in 1867.
The Congregation of Our Lady of Charity of the Good Shepherd is a branch
of the primitive institute Our Lady of Charity of the Refuge founded in 1641
by John Eudes (1601–1680), at Caen, France, for the purpose of caring for
prostitutes. Under the direction of Mother Mary Euphrasia Pelletier (1796–
1868), the ministry begun by Eudes was renewed. In 1835, she established a
central government and motherhouse in Angers, France. In the nineteenth and
twentieth centuries, the Sisters of the Good Shepherd extended their ministry
to prostitutes to various regions of the world. The first house in Brazil was
opened in 1892.

12. One of the traditional promises of socialism was the eradication of
economic poverty and, by extension, eradication of the need for oppressed
women to prostitute themselves in order to feed themselves and their children.
See August Bebel, *Women in the Past, Present and Future* (trans. H. B. Adams
Walther; New York: AMS, 1976).

13. Elite movements such as *Tradição, Familia, e Propriedade* ("Tradition, Family, and Property") emerged in the 1960s in reaction to the perceived
threat of communism. They placed great emphasis on traditional family values. In such a world view, prostitutes were identified as public sinners and
fallen women. The varied works of Plinio Corrêa de Oliveira, founder and
longstanding president of the *Conselho Nacional da Sociedade Brasileira de
Defesa da Tradição, Familia e Propriedade*, include *The Freedom of the
Church in the Communist State: The Church, the Decalogue, and the Right of*

was not a major preoccupation of the political left or the political right. If anything, reliance on prostitutes and the need for prostitution was one of the few social contracts upon which broad social consensus prevailed. For the most part, the church and its leaders followed the traditional practices of social toleration, moral exhortation, and charitable assistance.

Stage One: Incipiency (1967–1973)

Antônio Batista Fragoso was one of the first of the Brazilian bishops to pursue an active and liberative approach to pastoral assistance for prostitutes in the northeast of Brazil.[14] In 1950, during a visit to Brussels to commemorate the jubilee of Jovens Operários Católicos ("Young Catholic Workers"), he met with Father André Talvas, the co-founder of NID, a French movement approved by Cardinal Suhard and initially dedicated to ministry among prostitutes in Paris.[15] In 1957, while on his way to Rome to participate in an international meeting of Jovens Operários Católicos, the newly appointed auxiliary bishop of São Luís da Maranhão passed through Paris to invite members of the movement to the Brazilian northeast to serve in his diocese. In 1960, two women missionaries arrived.[16] Upon becoming bishop of Crateús in 1964, Dom Fragoso emerged as the first episco-

Ownership (4th amp. ed.; São Paulo: Boa Imprensa, 1964); *A Igreja ante a escalada da ameaça comunista: apelo aos bispos silenciosos* (São Paulo: Editora Vera Cruz, 1976); *Projeto de constituição angustia o pais* (São Paulo: Editora Vera Cruz, 1987). See also Thomas Case, "TFP: Catholic or Cult?" *Fidelity* 8 (1989) 22–29.

14. Dom Antônio Batista Fragoso, born in 1920, served as auxiliary bishop of São Luís do Maranhão from 1957 until 1964; in 1964, he was appointed bishop of Crateús, Ceará, a position that he still holds. See Dom Antônio Batista Fragoso, *O rosto de uma Igreja* (São Paulo: Loyola, 1982).

15. This initiative gave rise to a group of consecrated women called the *Équipières du Nid*. See Dom Antônio B. Fragoso, "Mulher marginalizada: diabo ou anjo?" in Hugues d'Ans, ed., *O grito de milhões de escravas: a cumplicidade do siléncio* (2d ed.; Petrópolis: Vozes, 1986) 98.

16. In Brazil, the secular institute adopted the name "Ninho," the Portuguese equivalent of the French word *nid* ("nest"). Over the years, the work of Ninho gave rise to pastoral teams in more than twenty-eight cities in the states of Pará, Pernambuco, Piauí, Ceará, Bahia, and Sergipe.

pal leader to incorporate the principles of Ação Católica ("Catholic Action") commonly identified as "see, judge, and act," into programs of pastoral outreach to prostitutes of his diocese.[17]

In subsequent years, other bishops demonstrated similar interest and concern for women in prostitution.[18] In reviewing the life histories of these bishops, it is not surprising to discover their names included among the vanguard of Brazil's eccesial hierarchy and the architects of the church of liberation.[19] There is no doubt that their heightened awareness and personal commitment contributed significantly to a new ecclesial consciousness about the phenomenon of prostitution.

17. It is important to note that the church movement Catholic Action gave rise to subsequent movements such as Jovens Operários Católicos and Juventude Universitaria Católica ("Young Catholic University Students"). For several years, as priest and as bishop, Dom Fragoso was identified with these movements and was a longstanding advocate of their activities, many of which the military government attacked as politically subversive.

18. Other bishops known for similar sorts of initiatives and approaches in support of outreach ministries to prostitutes include: Dom José Maria Pires, born in 1919 and bishop of Paraiba since 1965; Dom José Rodrigues de Souza, C.S.S.R., born in 1926 and bishop of Juazeiro, Bahia, since 1975; Dom Moacir Grechi, O.S.M., born in 1936 and bishop of Rio Branco, Acre, and Purus since 1973; Dom Avelar Brandão Vilela, born in 1912 and bishop of Petrolina from 1946 until 1955, bishop of Teresina, Piauí, from 1955 until 1970, cardinal archbishop of San Salvador, Bahia, from 1971 until 1987, and former primate of Brazil; Dom Aloisio Lorscheider, O.F.M., born in 1924 and bishop of Santo Angelo, Rio Grande do Sul, from 1962 until 1973 and cardinal archbishop of Forteleza, Ceará, since 1973; Don Antônio Celso Queiroz, born in 1933 and regional bishop of São Paulo since 1975; Dom Paulo Evaristo Arns, O.F.M., born in 1921 and bishop of São Paulo from 1966 until 1973 and cardinal archbishop of São Paulo since 1973; Dom Afonso Gregory, born in 1930 and director of the Centro de Estatistica Religiosa e Investigações Sociais from 1963 until 1980, and auxiliary bishop of Imperatriz, Maranhão, since 1987; Dom Luciano Duarte, born in 1925 and auxiliary bishop and archbishop of Aracajú, Sergipe, since 1966; Dom Angélico Sandalo Bernardino, born in 1933 and auxiliary bishop of São Paulo since 1975. See Conferência Nacional dos Bispos do Brasil, *Membros da Conferência Nacional dos Bispos do Brasil* (São Paulo: Paulinas, 1984); and *Annuario Pontificio per l'anno 1992* (Città de Vaticano: Libreria Editrice Vaticana, 1992).

19. See David Regan, *Church for Liberation: A Pastoral Portrait of the Church in Brazil* (Dublin: Dominican Publications, 1987).

In various regions of Brazil, missionary priests, usually with the encouragement and approval of their local ordinaries, committed themselves to ministries of advocacy and pastoral care of marginalized women. Prior to the arrival of these missionaries, limited numbers of Brazilian clergy, women religious, and lay persons,[20] such as Maria do Carmo R. Neves, sustained various ministerial commitments among prostitutes. Few of these commitments, however, received the same ecclesiastical attention as the pastoral activities undertaken by the foreign priests. Over time, their pastoral leadership, numerous publications, and international contacts earned them reputations as both informed authorities and recognized ecclesial spokespersons on the subject.

Much to the surprise of most of these foreign missionaries, their messages were heard not only in various regions of Brazil, but also in other parts of the world.[21] They became voices for the voiceless and brought their perspectives on the subjugated knowledge of marginalized women in Brazilian society to the attention of other pastoral agents. As advocates of abolitionism,[22] their stance was frequently cast in the language of sexual slavery. As foreign missionaries, they were particularly attuned to the dynamics of culture and religion and the ways in which such dynamics mutually reinforce the victimization and marginalization of women. Some of these missionaries are especially well known. Jean-Pierre Barruel Lagenest, a French Dominican and psychologist, served the local church of São Paulo both as a priest and human service professional. For several years, he was the president of the Associação Paulista de Amparo à Mulher,

20. Among the most significant of these lay leaders was Maria do Carmo R. Neves. She was internationally known as an advocate of abolitionism. For many years, she worked to influence and inform Brazilian church leaders about prostitution. Her death in mid-life was a major loss for those whom she challenged and inspired. Her legacy, however, continues. See Maria do Carmo R. Neves, "Prostituição: Abolicionismo, Regulamentarismo, Proibicionismo," *Revista Eclesiástica Brasileira* 36 (1976) 639–50.

21. Presentations were made before international groups and nongovernmental agencies of the United Nations. Selected books and articles were translated for audiences in countries outside of Brazil.

22. An explanation of this position and its origins is presented in the appendix, p. 179 n. 17.

("São Paulo Association for the Protection of Women") which was based in São Paulo and provided women with various forms of support and assistance.[23] Alfredo Kunz, a Son of Charity, was of Swiss origin, but also a native of France; in 1968 he came to serve the local church of Crateús in the northeastern state of Ceará.[24] Teodoro Helmut Rohner, a secular priest from Austria, worked in the formation of base communities in the interior of Maranhão and Ceará.[25] Hugues d'Ans, a secular priest from Belgium, served the local church of Lins in the state of São Paulo. For many years, he assumed the role of president for the Movimento de Libertação Mulher ("Movement for the Liberation of Women").[26]

When compared with the pastoral activities of Brazilian clergy, religious, and lay leaders, the efforts of these men must be understood in a broader missionary context.[27] As foreigners, as men, and as

23. Jean-Pierre Barruel de Lagenest's writings include *Lenocínio e prostituição no Brasil* (Rio de Janeiro: Agir, 1960); *Mulheres em leilão: um estudo da prostituição no Brasil* (Petrópolis: Vozes, 1973); "Migrações Internas, Trabalho Escravo, Desagregação Familiar, Prostituição na América Latina" (paper presented to the Human Rights Commission of the United Nations, 3–8 August 1987); reprinted by Programa Ação Cultural e Prostituição, Fundação Casa da Cultura Jundiai (São Paulo: Ministério da Cultura, 1987) 1–8; and "A Declaração Universal dos Direitos do Homem e a prostituição no Brasil," *Revista Eclesiástica Brasileira* 50 (1990) 433–36.

24. Alfredo Kunz's writings include *A burrinha de Balaão* (São Paulo: Loyola, 1977); and *A ovelha de Urias: o grito do justo oprimido* (São Paulo: Loyola, 1978). The former was censored by the Brazilian government.

25. Teodoro Rohner's writings include "As prostitutas podem receber os sacramentos?" *Revista Eclesiástica Brasileira* 45 (1985) 108–16; *Prostituição e libertação da mulher—Pastoral da Mulher Marginalizada: subsídios para a formação de agentes* (Petrópolis: Vozes, 1987); and *Atendimento pastoral às prostitutas* (São Paulo: Paulinas, 1988).

26. Hugues d'Ans's writings include "As prostitutas vos procederão no Reino de Deus," *Vida Pastoral* (1981); "O adolescente e prostituição" and "Prostituição: um pecado social," *Revista Eclesiástica Brasileira* 44 (1984) 564–72; he edited *O grito de milhões de escravas*. He also wrote "Pastoral da Mulher Marginalizada: 13 anos de caminhada libertadora," *Revista Eclesiástica Brasileira* 47 (1987) 651–53; and *Mulher: da escravidão à libertação* (São Paulo: Paulinas, 1989).

27. As is the case throughout much of the church's history, the names of countless coworkers of missionary priests frequently do not make their way into the historical record. In a similar fashion, successful efforts on the part

priests, they possessed a distinct advantage. They were not subject to local scrutiny in quite the same fashion as their Brazilian counterparts.[28] In accord with the scriptural allusion and often quoted Brazilian maxim, *profeta de casa não faz milagres* ("a prophet does not work miracles in his own house"; see Luke 4:24), these missionary priests did not encounter the same obstacles as those often faced by prophetic ministers in their native lands. Whether or not in practice the efforts of these priests were substantially more significant, enlightened, or effective than those of local pastoral agents is an open question. The fact does remain, however, that as a consequence of their notoriety and the influence that they were able to exercise, they succeeded in raising ecclesial consciousness about prostitution in ways that were unprecedented.

Stage Two: Coalescence (1974–1976)

The first visible sign of coalescence was displayed in 1974, during the first gathering of the Pastoral da Mulher Marginalizada, held in Rio de Janeiro.[29] It was the first indication that the church, as an institution, was prepared to take up the problem of prostitution at the national level. As the initial group met to discuss the realities of prostitution as well as the moral and pastoral responsibilities of the church, it sought to respond to three questions: What is sin? What is the church? What is a prostitute? The group concluded that prostitution was a collective social sin, that the church was the servant of the poor, and that the prostitute was a dehumanized person.

---

of high profile missionaries often supplant or overshadow preexisting or parallel efforts on the part of other clergy, religious, and laity, whether local or foreign. The priests highlighted in this study are subject to this reality, as is the study itself.

28. This observation is not meant to suggest that their efforts did not meet with criticism and resistance, but that as foreigners they were granted a certain measure of freedom to transgress cultural boundaries and norms before being penalized or ridiculed. Ordinarily, such freedom was not extended to Brazilians. This may best be exemplified in terms of the freedom to interact with prostitutes without being suspected of ulterior motives.

29. For translations, summaries, and commentaries on the proceedings of the First National Encounter of the Pastoral da Mulher Marginalizada, see the appendix, pp. 174–78.

In the course of deliberations, the group endeavored to respond to the question of what action should be taken toward women in prostitution. Members of the group identified three priorities: to encourage women to withdraw from the business of prostitution, to give value to the prostitute as a person, and to bring about the awareness of the prostitute's dignity as a child of God.

The needs of prostitutes were assessed from the perspectives of pastoral agents.[30] In the opinion of the participants, the majority of whom were involved in direct ministry among marginalized women, prostitutes needed three things: to be educated in order to abandon prostitution, to be made aware of their human rights, and to be understood not only individually, but in global and collective terms.

In considering the actions that should be taken by pastoral agents with regard to society, there was broad consensus about the urgent need to condemn and confront a social order that used and abused prostitutes, while simultaneously rejecting and marginalizing them. To this end, the group envisioned several strategies, including the conscientization of society; the use of media; the promotion of dialogue among people living in proximity to areas of prostitution; public education about the causes and consequences of prostitution; initial efforts to engage the imaginations of domestic workers, bishops, priests, pastoral agents, lay movements, and social service professionals; and the creation of a National Coordinating Committee. The group set for itself the long-term goals of preventative work with single mothers, the creation of information centers, securing further assistance and support from the National Conference of Brazilian Bishops, community service education, involvement in other pastoral ministries, and ecumenical dialogue with other ministers and religious leaders concerned with the problem of prostitution.

At the conclusion of the meeting, the group set forth numerous resolutions, including the need for more statistics and the need to combat tourism and sex trade within the country. Furthermore, they stated the need to break the silence surrounding the sexual exploita-

---

30. At this point, there was little awareness of the potentially distinct differences between the perspectives of pastoral agents thinking on behalf of prostitutes and the perspectives of prostitutes thinking on behalf of themselves.

tion of women through efforts aimed at peace and justice, the need to encourage responsible parenthood, and the need to determine a name for the organization.

As an outcome of the First National Encounter, members of the Brazilian ecclesiastical hierarchy, along with individuals representing various other sectors of church life, came to recognize the ways in which prostitution was an ecclesial problem, albeit one that was understood more in terms of impressions than firm statistics. Pastoral agents and their ecclesiastical advocates shared a common assumption that education was the key to social transformation. There was a firm conviction that women involved in prostitution were victims of oppression and warranted inclusion among the poor for whom the church had declared a preferential option. The prevention of prostitution was foreseen as a realistic goal connected to the emerging vision of the church as an agent of social change and transformation.

Over the course of the next two years, the P.M.M. incorporated into its agenda a new set of concerns. In 1976, the Second National Encounter took place, once again in Rio de Janeiro.[31] The overarching aim of the meeting was to set forth pastoral directives through a clear statement of identity, purpose, and objectives. Members of the group discussed at length the public debate about regulation, prohibition, and abolition of prostitution. Those directly involved in the matter highlighted for the group the contradiction between the Brazilian penal code and actual patterns of law enforcement that reflected the management of de facto regulation. The violation of the human rights of prostitutes, especially those in the *zonas*, was of particular concern. Ongoing preoccupation about the internal trafficking of women and adolescent girls surfaced with the presentation of evidence regarding the increased incidence of prostitution in areas of the rural interior— such as highways, factories, and mills—where development projects were underway.

These issues attracted a great deal of attention, in part because of active political lobbying to revise federal legislation regarding prostitution. It was noted that during 1975, efforts to establish a nation-

31. For translations, summaries, and commentaries on the proceedings of the Second National Encounter of the Pastoral da Mulher Marginalizada, see the appendix, pp. 178–83.

wide policy of regulation intensified. Although such initiatives met
with opposition at the time, due to the concerted efforts of various
national and international organizations, Brazilian society remained
largely indifferent to the politics of prostitution. With the exception
of a few voices, the church at diocesan and parish levels seemed to
follow suit. In light of this reality, participating pastoral agents expressed their powerlessness to effect change in a world where the
overwhelming odds were against them. They demanded more from
the bishops than a commitment to the pastoral care of prostitutes.
They charged the bishops with the moral duty, as a matter of faith
and justice, of defending the human rights of marginalized women.[32]

The gathering concluded by underscoring two important responsibilities of the P.M.M. The first emphasized the need for preventative
efforts, particularly among domestic workers, migrants, single mothers, juvenile offenders, and former prostitutes. The second highlighted
the need for ongoing ecclesial reflection on the part of pastoral ministers and Christian communities in order to facilitate the social reintegration of marginalized women.

In September of 1976, six months after the Second National Encounter of the Pastoral da Mulher Marginalizada, the C.N.B.B. responded to the expressed expectations and demands of the movement
with a detailed conference study document entitled *Prostitution: A
Challenge to the Society and to the Church*.[33] In the document, the
C.N.B.B. acknowledged its role in encouraging the pastoral initiatives
of the P.M.M. during the previous three years, highlighting how the
P.M.M. evolved under the auspices of the C.N.B.B., which provided
it with both episcopal support and some measure of financial assistance. In addition to setting forth in writing their renewed commitment to the Pastoral da Mulher Marginalizada, the bishops formally
incorporated the pastoral project into the national pastoral plan of the

---

32. In concrete terms, this meant alerting and exhorting leaders within the
Roman Catholic community to assume social and political responsibility for
upholding Brazil's commitment to the International Abolitionist Convention.
For further information, see Conferência Nacional dos Bispos do Brasil,
"Anexos," in idem, *Prostituição: desafio à sociedade e à Igreja* (Estudos da
C.N.B.B. 15; São Paulo: Paulinas, 1976) 89–125, 139–62.

33. Ibid.

C.N.B.B. and included the P.M.M. among the church's works of evangelization. The document provided the church in Brazil with a clear message about the bishops' commitment to promote the aims and objectives of the P.M.M. With the publication of such an unprecedented document, the bishops of Brazil prepared the way for the institutionalization of prostitution as an ecclesial problem.[34]

Stage Three: Institutionalization (1977–1986)

During the late 1970s, the church throughout Brazil was engaged in recognizing prostitution as an ecclesial problem. Growing numbers of bishops, clergy, religious, and lay leaders acknowledged the problem and began to grapple with the socioeconomic factors contributing to the plight of marginalized women in Brazilian society. Some pastoral agents, however, particularly those directly involved with prostitutes on a daily basis, felt the need to examine the phenomenon of prostitution more critically. As they came to know more about the life stories of the women among whom they ministered, it was no longer possible for them to focus exclusively on socioeconomic factors as the causes of prostitution. Culture and gender surfaced as new categories for analysis. As the focus shifted from economic poverty to other issues such as *machismo*, double standards for sexual behavior, and the power of men over women, the critiques of pastoral agents became more unsettling and ultimately more radical.

Growing numbers of pastoral agents asserted that the preferential option for the poor and oppressed could not be determined solely by categories of analysis that highlighted the disparity between the rich and the poor. The disempowerment and marginalization of women

34. In order to understand the radical nature of this publication, it is important to note that while twelve other countries with sizeable Roman Catholic populations and influential bishops (Argentina, Belgium, Bolivia, Equador, France, Spain, the Philippines, Haiti, Italy, Mexico, Poland, and Venezuela) have ratified the 1949 International Abolitionist Treaty, the action taken by the C.N.B.B. in 1976 was unprecedented. Although at times individual Roman Catholic bishops, acting alone or in small groups, have supported abolition, their numbers are few. For the most part, representatives of the church of Rome have distanced themselves from supporting abolition because of its historical association with feminism, socialism, and Protestantism.

were more than the consequences of an unjust economic order. They were indicators of systemic forms of oppression. Their myriad manifestations were embedded deep within the ethos of Brazilian culture. Prostitution was but one of the more flagrant examples.

Prostitution, they argued, was not a deviation from the norm, but rather an all too common example of the exploitation and degradation experienced by women in general. In effect, prostitution was the camouflage used to conceal the tragic reality of the dehumanization of women. For those who had eyes with which to see, the phenomenon of prostitution disclosed the interrelated dynamics of *machismo* and sexual discrimination within Brazilian culture.[35] Prostitution was a clear indicator of the ways in which cultural mores functioned so as to perpetuate the subordination and expendability of women within Brazilian society.

Insights such as these led members of the Pastoral da Mulher Marginalizada to assert that women were not born to be prostitutes. Female prostitution was only one aspect of a widespread prostitution that went on at every level of Brazilian culture and society. Many women, especially poor women, were held captive by taboos, exclusion, rejection, and lack of information about their own bodies. As long as the foundations upon which sexual discrimination was based remained intact, the daily realities experienced by millions of women would also remain unaltered and unquestioned.

In 1978, the deliberations of the Third National Encounter of the P.M.M. were guided by the following question: How could the church of liberation advance a preferential option for the poor and oppressed and leave the cultural underpinnings of sexism unexamined?[36] Participants continued to hold fast to the conviction that education was a critical force in bringing about the process of human liberation. In light of this conviction, strategies for dealing more adequately with the issue of sexism were explored. Proposals included the revision of

---

35. It should be noted that at this time ecclesial consciousness about racism had not yet surfaced in any explicit way.

36. For translations, summaries, and commentaries on the proceedings of the Third National Encounter of the Pastoral da Mulher Marginalizada, see the appendix, sec. 3.

school textbooks,[37] the availability and endorsement of sex education, the promotion of job training for women, and the guarantee of equal wages for equal work.[38]

At this gathering, the plight of marginalized women was linked not only to classism but also to sexism. Participants agreed that in order to address the problem of prostitution it was first necessary to address the root evil. This could only be accomplished by challenging the cultural assumption that men were more important than women. In effect, this would require both the church and the broader society to reexamine their operating anthropologies not only with regard to women, but with regard to men as well. The participants also concluded that the value and dignity of all human persons could not be guaranteed as long the predominant cultural viewpoint advanced the position that the sexual impulses and urges of men were beyond their control.

The group emphasized that women needed to become their own agents for change. It would be necessary to challenge the power relations between men and women and, to this end, to pressure political and business leaders alike. Concrete strategies for change included public education campaigns, securing and defending the rights of domestic workers, the creation of day care centers, and efforts to increase job opportunities for women. Along with these strategic initiatives, a thorough analysis of cultural and religious values was believed to be imperative.

Participants located the responsibility for promoting change with dioceses and *comunidades eclesiais de base* ("Christian base communities"). In doing so, the participants redirected their attention and their energies. In 1976, they celebrated the inclusion of the Pastoral da Mulher Marginalizada in the C.N.B.B. proposal of a national pas-

37. See Marta Suplicy, *De Mariazinha à Maria* (7th ed.; Petrópolis: Vozes, 1985) 219–21. See also Fúlvia Rosenberg, *A educação da mulher brasileira* (Rio de Janeiro: Global Editora, 1982); and idem, *Análise dos modelos culturais na literatura infanto-juvenil brasileira* (Rio de Janeiro: Fundação Carlos Chagas, 1980).

38. For statistical information on the inequality of salaries, see Heleieth Saffioti, *Mulher brasileira: opressão e exploração* (Rio de Janeiro: Aciamé, 1984) 97–129.

toral plan. By 1978, however, the concerns of the group shifted from responsible and inclusive pastoral planning on the part of bishops to responsible and inclusive pastoral implementation of the plan by local leaders and communities.

In order to ensure that efforts at implementation would be integrative, representative pastoral agents advanced the position that in effect prostitution was the reality of all women. In the lives of some women it took subtle and undetectable forms. In the lives of others, it was acute and exaggerated. In advancing this position, participants reasserted a basic tenet of the P.M.M., namely, that the experience of prostitutes was not very different from that of other women.[39] In light of this conviction, it was essential not to distinguish radically the pastoral agenda for prostitutes from the pastoral agenda for women. Many felt that if implementation followed the course of distinct pastoral agendas, such a practice would ultimately lead to a fundamental misrepresentation of reality and a perpetuation of false categories of difference.

Over the course of the next two years, many of the concerns expressed by members of the Pastoral da Mulher Marginalizada in 1978— especially those regarding the process of pastoral implementation —were heeded in some regions of Brazil. This was particularly true in dioceses where, under the leadership of certain cardinals, archbishops, and bishops, the church continued to deepen its pastoral and social commitment to the poorest and most marginalized people of Brazilian society.

At the Fourth National Encounter, held in 1980, participants directed themselves to three major tasks: a reexamination of abolition, an assessment of the work done in the course of the past two years, and, finally, a redefinition of the aims and objectives of the P.M.M.[40]

Throughout Brazil, the growth of the sex trade industry was out of control. There was clear consensus regarding the urgent need for church leaders to reassert the position that under Brazilian law, prostitution itself was not a crime. The crime was sex trade and trafficking. As a

39. For further discussion of this position, see the appendix, pp. 188–89.

40. For translations, summaries, and commentaries on the proceedings of the Fourth National Encounter of the Pastoral da Mulher Marginalizada, see the appendix, pp. 189–95.

matter of social justice, the church needed to shoulder greater responsibility for alerting society to the fact that the illegal prosecution of common prostitutes, which was often marked by police brutality and blackmail, deflected attention away from the real criminals—the barons and entrepreneurs of the sex trade industry. In calling for a renewed ecclesial commitment to uphold and defend the human rights of marginalized women, representatives of the Pastoral da Mulher Marginalizada endeavored to relate pastoral practice with political action as they appealed to the commitment of the C.N.B.B. to promote faith and justice. The defense of abolition was believed to be a concrete expression of such commitment.

Building upon this discussion, participants brought into focus broader ecclesial issues and concerns as they reiterated the need for the church to identify itself not only with the causes of prostitutes but also with those of women in general. Inasmuch as exploitation, precarious working conditions, and lack of education were realities that touched the lives of many women, participants encouraged church leaders to witness to their commitment to promoting evangelization and human dignity by helping women overcome the barriers and stigmas that kept them at the margins of society as victims of capitalism and *machismo*.[41]

In taking an active stance against the prevailing social order, the Pastoral da Mulher Marginalizada appealed to the church, as institution, to participate in public denunciations, to file law suits when appropriate, and to provide legal assistance for women victimized by the system. The inadequacy and failure of human services were highlighted as indicators of other serious crimes and injustices against women, such as sexual abuse and violence. Participants emphasized that it was not enough for pastoral agents to educate prostitutes for critical consciousness. Given the growing influence and agency of Christian base communities throughout Brazil, the church of liberation, broadly conceived, had to be involved in confronting the systems of oppression and injustice that militated against women's abilities to liberate themselves from the realities that often led to prostitution.

41. For an analysis of *machismo* in Brazilian society and culture, see Délcio Monteiro de Lima, *Comportamento sexual do Brasileiro* (Rio de Janeiro: F. Alves, 1976) 61–63.

In order to bring such action about, representatives of the P.M.M. underscored the need for the church to encourage broader networks of communication and participation.

In the aftermath of the 1980 National Encounter, it became clear that a new consciousness had emerged within the P.M.M. Pastoral agents began to realize that it was not enough for *them* to gather and talk about the problems faced by prostitutes. They perceived a need to include a greater representation of prostitutes at national and regional meetings of the P.M.M. This realization proved to be critical to the further institutionalization of prostitution as an ecclesial problem as well as to the ongoing evolution of the P.M.M. itself.

In 1982, the Fifth National Encounter of the P.M.M. began a more detailed examination of the relationships between the church, society, prostitution, and government authorities.[42] Unlike previous national encounters, the emphasis of the meeting was placed on process, rather than product.[43] The 1979 Puebla document—the product of the Third General Conference of Latin American Bishops, where bishops of Latin American reaffirmed and advanced their preferential option for the poor—was invoked as the group began to reconsider its own understanding of the preferential option for the poor.[44] While there was considerable agreement about what needed to be done, the group concluded that the works of evangelization and human liberation unfolded very slowly.

At this meeting, the testimonies of several prostitutes identified and confirmed the means by which the established social order op-

42. For translations, summaries, and commentaries on the proceedings of the Fifth National Encounter of the Pastoral da Mulher Marginalizada, see the appendix, pp. 195–96.

43. Given this fact, documentation on the proceedings of the meeting was limited to a few pages.

44. In 1979, the Consejo Episcopal Latinoamericano ("Latin American Episcopal Council") met in Puebla, Mexico for the Third General Conference of Latin American Bishops. In their final document, the following sections address selected concerns of women in Latin America: §§9, 126, 299, 317, 419, 834, 836, 839–45, 847, 849, 1134, 1174. References to prostitution in particular are found in §§577, 835, and 1261. For the English translation and commentaries, see John Eagleson and Philip Scharper, eds., *Puebla and Beyond* (Maryknoll: Orbis, 1979).

pressed and enslaved women in general and prostitutes in particular.[45] In this process, the group arrived at an almost complete articulation of the church's need to address the problem of prostitution not only as a social problem, but more precisely as an ecclesial problem.

Based on the experiences of dialogue and reflection that occurred as a result of the national meeting, several representatives returned to their respective regions and experimented with similar processes at local and regional levels. Over the course of the next two years, their commitment to a more process-oriented manner of interacting resulted in a greater level of participation and dialogue among bishops, pastoral agents, and prostitutes. It also led to enhanced networks of ongoing communication among the local, regional, and national representatives.[46]

In 1984, the Sixth National Encounter of the P.M.M. brought together participants from various regions of Brazil.[47] In addition to pastoral agents and bishops, participants included prostitutes, theologians, and representatives of various women's movements. Discussion focused on whether pastoral work was being done *to*, *with*, or *for* prostitutes. Documented testimonies from prostitutes underscored the need for greater consciousness regarding the incidence of child prostitution. Life stories made clear the fact that the growing phenomenon was not a recent development, and that many of the prostitutes in attendance themselves entered prostitution as children.

45. Testimonies representative of those given during the course of this meeting can be found in a series of fifteen interviews with prostitutes; these are compiled by Hugues d'Ans. See "Depoimentos," in d'Ans, *O grito de milhões de escravas*, 17–62. For the sake of comparison, it is important to note the relative similarities and occasional differences between testimonies given by prostitutes to church-based interviewers or audiences and those given to secular interviewers or audiences. See Amara Lúcia, *A difícil vida fácil: a prostituta e sua condição* (2d ed.; Petrópolis: Vozes, 1984).

46. Examples of such communication are included among the preparatory documents circulated prior to the Sixth National Encounter. They can be found in "Pastoral da Mulher Marginalizada," *Serviço de Documentação* 17 (1985) 804–57.

47. For translations, summaries, and commentaries on the proceedings of the Sixth National Encounter of the Pastoral da Mulher Marginalizada, see the appendix, pp. 196–206.

Critiques of social and ecclesial approaches to the problem of prostitution indicated the ways in which dependency, rather than personal agency, was likely to be fostered among prostitutes. There were favorable reports, however, regarding the integration of the P.M.M. with other popular movements. Greater communication, broader participation, and more complete representation were acknowledged to be influential factors in assisting the prostitutes to take ownership of the Pastoral da Mulher Marginalizada as their movement, and not just a movement of pastoral agents and bishops.

Reflections on the relationship between pastoral agents and prostitutes stressed the importance of presence, encouragement, and availability.[48] The pedagogy of Jesus, understood as "go and listen," was advanced as the most appropriate approach to foster conscientization, conversion, and compassion. Participants affirmed that the desired objective of achieving the integral liberation of all persons was contingent on the ways in which both personal sin and social sin were understood and addressed. Prostitutes noted that although the church desired to transform society and talked of embracing the cause of the poor, it in fact had a difficult time doing so.[49] In light of this reality, theologians responded by underscoring the essential need for pastoral practice to be guided by the attitudes of Jesus.[50]

Throughout the meeting, the prostitutes in attendance were both invited and encouraged by pastoral agents to participate as fully as possible. One unanticipated yet predictable outcome of such interaction was the manner in which representative prostitutes responded when challenged by another prostitute to organize among themselves so as to claim their own voice and agency: the response took the form of two written statements. The first was a letter sent to the Vatican in defense of the Franciscan theologian Leonardo Boff. The other was a letter addressed to the people of God in Brazil, alerting them to the

48. The significance of this for pastoral work among prostitutes will be discussed at length in chapter five.
49. See Gabriela Silva Leite, *Eu, mulher da vida* (Rio de Janeiro: Editora Rosa dos Tempos, 1992) 92–95.
50. See Leonardo Boff, "Deixar-nos questionar pelas atitudes de Jesus," *Serviço de Documentação* 17 (1985) 871–74.

fact that prostitutes sought to set themselves free and wanted their rights as persons restored. Inasmuch as it was believed that Brazilian society followed the lead of the church, the letter requested that the Roman Catholic church itself stop marginalizing prostitutes. The presence of Gabriela Silva Leite proved to be a catalyst for unprecedented action and awareness on the part of many participants.[51]

At this juncture, it became clear to bishops, pastoral agents, and prostitutes alike that the combined processes of conscientization, social analysis, and theological reflection that shaped the Pastoral da Mulher Marginalizada could lead to transformative action. What was not clear, however, was the extent to which a church that had actively participated in the construction of prostitution as an ecclesial problem was itself capable of conversion.

51. Gabriela Silva Leite is a significant figure in the struggle for the rights of prostitutes throughout Brazil. She was the first to speak out in the early 1980s. She came from the middle class, studied for a degree in social work at the University of São Paulo and entered the world of prostitution at twenty-five. Her background is considerably different from the women whom she has helped to organize in the past decade. She serves as an interlocutor between prostitutes, many of whom are unconnected to any organization, and national and international groups that provide various forms of economic and political support. In the mid-1980's Gabriela was in conversation with Leonardo Boff in conjunction with P.M.M. efforts in the *zonas* outside of Rio de Janeiro. As her activities become more political, she became less supportive of the strategies and activities of the P.M.M. She was convinced that despite the best intentions of pastoral agents, they were inextricably enmeshed in the belief structures of an institutional church that would never be capable of taking prostitutes on their own terms, precisely because of the internalized oppression that is reinforced by attitudes regarding women and human sexuality. The presence of Gabriela Silva Leite at this particular meeting proved to be a catalyst for calling into question the underlying assumptions and biases held by pastoral agents regarding sexual morality and human sexuality. By her example, she required the assembly to attend to the fact that she was no longer a victim, but a protagonist, as her work on the civil rights of prostitutes and the organization of prostitute movements throughout Brazil attests. See, Silva Leite, *Eu, mulher da vida* 161–64; and idem, "Women of Life, We Must Speak," in Gail Peterson, ed., *A Vindication of the Rights of Whores* (Seattle: Seal, 1989) 288–93.

Stage Four: Fragmentation (1987–1990)

In 1987, the Seventh National Encounter of the P.M.M. took place in the national capital of Brasilia.[52] It is important to note that other than an anticipatory announcement, this meeting received virtually no attention in the official communications networks of the church.[53] In comparison to previous years, this signified a departure from the type of documented ecclesiastical recognition given to national encounters of the P.M.M. in previous years. The major concerns upon which participants focused their attention included the growth of prostitution in Brazil, the professionalization of prostitutes,[54] the church's actual attitudes toward prostitutes, and the integration of P.M.M. into the life of a church in transition.

Throughout the course of this meeting, considerable time was given to group process. Unlike previous gatherings, prostitutes far outnumbered pastoral agents: the assembly was comprised of four groups of prostitutes and one group of pastoral agents. The group reports presented by prostitutes included several important observations. They noted that persons were not prostitutes but rather prostituted. Domestic employees were not workers, but slaves.[55] Together, the group reports of prostitutes and pastoral agents concurred that sexual violence, racism, and *machismo* were urgent issues that warranted ongoing reflection and discussion within the church and the broader society.

Throughout the course of the meeting, the church fell under criticism for being legalistic, moralistic, and lacking a human face. Furthermore, many participants were acutely aware that the important

52. For translations, summaries, and commentaries on the proceedings of the Seventh National Encounter of the Pastoral da Mulher Marginalizada, see the appendix, pp. 206–15.

53. Previously, notices about the meetings were published in *Serviço de Documentação* or *Revista Eclesiástica Brasileira*. See Hugues d'Ans, "Pastoral da Mulher Marginalizada: 13 anos de caminhada libertadora," *Revista Eclesiástica Brasileira* 47 (1987) 654.

54. In accord with actions taken by prostitutes in other countries, activist prostitutes in Brazil mobilized political forces in order to lobby for the recognition of prostitution as a profession. For a more detailed discussion of this point, see the appendix, pp. 206–7 n. 78.

55. For further information on the situation of domestic workers, see Saffioti, *Mulher brasileira*, 37–54.

claims and needs of other groups—such as persons with AIDS and homosexuals—were in direct competition with the claims of prostitutes. Prior to the emergence of demands by other sexually marginalized groups, prostitutes were already limited in terms of their access to human services. In the wake of competing claims of other groups, the allocation of resources was a definite preoccupation. In a similar vein, concerns were voiced about the long-term and short-term consequences of migration, drugs, and police repression.

In addition to giving consideration to the immediate concerns of prostitutes, the meeting also attended to the expressed concerns of ecclesial leaders. Three of the bishops in attendance, Dom José Rodrigues de Souza, Dom José Maria Pires, and Dom Afonso Gregory, urged participants to remember that despite the overwhelming realities, there were occasional signs of hope. Among such signs, they included reports indicating that in some areas of Brazil, prostitution was diminishing as a direct result of heightened consciousness about the causes of prostitution and an openness on the part of the church to deal with the problem. In identifying prostitution as a moral and social problem, they noted that the abuse and exploitation of women engaged in prostitution was an issue of human rights. Throughout the meeting they encouraged those involved in lives of prostitution to have courage and faith.[56]

In subsequent discussions, prostitutes proceeded to highlight more of their concerns, citing in particular the plight of street children as a desperately urgent problem. They expressed dismay over the fact that while they endeavored to deal with the concrete realities of their daily lives, pastoral agents tended to be oriented toward the future, preferring to focus on literacy and job training, along with other means of encouraging women to leave prostitution. They also chastised the church, as an institution, for its failure to treat women with care and respect.

As a consequence of heated discussion and debate, the prostitutes in attendance agreed to send an open letter to the Brazilian bishops demanding that the church grant equal rights to men *and* women. Prostitutes protested their traditional depiction as sinners and noted

56. See the appendix, p. 209.

that many of them were victims of oppression and injustice. They questioned why sacraments were denied to them and to their children. They questioned why they themselves were not allowed to be god-mothers. They recommended that in the future the liaison between the P.M.M. and the C.N.B.B. be selected by the P.M.M. rather than the bishops' conference. They also recommended that the bishops focus on the concerns of women as a theme for the 1990 Campanha da Fraternidade ("Brotherhood Campaign").[57]

Gabriela Silva Leite, who at the national meeting in 1984 urged the prostitutes in attendance to acknowledge the power of their own voice and vision within the P.M.M., returned to this meeting to present her views on the professionalization of prostitutes.[58] Once again, Silva Leite's views served as a catalyst for critical consciousness. Whether or not those gathered at the meeting agreed with her position, there was general consensus that the church needed to be more open to women, to address the problem of prostitution directly, and to face the issues that it encountered in dealing with prostitutes. The foundations and rationales that undergirded the general consensus, however, were multiple. While the consensus appeared to be common, the fundamental reasoning of individuals that led to consensual agreement was not only variant, but potentially conflictual. This was most clearly exemplified in how individuals made use of the Bible in supporting their particular positions.

57. Since 1964, the C.N.B.B. promoted broad national participation in the Campanha da Fraternidade. Each Lenten season, an annual theme was selected as a means of focusing the attention of the entire Brazilian church on a particular issue of concern. Through these annual campaigns, the bishops attempted to educate and form the social conscience of the Roman Catholic populace in accord with the social teachings of the church and the specific faith and justice concerns of bishops' conference. For more detailed information on the evolution of the campaign over the course of the first twenty years, see Conferência Nacional dos Bispos do Brasil, *Campanha da Fraternidade: vinte anos de serviço à missão da Igreja* (Estudos da C.N.B.B. no. 35; São Paulo: Paulinas, 1983).

58. At this point, Silva Leite was involved in the political organization of prostitutes in various regions of Brazil. The professionalization movement was an effort to unionize prostitutes, thereby requiring the state to recognize their services as "labor" and to guarantee them the rights afforded other workers.

Given the centrality of biblical narratives in the consciousness-raising process of base communities, a process that informed every level of pastoral action, it is important to note the potential for radically different interpretations and applications. This was best characterized by both the biblical foundations that participants appealed to at different parts of the meeting and the interpretations that were given to the story of the prodigal son (Luke 15:11–32) and that of the Samaritan woman (John 4). On the one hand, pastoral agents appealed to the prodigal son and the Samaritan woman as characters with whom women engaged in prostitution might identify. On the other hand, prostitutes appealed to the prodigal son and the Samaritan women as characters with whom the church and its pastoral agents should identify. In either case, the dynamics of interpretation highlighted the differences in perspective that emerged as the prostitutes began to claim their own authority in the interpretive process.

At the conclusion of the meeting, pastoral agents stressed the need for a renewed commitment to the P.M.M. and the need for the P.M.M. to act in a unified fashion, to be connected to other groups, and to be engaged in the enterprise of shaping an overarching pastoral plan. The bishops promised to continue their financial support of the P.M.M. Critiques of the meeting included concerns about preparation of representatives and the appropriateness of the level of discourse used throughout the meeting. On the one hand, some believed that pastoral agents did not sufficiently prepare the women representing prostitutes for full participation in the meeting. Other participants noted that the language of the meeting was beyond the comprehension of many of the women in attendance. It was agreed that efforts would be made to address these concerns at future gatherings. At the conclusion of the meeting, an administrative resolution was adopted to extend the P.M.M. to other countries in Latin America.

A careful review of the 1987 proceedings of the P.M.M. highlights the fragmentation of the church's understanding of prostitution as an ecclesial problem. Multiple concerns, issues, attitudes, priorities, and directions were not only in competition but at times in contradiction. The ability of the bishops, pastoral agents, and prostitutes to agree upon a common understanding of the problem of prostitution was no

longer possible inasmuch as the problem was more adequately understood as multifaceted and extremely complex in nature.

In 1990, the Eighth National Encounter of the P.M.M. was characterized by the influential presence of women not only as participants,
but also as facilitators.[59] The meeting opened with four creative presentations; through song, poetry, mime, and dramatizations, these
presentations captured the issues and concerns of women engaged in
prostitution. The overall encounter was guided by a woman lawyer
and a woman social worker. Prayer services were led by women,
some of whom were religious sisters. The presence of women from
other countries brought an added dimension of internationality to the
assembly. Although no members of the Bishops Conference were
present at the meeting, several longstanding advocates of the P.M.M.
sent letters of greeting and support.

At the 1990 encounter, two of the major topics addressed by participants were violence against women and the denial of women's
rights. Several women described and discussed the experiences of
violence to which they were subjected in the course of their lives.
During the meeting, emphasis was placed on the need to come to
terms with the devastating consequences of relationships of inequality. In this regard, particular attention was paid to the fact that through
the perpetuation of women's self-identification as victims, oppressive
systems and institutions conspire to ensure that women will not revolt.

Throughout the course of the gathering, the group repeatedly affirmed its desire to participate in the creation of a nonviolent society,
while underscoring the necessity for fostering relationships based on
love, rather than those based on domination and power. Participants
gave expression to an emerging conviction regarding the need to promote unified action among those marginalized, exploited, and disen-
franchised by society. Within the group there was a new consciousness
about violence and women, and about the failure of civil authorities
to enforce laws protecting women. There was also a stark realization

59. For translations, summaries, and commentaries on the proceedings of
the Eighth National Encounter of the Pastoral da Mulher Marginalizada, see
the appendix, pp. 215–23.

that many organizations explicitly committed to advocating the civil and human rights of women were not connected to the church.

At the conclusion of the meeting, a letter composed by the group was sent to the bishops of Brazil. Mindful of the ways in which the C.N.B.B. Campanha da Fraternidade for 1990, "Woman and Man: Image of God," proved to be limited in its capacity to address women's rights and issues of violence against women in tangible ways, the assembly called upon the bishops to provide leadership in supporting initiatives and activities specifically designed to respond to the urgency of women's claims and concerns. The group also affirmed the need for a regional reorganization of the P.M.M. Unlike the elections in previous years, those chosen to be directors of the local regions were all women. It was not only fitting but symbolic that the encounter ended with a celebration on the feast of Mary Magdalene.

In assessing the direction and outcome of the 1990 National Encounter, there are indications that the relationship between the C.N.B.B. and the P.M.M. was subject to the processes of change and renegotiation. Although it would be precipitous to conclude that interest in continuing to construct prostitution as an ecclesial problem was somewhat less certain than in the past, various indicators would suggest that its eventual demise was within the realm of possibility.

Insights and Observations

There are numerous insights and observations highlighted in the previous analysis, many of which lend themselves to further thought and exploration. Among the most important, however, are those that make it possible for outside observers to understand the role that episcopal leadership and foreign missionaries played in the construction of prostitution as an ecclesial problem for the church of liberation. Of equal importance is the manner in which these various insights and observations reveal the gradual process by which the church of liberation came to recognize that the problem of prostitution had as much to do with the oppression of women as it had to do with the oppression of the poor. Above all, the analysis illustrates how the church set in motion a process of evangelization and liberation that ultimately demanded the conversion of the church itself, or if not its

conversion, at least the admission of its complicity in the marginalization and oppression of all women.

Given that one of the primary aims of this study is to explain not
only *how* prostitution came to be constructed as an ecclesial problem,
but also what the ramifications of that construction were for the church
of liberation, the next chapter will give further consideration to other
factors and dynamics involved in the definition and selection of problems within the ecclesial arena. In order to do this, another method of
analysis, best described as an ecological approach, will be adopted in
the hope of demonstrating how the combined use of these approaches
results in a two-part method of analysis that is comprehensive in
nature and design.

4

The Church, Marginalized Women, and the Limits of Liberation

Prostitution is not vagrancy nor the result of savage capitalism, but rather the primary thread which holds together a society that is deathly afraid of addressing its sexuality and consequently feels profoundly threatened when a prostitute reveals herself, thus forcing others to acknowledge that in fact she is not very different from other women—much to the anguish of the moralists of our time.[1]

Gabriela Silva Leite

Your cause [the cause of prostitutes] is the cause of the Gospel. You are in the heart of Jesus. If we take seriously the word of Jesus—and we should take it seriously—marginalized women that believe and journey together for their own complete liberation and that of others, will arrive in the Kingdom of the Father before me, before the bishops and before the pope. . . . I know that this Gospel message was sequestered by the Pharisaic moralism of several sectors of the Church. It is befitting to you to set free the word of Jesus so that it may produce the fruits of fraternity, mutual understanding and support for each other.[2]

Leonardo Boff

1. Gabriela Silva Leite, "Coluna de Gabi," *Beijo da Rua* 1 (1988) 2.
2. This excerpt is taken from a reflection written by Leonardo Boff to the participants of a regional encounter of the P.M.M. held in Teófilo Otoni, Minas Gerais, in July 1985. The quotation is included in a report given by Hugues d'Ans in "Pastoral da Mulher Marginalizada: 13 anos de caminhada," *Revista Eclesiástica Brasileira* 47 (1987) 651. For the complete text, see *Mulher-Libertação* 3 (1985) 28.

In the previous chapter, knowledge about the church of liberation and the problem of prostitution was derived from a constructive developmental analysis of the origins and evolution of the Pastoral da Mulher Marginalizada. The fact remains, however, that idealized typologies, or "stage theories" such as the one employed in chapter three, have inherent limitations.[3] Although the evolutionary approach to analysis is helpful in understanding the interactions that occur among individuals and groups, it does not fully attend to the interactions between various problems. As a result, two dimensions of the analytical process can be skewed or overlooked. First, it is important to recognize that "social [ecclesial] problems exist in relation to other social [ecclesial] problems, and second, that social [ecclesial] problems are embedded within a complex institutionalized system of problem formulation and dissemination."[4] In an effort to include these critical insights in my research, this chapter uses an *ecological approach to analysis* as a means for broadening an overall understanding of the church of liberation and its capacity to carry prostitution as an ecclesial problem.

The ecological approach focuses attention on various types of interaction that occur within a given environmental arena. As such it is not an alternative approach to analysis, but rather it functions as a complementary approach for gathering and interpreting historical data that would otherwise be excluded. This approach to analysis "stresses the 'arenas' where social problem definitions evolve, examining the effect of those arenas on both the evolution of social problems and the actors who make claims about them."[5] Rather than focusing on the evolution of the problem, this approach focuses on how one problem—in this case prostitution—*competes* with other problems for the attention of a given constituency, such as the church of liberation. It takes into account the role of mass media, the networks of social

3. As noted by Hilgartner and Bosk ("The Rise and Fall of Social Problems," 54), "many problems exist simultaneously in several 'stages' of development, and patterns of progression from one stage to the next vary sufficiently to question the claim that a typical career exists." For this reason, one must compensate for the limitations of a singular method of analysis.

4. Ibid., 55.

5. Ibid. The method of analysis described in this section is derived from the public arenas model developed by Hilgartner and Bosk.

relationships, the resources available for mobilizing specific forces, and the political power necessary for setting an official ecclesial agenda. An ecological approach does not assume that any of these factors are determinative in and of themselves. Rather, it seeks to highlight the constraints that human actors face in identifying, selecting, and managing problems in a given arena such as the ecclesial arena.

To the extent that problem definitions are collective in nature, the approach proposes six main elements that are necessary in the process of problem definition. These include the identification of a problem within a particular arena, the problem-carrying capacity of the given arena, the dynamics of competition that exist among diverse problems within a given arena, the principles of selection that influence the visibility of a given problem, the feedback that a given arena receives from other arenas about a given problem, and the incorporation of a given problem into a macrocategory by an informal organizational structure that spans arenas.[6] Thus "the approach applies ecological concepts, such as competition, selection, and adaptation to public discourse about problems."[7] Its focus is the environment or arena in which the problem is constructed and defined as problem.

The following framework provides an interpretive adaptation of this approach for the purpose of examining how prostitution comes to be defined and selected as a problem within the ecclesial arena.

Defining and Selecting Problems Within the Ecclesial Arena: An Ecological Analysis[8]

The preliminary step in this type of analysis is that of *problem identification*. Prostitution, as an ecclesial problem, grows, declines,

6. Ibid., 70–72.

7. Ibid., 74. Terms such as "carrying capacity" are derived from the language of natural scientists. In short, this term refers to the limits of any given environment to provide for the needs of its inhabitants. For further discussion of the appropriation of these concepts by social scientists, see references cited in ibid., 55–61.

8. In the development of the following schema, I rely on the work of Hilgartner and Bosk. For purposes of clarity, I have adapted, and in some instances paraphrased, selected lines and paragraphs from their article "The Rise and Fall of Social Problems," 70–72.

and reemerges, receiving varying degrees of attention from selected groups of Christians in different historical periods. As a putative condition, it is not the objective reality of prostitution that accounts for the attention devoted to it, but rather, a process of collective definition that emerges from within the ecclesial community.

In terms of the second element, the *carrying capacity of the ecclesial arena*, the arena is limited in the number of ecclesial problems to which it can attend during any given period of time. Prostitution is one of many potential ecclesial problems that compete for space in the ecclesial arena. Whether or not prostitution becomes an ecclesial problem is not a function of its being a harmful or dangerous condition, but rather is a function of whether or not the ecclesial arena has the capacity to carry prostitution at a given historical moment.

The dynamics of competition within the ecclesial arena is the third element in this framework. In order for prostitution to be carried as a problem in the ecclesial arena, it must compete for attention at two different levels. First, prostitution must be given priority and perceived to be *more* important than a wide range of other putative conditions. Second, since there are alternative ways in which prostitution can be framed, the exact formulation of the problem is subject to competing claims and concerns. The attention that Christians give to ecclesial problems is uneven. Very few ecclesial problems become dominant topics of Christian discourse. The amount of attention received by prostitution in any given period of time varies. Like other ecclesial problems it does not sustain a high level of attention over several years. Its ascent and decline tends to change in the ecclesial arena.

Fourth, *principles of problem selection* exist within the ecclesial arena; these influence the probability of prostitution appearing as an ecclesial problem. A premium is placed on drama; when prostitution is presented in a dramatic way, it is better able to compete as a problem in the ecclesial arena. However, repetitious claims, redundant symbols, and bombardment of the Christian community with the same message can create boredom. To remain high on the ecclesial agenda, prostitution must remain dramatic. For this reason, prostitution must tap into broad cultural preoccupations and biblical themes. To the extent that the ecclesial arena is influenced by dominant theological, historical, moral and pastoral views that set the acceptable range of discourse in the ecclesial arena, changes in any of these areas could affect the selection by altering the range of acceptable ecclesial discourse. The ecclesial arena has its own organizational rhythms which influence the timing of its interaction with social problems. The ecclesial arena, broadly conceived, is also under the influence of local factors related to the institutional characteristics, political allegiances, and cultural affinities of church leaders and members. Finally, the ecclesial arena, inasmuch as its actions are negotiable, can be influenced by other arenas in its selection and definition of prostitution as an ecclesial problem.

The fifth element is *feedback to the ecclesial arena from other public arenas*. Social networks and patterned institutional relationships link the ecclesial arena with other public arenas. There is a tendency for problems that rise in one arena to spread to another. In the shift from one arena to another the problem definition may be significantly altered. There are some ecclesial problems that successfully compete in other arenas, and some that survive only in the ecclesial arena. This variability is frequently influenced by the broader social context in which the arenas exist.

The sixth and final element is found in the coelesence of related microcategory problems, [*the emergence of macrocategory problems, the formation of communities of operatives, and the development of macrocategory departments*]. In this dynamic, interrelated microcategory problems, such as prostitution and violence against women, are recognized as manifestations of macrocategory problems such as poverty and human rights. Over time, representatives from different arenas concerned about similar or related microcategory problems shift their attention to a macrocategory problem. Although their reasons for doing so may be guided by very different motivations, these so-called communities of operatives take up society's well-established macrocategory problems, such as human rights, poverty, and war. This leads to the development of what could be called a macrocategory department. Given the diverse opinions and orientations that exist among various actors in the macrocategory department, consensus or conflict may prevail. In either case, the macrocategory department draws to itself the problems and perspectives that fall under its domain. Even when communities of operatives within a macrocategory department are on opposing sides of a problem, unexpected working relationships have been known to develop as a result of ongoing interaction.

The following sections of this chapter are patterned after this framework. Each section uses one of the six dynamics described above as a paradigm for further investigation into the interactive processes that informed and influenced the church of liberation and its efforts to address the problem of prostitution and the plight of marginalized women. I begin the analysis with a preliminary discussion of the dynamics that were involved in the process of identifying prostitution as a problem within the ecclesial arena.

The Dynamics of Problem Identification

As noted in previous chapters, the 1960s proved to be a critical turning point in the modern history of Brazil. In particular, the country was shaken by the repressive actions taken by the military regime against students, union leaders, journalists, intellectuals, and anyone suspected of subversion.[9] The northeastern region of Brazil was a decided target for such tactics, due in part to the coalescence of political activity and the consciousness raising that already had taken place within certain segments of the Roman Catholic church.[10]

It was in the northeast that the revolutionary educative methods articulated by Paulo Friere in *Pedagogy of the Oppressed* were first introduced.[11] Given the political orientation of Catholic radicals[12] and progressive political reformers,[13] as well as the influence of neo-Marxist economic analyses of Brazilian reality, it is no wonder that one of the alleged benefits of socialism—namely, the elimination of

9. See Bruneau, *The Political Transformation*, 177–216.

10. See Luiz Alberto Gómez de Sousa, *A JUC: os estudantes católicos e a política* (Petrópolis: Vozes, 1984); Luiz Gonzaga de Sousa Lima, *Evolução política dos Católicos e da Igreja no Brasil* (Petróplis: Vozes, 1979); and Cândido Mendes de Almeida, *Memento dos vivos: a esquerda católica no Brasil* (Rio de Janeiro: n.p., 1966).

11. See Freire, *Pedagogy of the Oppressed*, 75–118.

12. See Emanuel de Kadt, *Catholic Radicals in Brazil* (London: Oxford University Press, 1970).

13. See Alfonso García Rubio, *Teologia da Libertação: politica ou profetismo?* (São Paulo: n.p., 1977).

prostitution—was posited as a desired end. Inasmuch as prostitutes were considered to be among the most alienated of individuals within the capitalistic economic structures, some advocates of the church of liberation saw efforts to remedy the abject poverty and exploitation of these women as one concrete step toward realizing a new vision for society.

Because the socioeconomic analysis focused primarily on the material causes of prostitution, the primary cause of the problem was identified as an unjust capitalist economic order.[14] While this order was upheld within Brazil by a repressive military dictatorship, many believed that the order was internationally orchestrated to ensure so-called First World interests and investments.[15] Given that the ravages of unbridled capitalism were exposed most brutally in the abject material poverty of exploited workers and peasants, dire economic need was identified as the causal factor that drove countless numbers of women into lives of desperation and prostitution.[16] In light of the church's heightened understanding of its evangelical commitment to bear witness to the gospel of peace and justice, and in accord with the spirit of the times, the church articulated a preferential option for the poor, denouncing the oppressive economic system that caused others to sin. Within this ecclesial world view, the traditional problem construction of prostitution as a "necessary evil" was reconstructed. The prostitute ceased to be regarded as a sinner. Instead, she was included among the poor and oppressed and was ascribed the status of victim.

It could also be posited that the militarization of the country exacerbated the problem of prostitution. As the national militia increased in number and strength, the training and stationing of military police frequently resulted in the assignment and relocation of large numbers of young men to various regions of Brazil. Such movement had ramifications for the sex trade industry. Prostitution was diversified to meet a wide variety of needs and circumstances. The number of pros-

14. See Hugues d'Ans, "Prostituição: um pecado social," *Revista Eclesiástica Brasileira* 44 (1984) 564–72.

15. See Bruneau, *The Political Transformation*, 178–182; and Alfred C. Stepan, *The Military in Politics: Changing Patterns in Brazil* (Princeton: Princeton University Press, 1971).

16. See Rohner, *Prostituição e libertação da mulher*, 39–41.

titutes increased exponentially in accord with the age-old pattern of supply and demand. Oddly enough, as growing numbers of young men were conscripted into national service, so were growing numbers of young women. The female form of national service, however, was prostitution. It could be said that the same was true for men, only that their form of prostitution was of another order.[17] Maintaining lesser evils in order to ensure national security was a persuasive rationale.

Given the church's expressed desire to witness to the gospel mandate of Jesus Christ by acting as a saving and liberating presence among the victims of poverty and oppression, it sought to renew itself as the church of the poor and to identify itself with the plight of the poor and oppressed. Prostitutes were included in the same category with other marginalized people in Brazilian society. Internal migrations caused by poverty, loss of land, and fear of repression led to the displacement of thousands of people from the rural interior of the country to capital cities and major urban areas along the coast. For some women and girls, prostitution promised—and sometimes provided—a means of survival for themselves and often for their dependents, when other options were either unavailable or insufficient. In light of this grim reality, it was possible for the church to arrive at a collective definition of the prostitute as poor, powerless, and oppressed. Within the ecclesial context of Brazil, the problem of prostitution was linked explicitly to the problem of poverty. Thus, the same world view that enabled the church to understand the poor as victims allowed for the ecclesial definition of the prostitute as victim.[18]

It is important to recall, however, that the world view held by the church of liberation was not universally regarded or supported throughout all sectors of the Roman Catholic church in Brazil. In many re-

17. The activities of the military police often included surveillance, repression, and torture. Young men were controlled and paid by the government to engage in various acts of violence and dehumanization. Like prostitution, such actions were justified as lesser and necessary evils, the greater evil being the threat of communism. Like prostitutes, many of the young men were expendable pawns, who willingly or unwillingly sold their bodies in order to serve the interests of those who funded their deeds.

18. Conferência Nacional dos Bispos do Brasil, *Prostituição: desafio à sociedade e à Igreja* (São Paulo: Paulinas, 1976) 7–12.

gions, particularly in those areas where the church had not yet been the target of antisubversive activity, where modern feudalism prevailed on large *fazendas* and literacy campaigns had barely made a dent, sex role differentiation was still securely in place,[19] as were all other role differentiations, including those of bishops, clergy, and religious. In these areas, it was difficult for the church to recast the prostitute as victim. In part, this was due to the fact that the church had long been the defender of the moral and religious underpinnings of traditional family values and structures. The church had contributed to the double standards of sexual morality that solidified society's need to keep the prostitute marginalized, scorned, or objectified in her "otherness."

In many interior towns and cities, the "cult of virginity" and the "cult of virility" continued mutually to reinforce each other.[20] Within this context, prostitution was a well established means for safeguarding family life and personal honor. Prostitutes were considered "expendable women" whose sexual availability not only served to satisfy the alleged indefatigable sexual urges of men,[21] but also to ensure that the honor and integrity of other women would not be threatened. In accord with the patriarchal system of values, lechery on the part of men went unquestioned. Seduction, coercion, and even rape were often constructed in such a way that the man was seldom deemed culpable, while the woman, no matter how young or vulnerable, was held responsible for whatever sexual exploitation befell her.

Within traditional patriarchal family structures, damaged property held little market value.[22] Virginity was a high commodity. If virginity was lost before marriage, the "fallen woman" ran the risk of being marginalized. The contagion of her dishonor and shame frequently

---

19. See Délcio Monteiro de Lima, *Comportamento sexual do Brasileiro* (Rio de Janeiro: Francisco Alves, 1976) 20–22.

20. See Emilio Willems, "The Structure of the Brazilian Family," *Social Forces* 31 (1953) 339–45.

21. See Renan Springer de Freitas, *Bordel, bordéis: negociando identidades* (Petrópolis: Vozes, 1985) 92–95.

22. See José Alberto da S. Curado, "A mulher de 'vida facil' numa conjuntura dificil," in Assis Angelo, ed., *A prostituição em debate* (São Paulo: Paulinas, 1982) 25–26.

had serious implications for her entire family.[23] This reality proved to be particularly harsh on young domestic workers, who frequently were violated—and at times impregnated—by their employers or their employer's relatives. In many instances, the girl was dismissed from her job and sometimes excluded from her own family.[24] In a moral universe where access to prostitutes was accepted, a pregnant adolescent bore the brunt of the responsibility and blame for the condition in which she found herself. Cast as a sinner or seductress, the young woman, regardless of evidence to the contrary, was tried and judged to be at fault. Oftentimes because of class distinctions, her father, if present, was in no position to argue with his daughter's employer. Paternal anger was thus taken out on the daughter, rather than the man of the household where she was employed.

By placing such a high value on female virginity and such a low tolerance for its loss, particularly when accompanied by an illegitimate pregnancy, the church itself cultivated the very attitudes that gave rise to punitive actions such as the exclusion and marginalization of countless girls and women. According to such a theory, in circumstances where men had access to prostitutes, there was no excuse for women falling prey to the sexual advances of men unless of course it was the woman's fault. Prostitutes were there to be used, thus providing a guarantee that other women would not be. The theory, in fact, did not work. Still, the church, like society, upheld the pretense that it did. Regardless of how a girl or woman lost her virginity or her reputation, she was to be blamed and treated as if she were a prostitute. As the life histories and personal testimonies of prostitutes repeatedly confirmed, such women rarely had fallen into prostitution. More often than not, they had been pushed.

Despite the fact that a new world view was envisioned by certain church leaders who identified themselves with the struggle for human liberation, such a view was not widely shared or understood by many Brazilians. In an era of national security, marked by political repres-

23. See Jéferson Afonso Bacelar, "Família, normas sociais e prostitutas," in *A família da prostituta* (São Paulo: Atica, 1982) 3–14.
24. See Hugues d'Ans, "Os guetos prostitutionais," in idem, *O grito de milhões de escravas*, 123.

sion and military dictatorship, everything possible was being done to defend not only the social order of Brazilian society, but the sexual order as well. To question the rationality of longstanding attitudes and practices in either order was an act of subversion.

As forms of prostitution became more diversified, due to development projects in the interior, such as highways, factories, refineries, mines, mills,[25] and internal migrations to large cities,[26] the characterizations of prostitutes as easy women and entrepreneurs were often reinforced. Although prostitution districts known as *zonas* continued to confine prostitution to designated areas in cities and villages throughout Brazil, the rapid growth and diversification of the sex trade industry spun out of control. With little knowledge of how the sex trade industry operated, traditional clergy tended to rail against the prostitutes as seductresses who had crossed the boundaries of custom and propriety. Local church leaders made demands on police to control vice. As growing numbers of women engaged in various forms of prostitution outside of the *zona*, the limits of toleration were tested as were the limits of understanding. Overall, most sectors of the church, even those considered to be progressive, knew little about the migrant women and girls involved in lives of prostitution at truck stops and highway crossroads, motels and massage parlors, street corners and alleyways, *fazendas* and factories. In many ways, the church did not know how much it did not know.

In summary, any effort on the part of the church to define the prostitute as victim was dependent ultimately on a world view that was informed by a critical social consciousness directed toward and by the project of human liberation. Where this world view was not in place, the traditional Christian understanding of the prostitute as sinner and source of familial dishonor remained intact. Although the church of liberation was in a position to identify, select, and define prostitution as an ecclesial problem, it was not in a position to determine how many problems in the ecclesial arena could be addressed.

25. See Maria Geralda Resende, "Luta pela terra e prostituição no Centro-oeste," in d'Ans, *Mulher: da escravidão à libertação*, 21–25.

26. For a description of this phenomenon in Salvador, Bahia, see the sociological analysis of Gey Espinheira, *Divergência e prostituição* (Rio de Janeiro: Tempo Brasileiro, 1984).

The Carrying Capacity of the Ecclesial Arena

In examining prostitution as an ecclesial problem and in studying its evolution over the course of nearly three decades, it is important to note that only in situations where prostitution destabilized the church did it come to the fore as an ecclesial problem. For the most part, the evaluation of prostitution as an ecclesial problem could happen only in circumstances where church leaders and church members were in agreement that prostitutes were victims rather than sinners. Furthermore, even when the prostitute was defined as a victim, it could be expected that any given community would rank the plight of prostitutes below that of other victims, thus limiting the extent to which prostitutes received attention and support.

Throughout Brazil the church of liberation occupied itself with the defense of individuals whose human rights were being violated during the years of repression. The harassment, kidnapping, imprisonment, torture, and assassination of labor leaders, union organizers, political activists, students, journalists, and all those who declared themselves to be on the side of the poor and oppressed received the special attention of the hierarchy. The abuse, exploitation, and displacement of laborers and peasants,[27] whether random or systematic, became issues of concern as well.

Exactly who the poor and oppressed were, however, was a question rarely answered in any specific fashion. It was not until the late 1970s that the face of the poor began to be distinguished with greater specificity. Until that time, the generic *pobre* ("poor one") was the *trabalhador* ("male worker"), emasculated by society and unable to provide for his family—in short, the patriarchal ideal gone awry.[28] It

27. See Vanilda Paiva, ed., *Igreja e questão agrária* (São Paulo: Loyola, 1985).

28. This generic *pobre* is characterized in an address given by Dom Helder Câmara on the occasion of his installation as bishop in 1964. See "Mensagem de D. Helder Câmara na tomada de posse como Arcebispo de Olinda e Recife," *Revista Eclesiástica Brasileira* 24 (1964) 384. Repeatedly, this characterization was depicted in illustrations and photographs used in printed materials for bible study, seasonal reflections for Advent and Lent, and diocesan newsletters.

took over a decade before the church began to come to terms not only with the fact that the poor were many but also that the idealization of the poor man had to be extended to poor women and children abandoned by the men who could not or would not provide for them.

The numbers of single and abandoned mothers exploded in direct correspondence to the development projects in the interior states. The price of marriage licenses was prohibitive for many, making common law marriages of convenience the rule. Because of Brazil's stringent prohibition of divorce, illegitimate children—who abounded—rarely had any claim to their father's resources. Hastened by migration, the general breakdown in the extended patriarchal family removed the burden of responsibility from those few men who, under other circumstances, would have been forced as a question of honor to provide for the children they fathered.

Because of its focus on sociopolitical and socioeconomic concerns, the ecclesial arena had little carrying capacity for sociosexual concerns. The social conscience of the Brazilian church was shaped in large part by its own efforts to implement the social teachings of the church in accord with the recommendations of advisors, researchers, and theologians, many of whom were influenced by socioeconomic analysis. For the most part, other forms of sociocritical analysis, such as those focused on race, gender, culture, or ethnicity, were limited, suppressed, or altogether lacking.

Given Brazil's repressive climate, it is important to remember that in the late sixties and early seventies, the country had lost many of its intellectuals, social analysts, and political theorists, due to exile, imprisonment, censorship, or assasination. In light of this reality, we can understand more clearly why issues of race and gender failed to surface in the ecclesial discourse of the day.[29] Despite the rise of international solidarity movements against racism and sexism in other regions of the world, the focus of Brazilian social activism by necessity remained singular. Opposition forces of every stripe set aside

29. Individuals inclined toward a more radical critique of Brazilian society, such as militant Afro-Brazilians, radical feminists, and other types of cultural revolutionaries, were effectively silenced by government censorship and political persecution.

ideological differences[30] and united themselves along with the church in a common and principled effort to bring down the repressive military regime and restore democratic freedoms. Within the Brazilian context, the primary cause of oppression was usually thought to be the class interests of wealthy conservative forces supported by a military dictatorship that mounted a national security state in order to defend the political and economic power of national elites, large landowners, and international collaborators. Under such circumstances, distinct forms of structural oppression related to race and/or gender remained largely undifferentiated.

By the mid-1970s, the collective efforts of the opposition began to manifest themselves in numerous ways. The power base of the military dictatorship began to lose its stranglehold on the country. Winds of change began to blow. Measured expectations for social justice found expression in the promotion and defense of human rights. Under these circumstances, the announcement of the United Nations' International Year of Women proved to be both a challenge and an opportunity, particularly for those who were conscious of the toll that a decade of human rights abuses had taken on Brazilian women and their children.[31]

One particular example of this concern focused on the plight of prostitutes. Debates about proposed changes in the penal code relating to prostitution gave the illusion that there was a legislative and judicial power still at work in Brazil. If nothing else, such debates were indicators of the fact that the country had more problems than the repression of subversives. In addition, these debates served to engage the moral imagination of the Brazilian bishops, so much so that they committed themselves to the formulation and publication of an epis-

30. As noted earlier, the Roman Catholic church proved to be the strongest of the opposition forces and the least assailable. In light of this fact, even those holding ideological positions in absolute contradiction to the church's traditional teachings and practices stood with the church of liberation and her progressive leaders in an effort to create a critical mass and unified block of organized protest and popular resistance.

31. See Maria Lygia Quartim de Moraes, *Mulheres em movimento: o balanço da Década da Mulher do ponto de vista de feminismo, das religiões e da política* (São Paulo: Nobel: Conselho Estadual da Condição Feminina, 1985) 1–33.

copal document about prostitution.[32] Prostitution was not only a moral issue but also a political and legal one. The bishops' statement was courageous inasmuch as it challenged Brazilian society and culture on an issue of social justice for women.

The irony, however, is that the church of liberation set itself on the side of the oppressed—namely, those exploited by prostitution—without fully acknowledging or comprehending its own institutional complicity in creating and tolerating sexual forms of oppression.[33] Given that the bishops and pastoral agents involved in the drafting of the document were among the most progressive in the country, the statement made it possible for them to demonstrate the coherence of their struggle to defend human rights and to focus, in light of the International Year of Women, on a topic of international significance.[34] In any event, the bishops of Brazil explicitly took up the cause and defense of poor and marginalized women, an action that was at once pastoral and, consciously or unconsciously, protagonistic.

The Dynamics of Competition

The Brazilian bishops merit considerable recognition for responding to the problem of prostitution through the publication of *Prostituição: desafio à sociedade e à Igreja*. The promulgation and reception of the document, however, were somewhat problematic. In effect, the document affirmed the work of those already committed to pastoral outreach among prostitutes. It was limited, however, in its ability to challenge or persuade those outside the conversation to embrace a more radical commitment to the cause of marginalized women. The reasons were numerous.

As noted earlier, resistance on the part of traditional clergy and laity was only one reason why the document was not widely received.

32. See Conferência Nacional dos Bispos do Brasil, *Prostituição*.
33. See Teodoro Helmut Rohner, "As prostitutas podem receber os sacramentos?" *Revista Eclesiástica Brasileira* 45 (1985) 108–16.
34. As highlighted in chapter three, such actions were supported and influenced, at least in part, by expatriot pastoral agents involved in outreach ministries to prostitutes. It should also be noted that many of these missionaries came from countries where the defense of women's rights was a major concern.

Another explanation worthy of consideration is the way in which the relative significance of the document was eclipsed or supplanted by other episcopal documents published during the mid- and late 1970s. Above all, it must be remembered that the document appealed to a limited audience. Unlike other pressing ecclesial concerns of the day, it did not arise out of a prior discussion that was common and broadly based.

In the light of insights derived from research on methods of communication representative of both oral and literate cultures, it can be argued that the document lacked a corresponding experiential narrative within the general population. In short, few base communities were focusing their energies and reflections on the plight of girls and women in prostitution. Although the document became an impressive matter of public and ecclesial record, it is not clear whether it succeeded in engaging the hearts and minds of those it was meant to inspire and inform[35] or whether it simply enhanced the impressive collection of C.N.B.B. documents.

In this regard, attending to the dynamics of competition is consequential for understanding the ebb and flow of ecclesial consciousness regarding prostitution. In the larger picture, preoccupation with the apparent failure of the *milagre brasileira* ("Brazilian miracle") to trickle down to the masses was evidenced in ongoing ecclesial concern about education, health care, employment, and housing. The human service needs of a rapidly growing sector of the population, namely, children under the age of sixteen, added to the urgency of the situation. At the same time the spread of agricultural business and the industrial expansion of multinational corporations contributed in many cases to more brutal forms of human exploitation.[36]

35. For a more detailed explanation of the dynamics involved in this process, see Tereza Lúcia Halliday, "Atos retóricos: discurso e circumstâncias," in idem, ed., *Atos retóricos: mensagens estratégicas de politicos e igrejas* (São Paulo: Summus Editorial, 1987) 121–31.

36. In rural areas, the reckless and widespread use of insecticides, fertilizers, and defoliants resulted in the exposure of countless men, women, and children to hazardous chemical agents. In a similar fashion, factory workers were exposed to toxic industrial pollutants and precarious working environments. As the incidence of work-related illnesses, disabilities, and deaths increased among peasant laborers and unskilled workers, the expendability of the poor was given a modernized expression.

Efforts to address issues related to agrarian reform and urban migration highlighted the increase of organized violence and corruption throughout the country. Although the vision of redemocratization promised to be a light at the end of the tunnel, it too carried a number of new considerations associated with the organization, selection, and endorsement of political parties. With so many concerns competing for the attention of ecclesial leaders, base communities, and the Roman Catholic population in general, it is not surprising that the problem of prostitution, although included in the ecclesial arena, had a difficult time securing and maintaining a competitive edge in comparison with other problems. Still, it managed to compete effectively enough and was not eliminated from the arena altogether.

Initially, it would appear that the problem of prostitution held its ground in the ecclesial arena because of the efforts and high profiles of pastoral agents and bishops committed to redressing the situation. As their interests and energies peaked, so did the broader awareness of the problem of prostitution. Although many problems occupied space in the ecclesial arena, some of the problems associated with the military dictatorship gradually waned. This meant that the problem of prostitution could be given more attention. Research statistics on the number of prostitutes in Brazil paralleled research studies on the causes and consequences of prostitution.[37] No longer was the church responding solely to the impressionistic evidence of a few dedicated pastoral agents. Rather, every sector of the church was forced to grapple with the disturbing demographic fact that growing numbers of women and children, in every region of the country, were caught up in some form of prostitution.[38] The implications of such statistics for the largest Roman Catholic country in the world were grave.

In short, the ecclesial nature of the problem could not go unacknowledged indefinitely. The invisibility of prostitution ceased in some

37. Under the leadership of Dom Afonso Gregory, these research findings were gathered and interpreted by the *Centro de Estatística Religiosa e Investigações Sociais.*

38. In 1983, the national estimate was roughly four million women and children engaged in prostitution in a population of one hundred and ten million habitants (see d'Ans, *O grito de milhões de escravas,* back cover). Although contested by some, these figures represent rough estimates indicative of the severe and widespread nature of the problem.

quarters. Women and children emerged from the shadows of *zonas*; their presence became obvious on street corners, at bus stations, and in open markets. The establishment of growing numbers of motels and dancing bars was rapid and diversified in terms of location and clientele. Casual forms of prostitution were on the rise as well. The face of prostitution appeared everywhere, as did the prostitutes themselves.[39] No longer were they unseen, anonymous, and unattached. Not only did they constitute a significant percentage of the female population between the ages of fifteen and thirty-five, but they also were mothers, daughters, sisters, neighbors, co-workers, laborers, teachers, nurses, and wives. The basis for distinguishing a difference between prostitutes and other women was no longer secure.

Parallel to the heightened social visibility of prostitutes came the development and expansion of telecommunication networks and the film industry. The many facets of prostitution began to be considered in public discourse and cultural consciousness. In the past, the life stories of prostitutes and abandoned women had reached the general population primarily through books, radio, magazines, recordings, and performing artists of various sorts. In time, however, the unprecedented influence of visual media took the country by storm.

Rede Globo, the national television network, contributed to the process by which the imagination and curiosity of the nation were engaged through its broadcast of novellas such as *Gabriella cravo e canella*, a soap opera, based on a novel by Jorge Amado, that depicted the life of a public woman in northeastern Brazil.[40] Directors

39. As Jéferson Afonso Bacelar notes in his study of the city of Maciel (*A família da prostituta*, 121), women in prostitution, although often affected by social stigma, are not isolated socially or physically from life in general. For the most part, they exercise many other social functions and roles in addition to those identified exclusively with their lives as prostitutes. They are involved with other social groups and with individuals from a variety of social locations. They go shopping, they participate in religious activities, they are sport fans and sun bathers. They go to parks, they read magazines and newspapers, they know what is going on in the world, they listen to the radio and watch television.

40. See Jorge Amado, *Gabriela Clove and Cinnamon* (trans. James L. Taylor and William Grossman; New York: Knopf, 1962).

such as Carlos Diegues and Hector Babenco took up the theme of prostitution in several of their films, not for the sake of advancing a lucrative pornographic film industry, but for the purpose of forming the social conscience of Brazil through accurate portrayals of Brazilian reality in internationally renowned films such as *Bye, Bye Brasil* and *Pixote*. Likewise, filmed depictions of literary works, such as *A Hora da Estrela* by the Brazilian writer Clarice Lispector, illustrated the complexities of women's reality and the seeming inevitability of prostitution for those endeavoring to improve their lot in life.[41]

Unfortunately, however, few church leaders used the media as a tool for education and evangelization.[42] Instead, the media became the frequent target of undifferentiated criticism and religious censorship;[43] more frequently than not, priests and pastoral agents failed to recognize that the issues and concerns depicted in the media provided them with powerful narratives for examining the relationship between what people viewed on television or in the movies and what they experienced in their daily lives. Had the church engaged the methods of critical social analysis in an effort to understand why such depictions held the attention of their audiences in ways that bordered on the addictive, it might have better understood why people abandoned evening education and why makeshift television antennas could be found even on the roofs of *favellas* ("shanties"). As the public voice of the church spoke out against the media and the immoralities that the media portrayed with regularity, the private television viewing habits of clergy, religious, and lay leaders closely paralleled those of other Brazilians.

41. See Clarice Lispector, *The Hour of the Star* (trans. Giovanni Ponteiro; Manchester: Carcanet, 1986).

42. See Ralph Della Cava, "The Catholic Church and the Mass Media in Brazil: Some Theoretical Considerations," *Studies in Latin American Popular Culture* 7 (1988).

43. It should be noted that during this period Brazilian society was inundated with the products of a national pornographic industry that had few parallels in other countries of the world. For further information, see Hugues d'Ans, "Pornografía: ideologia, indústria e comércio," in idem, *Mulher: da escravidão à libertação*, 38–50. Although unfortunate, the church's inability or unwillingness to distinguish pornography from diverse forms of cultural expression that merited serious reflection and consideration was predictable.

Although stories, ballads, and songs had long recounted the plight of women, the intrigues of prostitution, and the conquests of *machismo*, television and film had a power greater than that of the written word, the artistic performance or the radio. For the first time, people unable to objectify—to stand apart from a situation, thus gaining the distance necessary for critical thinking—the realities of their lives for reasons of fear and taboo, watched as television and film characters gave voice to their pain and their aspirations, their fantasies and their anxieties. For better or for worse, novellas and movies took Brazilian cultural reality on its own terms, not as it should have been or as it could have been, but frequently as it was. They exposed in an unequivocal way the double standards of morality that operated within the culture.

In effect, there was no way the church could begin to address the issues raised by these visual narratives in any credible fashion, unless of course it was prepared to engage in dialogue regarding ecclesial hypocrisy, complicity, and irresponsibility with regard to the sexual oppression of women. It was far easier to discourage viewing than to acknowledge the element of truth that fiction disclosed to those who had eyes with which to see.

In spite of the church's limitations in other regards, the ecclesial arena allowed the problem of prostitution to hold its own. In part, this can be attributed to the advocacy work of pastoral agents as well as to the interest and ongoing support of influential bishops. Such viability, however, unquestionably was shored up by the coincidence of many factors, of which ecclesial concern was only one. In large part, the staying power of the problem was dependent on the heightened visibility of prostitution, the proliferation of prostitutes, and the captivating power of the media to provide the common narratives that both controlled and liberated the imaginations of the people and the church.

The Principles of Problem Selection

There are numerous principles of selection involved in the church's decision to address prostitution as an ecclesial problem. These principles are related in part to a number of points highlighted in the previous section. It should be noted, however, that the magnitude of the problem of prostitution was not the only criterion for determining whether or not it would be recognized as a problem within the ecclesial arena. Rather, what secured for prostitution a privileged place as an ecclesial problem were the ecclesial purposes served by selecting the problem of prostitution over other problems.

By casting the problem of prostitution in the language of sexual slavery, the church of liberation had something to offer and something to gain. The notion of sexual slavery appealed to a specific ideal in the collective ecclesial consciousness, namely, the desire to set the captives free. In drawing upon biblical and theological foundations as well as political philosophy, the church embraced a liberationist perspective and set as its goal the abolition of all forms of human slavery.[44] Sexual slavery,[45] understood as the exploitation of poor women by sex trade traffickers and sex industry magnates, located the origins of the problem squarely within the capitalist economic order and, to some extent, in the patriarchal order as well. Ironically, however, it failed in general to note the racial underpinnings of sexual slavery.[46]

44. In taking such an action, the church set itself on the side of hope. Although judged by some to be utopian in orientation, the church's views also resonated with those of Maurice Blondel, who wrote (*Action [1893]: Essay on a Critique of Life and a Science of Practice* [trans. Oliva Blanchette; Notre Dame: University of Notre Dame Press, 1984] 261): "It seemed impossible that the social need for slavery could ever be eliminated: it has been. It seemed impossible that, toward an enemy on the battlefield, any consideration could be given; little by little a law of nations is being established which, violated though it may be, is forcing itself on the judgement of peoples."

45. The images and insights that accompany the notion of sexual slavery are described at length in d'Ans, *O grito de milhões de escravas*. In this volume the relationship between the church's concern for prostitutes is linked explicitly to ecclesial support for the International Abolitionist Treaty.

46. Brazil was one of the last countries in the Western hemisphere to abolish the trade of African slaves. It is surprising to find the extent to which antislavery rhetoric shaped the discourse surrounding the problem of prostitution without taking into serious account the large number of prostitutes that were Afro-Brazilian. For further information on the historical background related to this point see Sonia Maria Giacomini, *Mulher e escrava: uma introdução histórica ao estudo da mulher negra no Brasil* (Petrópolis: Vozes, 1988).

The principles involved in the continued selection of prostitution as an ecclesial problem in the 1980s, although coherent with the principles of the 1970s, were distinguished by historical circumstances. In short, the era was one of redemocratization, rather than political repression. The return of exiles, the establishment of new political parties, and the envisioning of a new Brazilian social order through constituent assemblies and the ratification of a new national constitution brought to the forefront of Brazilian culture and society questions and concerns about structural forms of oppression other than classism and militarism.

Ecclesial discourse about racism and sexism was negligible until the late 1970s. In the 1980s, however, the integrity of the church's commitment to the poor and the oppressed was dependent upon the church's ability to take seriously additional categories of analysis. Ecclesial concern for victims of sexual slavery accompanied a growing historical consciousness about the tragic legacy of African and Indian slavery in Brazil. Although the church was not in a position to apply its liberation ethic to pressing issues that women raised,[47] such as divorce, reproductive rights, and in some instances, domestic abuse, it offered a gesture of ecclesial solidarity with women through its efforts to address the victimization of the marginalized woman engaged in prostitution. In identifying prostitution as an ecclesial problem, the church proved itself to be concerned about the exploitation of women through sexual slavery.

In accord with the liberation methodology of accompanying the poor and oppressed to gain both voice and visibility, the church of liberation encouraged marginalized women to recognize their own power, authority, and personal agency. The extent to which the church fully realized the potential consequences of its commitment is not clear. What is clear, however, is the fact that for centuries the church contributed to a cultural milieu that tolerated women's sexual enslavement, victimization, and expendability. Then, in the 1960s and 1970s, the church of liberation gave itself over to the process of conscientization. Over the course of more than two decades, the church assumed a radically different posture and course of action; not only did it

47. For a descriptive analysis of the issues raised by Brazilian women in the early 1980s, see Projeto-Mulher do Instituto de Ação Cultural, *As mulheres em movimento* (Rio de Janeiro: Marco Zero, 1981).

become an advocate for marginalized women, but it also initiated efforts to secure and defend their human dignity. The church's commitment, although edifying in many respects, had a major flaw. For the most part, the church thought about the plight of prostitutes within a specific category, namely, the category of the marginalized. What the church was unable to perceive, at least initially, was that the plight of marginalized women needed to be understood in terms of an even broader category, namely that of women in general.

In the course of encouraging prostitutes to tell their own stories, the church was required to listen to more than it expected to hear. Not only was it entrusted with stories of the poor, it was also entrusted with the stories of women. Over time, the narratives of prostitutes persuaded the church of liberation to recognize the fact that its primary preoccupation with the economic causes of prostitution was limited in scope and vision. In accord with insights derived from these narratives, the church was challenged to include in its social analysis not only issues of class, but issues of gender and race as well. As prostitutes began to examine the nature of moral culpability and moral agency as presented within the Christian tradition, they astutely recognized the multiple ways in which the church itself exacerbated sexism and racism through its teachings and practices. Speaking the truth as they perceived it, prostitutes demanded that the church of liberation be honest with itself.

Recognized as the largest Roman Catholic country in the world, Brazil had one of the three largest episcopal conferences in the Roman Catholic church and, by international standards, one of the most progressive and influential. Although it had a larger black Catholic population than Nigeria, the largest Catholic country in Africa, Brazil had only six Afro-Brazilian bishops and, as a nation, Brazil had a relatively high incidence of prostitution. From the perspective of women prostitutes, there was no way that the church could dissociate itself from some measure of responsibility for the rationalization and toleration of racism and sexism within Brazilian culture and society. How could the church admonish individuals and institutions, when the church itself was actively or passively complicit?

As consciousness about sexism and racism heightened, the equilibrium of the church of liberation was destabilized. The church that cast itself as the advocate of prostitutes now found itself in the uncomfortable position of being, at best, a sympathetic care giver and, at worst, a causal agent. As the problem of prostitution ceased to be understood exclusively in terms of economics, the definition of the problem had to be reconceived. If the church acknowledged the fact that women did not engage in prostitution solely because they were victims of an unjust economic system, it ran the risk of being placed in the unsettling position of recognizing that such women were, above all, victims of an unjust cultural system that had its moral moorings in a Luso-Brazilian patriarchal social order that identified itself as Christian.

As the church of liberation began to perceive the problem of prostitution as a convergence of structural forms of oppression—namely, the coalescence of sexism, racism, and classism—the church lost control of its power to define the problem in its own way and on its own terms. As issues of domestic abuse, incest, sexual exploitation, discrimination, and violence against women became more visible in the life histories of women prostitutes, poverty could no longer be advanced by the church or any institution as the primary causal factor, much less the only one. Within the ecclesial arena, many were concerned about how the church had defined and selected the problem of prostitution. Such concern hinged upon three questions. First, if poverty were the primary reason why women became prostitutes, why were only *some* poor women prostitutes and not all? Second, if the church of liberation acknowledged causal factors other than abject poverty, why did it hesitate to take a more aggressive public stand regarding crimes against women? Finally, how would the church of liberation relate to prostitutes whose tongues were loosed in the passage from victimization to conscientization?

Feedback to the Ecclesial Arena

In 1968, when the church of liberation began to articulate its preferential option for the poor and oppressed, it sought to distance itself from the power and privilege it once enjoyed as a beneficiary of both feudal and capitalist economic orders.[48] In doing so, it became aligned,

48. See J. F. Régis de Moraes, *Os bispos e a política no Brasil: pensamento social da CNBB* (São Paulo: Cortez, 1982) 71–95, 99–128.

intentionally or unintentionally, with other social and political forces at odds with the dominant social order. The church consistently gave as its foundation and justification for such action the gospel of Jesus Christ and the social teachings of the Roman Catholic church.[49] Although similarities existed between these convictions and insights, and those ascribed to Marx, Hegel, Gramsci, Bloch, Mao, and any number of movements identified with a more just distribution of the world's resources, the church repeatedly asserted and affirmed the evangelical basis for its values and claims.

In the 1970s and 1980s, the church, like other social and political actors committed to the struggle for human liberation, came face to face with the challenges posed by the particular struggles associated with the liberation of women. The church of liberation found itself listening not only to the cries of the marginalized, but more specifically to the cries of marginalized women. Leaders of the church, particularly those respected for their unwavering commitment to the defense of human rights, could not listen to these cries indefinitely without offering some response. In order to be credible advocates for marginalized women, however, they needed to distance themselves not only from the power and privilege they enjoyed as beneficiaries of a capitalist economic order, but also from the power and privilege they enjoyed as beneficiaries of the patriarchal social order. Without such distance, the church could not stand against machismo with the same integrity and conviction with which it stood against the class privilege of the elite.

As one among many influential social institutions within Brazilian society, the church of liberation was not exempt from the challenges and criticisms that advocates of women's rights voiced in every arena. What was unusual, however, was that such challenges and criticisms did not come to the church of liberation through the intellectual vanguard of privileged women. It came instead from marginalized women convinced that the church of liberation was worthy of their trust and thus a trustee of their personal and collective struggles for liberation.

Despite this reality, however, prostitutes were instinctively aware of the fact that not even the church of liberation could easily extricate itself from a traditional ecclesial outlook conditioned by fear of the

49. Ibid., 44–67.

body and sexuality, and, above all, fear of women. Dualism, patriarchy, and misogyny were ingrained too deeply in the religious ethos and social culture of the church. The fact that the Roman Catholic church at large held Brazilian church leaders responsible for identifying and nuancing the elements of the women's rights movement that were irreconcilable with the gospel came as no surprise. What was troublesome, however, was that many church leaders hesitated to take issue with certain *machista* elements of *Cristianismo* that were also irreconcilable with the gospel.

Inasmuch as the wider church frequently found it difficult to redress the marginalization and the exclusion of women from full participation in the life of the institution,[50] the marginalized and the oppressed found it increasingly more difficult—if not altogether impossible—to imagine the full realization of the gospel message of inclusion, liberation, and salvation. Although the marginalized and oppressed were counted among Jesus' chosen ones, far too often in the church's history they were judged, condemned, and excluded by the very institution that claimed authority over and responsibility for the process of evangelization.

Despite its best efforts to overcome such disparity, the church of liberation was caught between its commitment to the oppressed as expressed in its teachings on social justice *and* its commitment to promote and uphold traditional family values as expressed in its teachings on the family and human sexuality. As might be expected, the church of liberation found itself on a collision course. As an ecclesial institution, already under the scrutiny of the Vatican, it had to weigh carefully all of its actions. To call into question its own complicity in the exacerbation of *machismo* would be to call into question the patriarchal ethos of the Roman Catholic church. By any stretch of the ecclesial imagination, the church of liberation could not dare to go that far—or could it?

---

50. As noted earlier in this chapter, the exclusion of individuals from the sacramental life of the church was a particular issue for prostitutes. See Rohner, *Prostituição e libertação da mulher*, 21–34, 71–88. The work of Rohner represents an effort to reexamine the church's practices in order to prepare pastoral agents for a more adequate understanding of the principles of individual conscience that must be honored by the church.

Although it can be argued that at some level the church's commitment to women in prostitution served as a means of avoiding or
circumventing other important women's issues, the inclusion of the
problem of prostitution within the ecclesial arena required the church
to recognize that the emergence of a critical social consciousness
among women in various regions of Brazil could not be dismissed as
the work of subversives.[51] As a consequence of its ongoing interaction with marginalized women, the church realized that there were
many other "artisans of a new humanity" concerned with the plight of
prostitutes, not only as prostitutes, but as women. With this acknowl-
edgment came the recognition that the struggle for women's liberation
within Brazilian society could not be caricatured as the fascination of
secularized bourgeois women reading Simone de Beauvoir.

51. In the minds of some critics, the promotion of women's rights was
identified with upper-class elites who were influenced largely by the "pleasure principles" of French feminism. However, a more diffuse form of feminism took hold in three other social groupings as well. First, militant feminist
autonomous organizations brought the country's attention to the realities of
domestic violence and sexual abuse. For example, these women took to the
streets protesting legal practices that defended "the honor of men" by letting
murderers go free after brutally beating, knifing, or shooting their wives to
death for suspected infidelity. Their slogans included: "He who loves does not
kill! Down with the farce of honor!" and "How many more corpses until
women's oppression is acknowledged?" Second, feminist groups with ties to
political parties identified with the "new Brazilian feminism" which
deemphasized issues such as abortion, sexual repression, and sexist education, while stressing the need for day care facilities, better wages, and mater-
nity benefits. These groups were closer to addressing the realities and needs
of the majority of women than any of the extreme groups of the political Left
or the political Right. Third, the intellectuals included a variety of social
scientists and philosophers, who for the most part—in practice, more than in
theory—remained separate from activists. They were the most outspoken critics of French, German, and North American feminism, considering it another
imperialist "export" imposed upon Third World women. It was believed that
this form of imperialist feminism presumed that Third World women were
incapable of determining their own futures without the insights and assistance
of North Atlantic women. See Danda Prado, "Brazil: A Fertile but Ambiguous
Feminist Terrain," in Robin Morgan, ed., *Sisterhood is Global: The International Women's Movement Anthology* (trans. Magda Bogin; Garden City, NY:
Anchor, 1984) 80–88.

Coming to Terms with the Social Processes Involved in the Categorization and Management of Ecclesial Problems

Over the course of three decades, the church of liberation was constantly scrutinized by political, economic, and religious leaders who feared an unholy alliance between Christian utopians and socialist revolutionaries. Despite the dissolution of military dictatorships and the collapse of communism, the scrutinies continued and in some cases increased. Concerns about the orientation and activities of the church of liberation and its participation in various so-called *communities of operatives*, took on new dimensions, in part because of the social changes that accompanied the process of redemocratization, and in part because of the ecclesial changes associated with the growth of neoconservatism.[52] Pressing issues related to politics and economics remained a source of ongoing preoccupation for the church of liberation, particularly since the plight of the poor continued to grow worse over time. These issues often coalesced and took the form of complex *macrocategory problems* related to human rights, public welfare, and family values. One brief comparison between the late 1960s and the late 1980s illustrates the Brazilian reality in which the church of liberation emerged and developed: during the years of repression, death squads assassinated sociopolitical activists;[53] in the years of redemocratization, death squads assassinated street children.[54]

As the church in Brazil faced the limits of its commitment to women engaged in prostitution, the social and political agendas of secular advocates of women's rights converged in a supportive way with the aspirations of prostitutes who had been encouraged by pas-

52. See Ralph Della Cava, "The 'People's Church,' the Vatican and *Abertura*" in Alfred Stepan, ed., *Democratizing Brazil: Problems of Transition and Consolidation* (New York: Oxford University Press, 1989) 158–60; and José Comblin, "O ressurgimento do tradicionalismo na teologia latino-americana," *Revista Eclesiástica Brasileira* 50 (1990) 44–75.

53. See *Brasil nunca mais* (10th ed.; Petrópolis: Vozes, 1985).

54. See Mario Simas Filho, Elaine Azevedo, and Lula Costa Pinto, "Infancia de raiva, dor e sangue," *Veja*, 29 May 1991, 34–44; and Marinho Pacheco, Menezes de Morais, and Jason Tércio, "A guerra brasileira," *Visão*, 6 March 1991, 42–43.

toral agents to take up their own cause and exercise personal agency. By the late 1980s, particularly during the drafting of the new constitution, the church found itself in a so-called *macrocategory department* and in a serious dilemma. On the one hand, the church was an advocate of human liberation, yet, on the other, it was unable or unwilling to support many of the projects advanced by women's rights advocates as being in the best interest of women, particularly poor women. In short, the church could stand on the side of women who were victims, but it often could not support many of the strategies for liberation advanced by victims turned protagonists.

In 1987, it was women prostitutes who challenged the bishops of Brazil to make sexism the focus of the 1990 Campanha da Fraternidade. They even went so far as to propose a campaign theme that alluded to John 8:11 with the phrase, "Woman arise, assume your liberation." Forced to negotiate between the challenges of women and the challenges of the Vatican, the bishops attempted to steer a middle course. They acknowledged the role of women in the building up of the Christian community and the victimization of women in Brazilian society, but the majority stopped short of acknowledging any error or complicity on the part of the church in contributing to the oppression of women. In selecting the campaign theme: "Woman and Man: The Image of God," they dared to do more than most episcopal conferences, yet in some respects, their words were measured and their voices constrained. The spirit of courage and tenacity that had distinguished them in previous years was more cautious and tentative.[55]

By 1990, the problem of prostitution was reconceived by the church of liberation as a part of two larger problems: marginalization and women's rights. As a result of such redefinition, the problem of prostitution per se began to be eased out of the ecclesial arena. In the effort to uphold its preferential option for the poor and the oppressed, the church of liberation endeavored to keep its focus on all those who

---

55. Upon hearing of the decision of the C.N.B.B. to recast the theme, regional groups of the Pastoral da Mulher Marginalizada voiced their opposition to such a move. They reiterated the importance of the original theme and expressed their frustration with the C.N.B.B.'s hesitation and reluctance to endorse it. See letter from the Pastoral da Mulher Marginalizada, Região oueste/sul to Padre Dagoberto Boím, *Mulher-Libertação* 15 (1988) 11.

were marginalized by the existing socioeconomic order and to avoid as much as possible driving headlong into conflict with the Vatican over issues and activities that challenged magisterial teachings on women and human sexuality.

The church of liberation, however, could not help but admit that the systemic oppression at work within Brazilian society was driven by more than free market capitalism. As the church attempted to reconceive the problem of prostitution, it found its appeals to the social teachings of the church to be insufficient. There was little chance that the problem of prostitution could be redressed without a critical reconsideration of the church's teachings, attitudes, and practices regarding human sexuality and the humanity of women.

In time, the church became acutely aware of the ramifications involved in taking a preferential option for poor and oppressed women. Concerns related to the rights of women, particularly with regard to their lives and their bodies, were known to be controversial and contentious. The church in Brazil was already subject to the scrutinies of the Vatican regarding questions of orthodoxy related to theology and ecclesiology. Inasmuch as the ultimate litmus test for orthodoxy was to be found in an unwavering commitment to defend the church's teachings on human sexuality and the essential nature of women, the expectations were direct and unambiguous.

The church was limited as an institution in terms of how far it could go in its pastoral care of prostitutes. At a certain point, it would be forced to choose between its preferential option for the poor and its deferential obligations to the Vatican. In committing itself to the cause of poor women, the church in Brazil set itself on a collision course with patriarchy that would be difficult, if not virtually impossible, to ride out.

By the late 1980s, the problem of AIDS added yet another dimension to the problem of prostitution, not only in terms of the potential threat posed by infected women prostitutes, but even more dramatically, by the threat posed by growing numbers of infected transvestite male prostitutes.[56] Previous efforts on the part of the church to cast

56. This is best described in various issues of *Beijo da Rua*, a quarterly publication of the Instituto de Estudos de Religião ("Institute for Studies in Religion") and its program on "Prostituição e Direitos Civis" ("Prostitution

prostitutes as sexual slaves and victims were quickly supplanted by the efforts of those who, threatened with the spread of AIDS, saw fit to scapegoat prostitutes not only as public enemies, but once again as public sinners.

The social and ecclesial conditions that once made it possible for the church to include prostitutes in its preferential option for the poor and oppressed were replaced by a new set of conditions that were driven by panic and hostility. Public fear and moral judgments fueled by broader awareness regarding the sexual transmission of AIDS required the church to acknowledge the power of the competing forces at work in the definition and selection of ecclesial problems. Increasing polarization among factions within the bishops' conference, concern about the widespread growth of Pentecostal churches[57] and para-Christian sects, and efforts on the part of the World Council of Churches to support financially the promotion of prostitutes' rights were only but a few of the realities that contributed to the gradual decline of prostitution as a high-profile ecclesial problem.

By 1990, it became clear that the church was at a critical point in its relationship to the Pastoral da Mulher Marginalizada. Given the growth and direction of the movement, the church negotiated a means for securing the financial stability and ongoing viability of the P. M. M. by helping to provide resources to set in place an administrative staff and center in São Paulo known as Serviço à Mulher Marginalizada (S.M.M.). Although certain members of the Brazilian heirarchy continued their vocal and visible commitment to the P. M. M., impressionistic evidence suggests that broadbased support was diminished in comparison to previous years. Given that many of the church leaders who supported the P. M. M. in its early years were among those who bore the heaviest burden of Vatican scrutiny in the the 1980s, it would be unreasonable to criticize them for not going farther than they struggled to go. Most went as far as they could, and many went much further than the majority of their brothers throughout the world.

It is unquestionable that the ongoing support and encouragement of significant church leaders made it possible for the vision of the P.M.M.

and Civil Rights"). Since its inauguration in 1988, Gabriela Silva Leite has served as the general editor of the publication.

57. See "A fé que move multidões avança no país," *Veja* 23 (1990) 40–52.

to be realized, at least in part. By the early 1990s the P.M.M. had its own network, its own building, its own organization and was primarily under the direction of women. In the beginning, a few courageous bishops, in the company of priests, religious, and lay leaders, dared to put their power and resources at the service of this pastoral movement. They contributed greatly to the rise in consciousness that brought the multifaceted problem of prostitution into the ecclesial arena. Exactly what the future holds, however, is uncertain. Aware of the forces of time and circumstance, it is not immediately clear how the church in Brazil will relate to women in prostitution or respond to their challenges and ongoing concerns. Regardless of what the future may hold, the history of the P.M.M. remains an important illustration of how the church of liberation, in spite of limitations, initiated and accompanied the process of evangelization and human liberation that led women defined by their victimization to redefine themselves as protagonists and witnesses of a faith that does justice.

Conclusion

The analysis of the origins and evolution of the Pastoral da Mulher Marginalizada illustrates how the predominant practice of institutional silence regarding the plight of prostitutes was broken, how the concerns of marginalized women were given some measure of voice and visibility within the official structures of the church, and ultimately how prostitutes came to be formally included in the ecclesial agenda for evangelization and human liberation.[58]

At first glance, the apparent results of the Pastoral da Mulher Marginalizada seem to affirm the transformative power of liberating pastoral practice. Still, the critical observer must not lose sight of the real limits and constraints experienced by the church in Brazil. These limits and constraints are not only ecclesial but cultural, political, social, economic, and demographic. Coming to terms with the dynamics of interactive processes, whether social or symbolic, requires a recognition of the ongoing potential for change that is inherent in the

58. See Conferência Nacional dos Bispos do Brasil, "Programa 19: Pastoral da Mulher Marginalizada (PE-19)," in idem, ed., *9 Plano bienal dos organismos nacionais 1987/1988* (Documentos da CNBB no. 39; São Paulo: Paulinas, 1987) 191.

historical projects of human persons and institutions as well as the ongoing potential for resistance. In the past, failure to attend to these dynamics has fueled the presumption of some and has reinforced the despair of others. For those intent on advancing an ecclesial bias for hope, it is not enough that the church merely understands such dynamics; it must learn from them as well.

In assessing the overall situation, it seems reasonable to conclude that pastoral concern for the lives of a few million Brazilian prostitutes, thousands of whom are children,[59] would be sufficient reason for engaging in systematic reflection upon the dynamics of the past three decades. To this end—namely, that of systematic reflection on ecclesial practice—these two chapters attempt to demonstrate how a particular problem, such as prostitution, rises and falls within the ecclesial arena. The task of the next chapter is to think theologically about the implications of such dynamics for pastoral practice in the world church.

59. See Maryknoll Brazil Unit, *O Brasil* March (1992) 1. For further statistical information see a report given by Ana Maria Brasileiro, coordinator of UNICEF's Women's Program in Brazil. See also, Raimundo Rodrigues Pereira, "Em busca da infância perdida," *Veja* 16 March, 1994 66–75.

5

Toward a Theology of Incarnate Presence for the World Church

We only understood on the basis of what we are.[1]

Gabriel Marcel

When they had given her *The Imitation of Christ* to read, with the zeal of a donkey she had gone through the book without understanding it, but may God forgive her, she had felt that anyone who imitated Christ would be lost—lost in the light, but dangerously lost. Christ was the worst temptation.[2]

Clarice Lispector
Imitation of the Rose

I say that the incarnation of Christ was not foreseen as occasioned by sin, but was immediately foreseen from all eternity by God as a good more proximate end.[3]

John Duns Scotus

The aim of this final chapter is to reflect theologically on the meaning of mission and ministry in the world church in light of the insights derived from the preceding chapters. Given this aim, I

1. Gabriel Marcel, *Being and Having* (trans. Katherine Fanei; Boston: Beacon, 1951) 81.

2. Clarice Lispector, *Imitation of the Rose*, in Alberto Manguel, ed., *Other Fires: Short Fiction by Latin American Women* (trans. Giovanni Ponteiro; Toronto: Lester & Orpen Dennys, 1986) 44; for original, see Clarise Lispector, *Imitação da Rosa* (Brasil: Artenova, 1973) 33.

3. John Duns Scotus, *Ordinatio* 3 (sup.) dist. 19 (Assisi com. 137, fol. 161vb); quoted and translated in Allan B. Wolter, "John Duns Scotus on the Primacy and Personality of Christ," in Damian McElrath, ed., *Franciscan Christology* (St. Bonaventure, NY: Franciscan Institute of St. Bonaventure, 1980) 153.

here set out to accomplish three objectives. First, I propose to demonstrate the relevance of this Brazilian case study for Christian missionaries and ministers who find themselves drawn to ministries of faith and justice among women involved in prostitution. Second, I seek to engage the imaginations of those entrusted with the theological task of reflecting on the nature of the *missio dei* and the *missio ecclesiae*. I do so by advancing the need for a reconsideration of the *imitatio Christi*, in terms of both its theological foundations and its ecclesial expressions. Finally, I give my rationale for advancing a theology of incarnate presence and explain the pastoral significance of such a theology for ministry in what may be best described as the underworld of the world church. It is my hope that such a theological orientation will prove to be particularly affirming and relevant for individuals and communities involved in ministries of presence among women marginalized by abuse, exploitation, and the commercialization of human sexuality.

Unquestionably, there are many lessons to be learned from this overall study, particularly with regard to the church in Brazil and the evolution of the Pastoral da Mulher Marginalizada. Among these lessons, one of the most important to remember is this: as the Roman Catholic church took seriously its obligation to discern the competing claims of the oppressors and the oppressed, it also found itself discerning the competing claims of the poor and marginalized who were no longer one, but many.[4] Despite its broadly based commitment to affirm the "preferential option for the poor" as a constituitive part of its identity and mission, the church found itself in the difficult position of having to choose among the poor, because of the prioritization of specific needs and the availability of ecclesial resources, including personnel.

4. Since 1971, the National Conference of Brazilian Bishops has issued biennial plans that have outlined and described the development of various pastoral and ecclesial movements of the church in Brazil, of the church in Latin America, and of the church universal. An analysis of the past ten biennial plans (1971–1990) demonstrates the multiplication and diversification of ecclesial interests and concerns over the course of twenty years. See in particular, Conferência Nacional dos Bispos do Brasil, *Documentos da C.N.B.B.* (São Paulo: Paulinas, 1975–1990) vols. 5, 9, 16, 21, 28, 29, 34, 38, 39, and 40.

By the end of the 1980s, church leaders throughout Brazil were challenged by prostitutes as well as women in general to come to terms with the fact that the church was better positioned theologically *and* ideologically to exercise a preferential option for some poor than for others.[5] In the process, it discovered that the presence of a plurality of visions and voices within the ecclesial arena—although essential to the articulation of a broad and integrated pastoral plan—could not guarantee, in and of itself, an equity of resource distribution, personal involvement, and ecclesial investment. Although the implementation of national pastoral plans was always subject to local conditions, interests, and energies, ecclesial cohesion grew increasingly more difficult to sustain as the plans themselves became more complex and controversial.[6] Progressive documents and discourse alone could not control the powers of discrimination at work within an ecclesial institution that, despite its occasional protestations to the contrary, was affected both from within and without by a diversity of opinion that posed a constant threat to broad consensus.[7]

5. Inasmuch as the social oppression of marginalized women could not be addressed without specific concerns regarding women's health and welfare coming to the fore, the church was in a particularly difficult position in terms of its efforts to defend in a selective fashion the human rights of poor women. Secular advocates of women's rights challenged the church's complicity in the oppression of poor women given its unwavering position on controversial issues related to reproductive rights, public safety, and health care. See Ana Maria Portugal, ed., *Mujeres e Iglesia* (Col. Coyoacan, Mexico: Distribuciones Fontamara, 1989). See also various issues of the periodical *Mujer/Fempress*, which is published in Santiago, Chile.

6. See Mainwaring, *The Catholic Church and Politics in Brazil*, 237–53.

7. The work of Paul E. Sigmund is particularly helpful in illustrating how the evolution of sociopolitical consciousness required representatives of the church to rethink their understanding of the process of human liberation. He asks (*Liberation Theology at the Crossroads* [New York: Oxford University Press, 1990] 43) whether the ultimate objective was to be achieved by "the overthrow of capitalism and the abolition of private ownership of the means of production" or the "extension of democracy and equality to all human beings, regardless of sex, race or social class." He maintains that over time, it was not anticapitalist revolution, but rather grass roots democracy that was in need of religious support as well as a "spirituality of socially concerned democracy."

In light of this reality, charting the rise and fall of the problem of prostitution within the ecclesial arena of Brazil provides several insights into the dynamics affecting other local churches committed to the struggle for human liberation. Above all, the example of Brazil illustrates how ecclesial institutions are constrained not only by dilemmas and conflicts of various sorts and origins, but also by the inevitable changes that accompany the natural course of human history. Despite the church's desire and commitment to redress and solve specific problems associated with oppression and injustice, it was, is, and most likely will always be unable to realize fully its aspirations and longings because of any number of causes and conditions outside of its control.

Although the frameworks for analysis used in chapters three and four assist in providing a social-psychological explanation of this ecclesial reality, the explanation leaves the task of thinking theologically about this reality to those who devote their energies to reflecting upon God's action in the world. The question implicit in such interpretation is not new; those who profess to follow Jesus Christ have had to grapple with it since the early beginnings of Christianity. In effect the question asks: What must the church do when it cannot ameliorate the situations that it identifies for itself as problems?

History reveals that the church copes with the practical and theoretical implications of this question in a variety of ways, one of which is to adapt its theology. Despite these adaptations, however, the church carries on in a problem-solving mode. This mode is reflected in the way the church redefines problems, renegotiates solutions, and reconstructs theologies. Rather than questioning whether there is an inherent limitation in the fundamental theological orientation that the church takes as its starting point for understanding its purpose and mission, namely, the mystery of God's saving action in the world, the church devotes itself to questioning whether or not salvation and liberation will be realized here on earth or only in the hereafter. In light of the church's pervasive orientation and the realities of our world, it is my conviction that it is no longer enough to adapt old theologies or elaborate new ones. What is needed is a radical change in the church's fundamental theological orientation.

The contemporary ecclesial problem of prostitution as examined within the Brazilian context challenges the purpose and mission of the church in the world. Mindful of this fact, we must note how parallels, in other contexts from around the world,[8] while characteristically distinct, serve to illustrate that regardless of how the problem of prostitution is acknowledged or addressed by a local church, it tends to defy solution. Such parallels also demonstrate that although the church, over time, may prove to be incapable of bringing about or sustaining a high-profile *commitment to* and *concern for* women in prostitution, the challenges and claims that marginalized women continually place before Christian communities do not go away.

Warrants for Rethinking the Identity of the Church as Problem Solver

Although all of the previous observations merit further attention and discussion, the immediate purpose of highlighting them is to show how each calls into question the nature and character of a church that views its primary relationship to the world as that of problem solver. To the extent that such questioning is the responsibility of those entrusted with the task of thinking theologically about the *missio ecclesiae*, it is important to underscore that there is more to be learned from this Brazilian case study than information about how the problem of prostitution is defined, how it rises and falls in the ecclesial arena, and how the church negotiates between its complicity and its commitment.

The most consequential lesson that the evolution of the Pastoral da Mulher Marginalizada has to teach the world church about its relationship to those engaged in lives of prostitution is not a lesson about how the church might better respond to the problem of their marginalization. Rather, it is a lesson about the mystery of how the church itself may be transformed through the process of participation in the lives of marginalized women. Acknowledging the fact that in certain instances the church, as an institution, can learn only through

8. For examples, see Nadeau, *La prostitution*; Mary Soledad Perpinan, "One Journey Among Others: Work for Justice and Women's Concerns in the Philippines," *International Review of Mission* 73 (1984) 317–23; and Mil Roekaerts and Kris Savat, "Mass Tourism in South and Southeast Asia: A Challenge to Christians and the Churches," *Pro Mundi Vita—Asia Australasia Dossier* 24 (1983) 2–33.

participative action and human encounter does not come easily for a church that is all too accustomed to a theoretical and disembodied existence. While such an existence does not necessarily impede the church from reflecting on its actions, it does preclude the church's openness to thinking in process, to thinking *within* the body, rather than *outside* of it or in spite of it.[9] Despite the fact that the church has long upheld the transformative power of education, it often has had difficulty conceiving of the educative process in terms of relationship and reciprocity.

As already noted, the evolution of the Pastoral da Mulher Marginalizada draws attention to the warrants that summon the church to rethink the theological foundations that uphold its identity as a problem solver. Building upon this awareness, the following reflection advances the need for a theology that explores the dynamic relationship between christology and ministerial identity as a means for transforming the church's understanding of mission in a postmodern world. Such a theology is grounded not only in convictions about the nature of salvation and liberation but also in a conviction about the nature of incarnate presence.[10]

Reconsidering the Desire to Save: *Imitatio Christi* or *Tentatio humana*

In the novel *Imitação da Rosa* ("Imitation of the Rose"), the well-known Brazilian author Clarice Lispector alludes to a number of re-

9. The notion of "thinking in process" is taken from Gabriel Marcel, who derived the idea from Maurice Blondel. See Gabriel Marcel, *The Existential Background of Human Dignity* (Cambridge, MA: Harvard University Press, 1963) 23. According to Fischer-Barnicol, Marcel distinguishes the concept of *pensée pensée* ("closed thought") from *pensée pensante* ("open thought"). For a more detailed discussion of this point, see Hans A. Fischer-Barnicol, "Systematic Motifs in Marcel's Thought: Toward a Philosophical Theory of Composition," in Paul Arthur Schilpp and Lewis Edwin Hahn, eds., *The Philosophy of Gabriel Marcel* (trans. James S. Morgan et al.; La Salle, IL: Open Court, 1984) 440, 452 n. 49; and Kenneth T. Gallagher, *The Philosophy of Gabriel Marcel* (New York: Fordham University Press, 1962) 41.

10. Fischer-Barnicol, "Systematic Motifs in Marcel's Thought," 440–41. The notion of incarnate presence (*être incarné*) is taken from the work of

ligious symbols and metaphors as she writes about the evolution of one woman's consciousness in a world of dualities. One allusion that is of particular significance refers to the ambiguities involved in the imitation of Christ.[11] The quotation used to introduce this chapter sets in relief one of the major considerations of this reflection, namely, the limits and dangers of an *imitatio Christi* that is grounded in the desire to save others. The quotation that introduces this chapter gives expression to a provocative and unsettling perspective that calls into question the very foundations of Christian life and practice. Yet it is only by considering the possibility that the imitation of Christ could well be the "worst temptation" that Christians throughout the world can begin to discover how the *desire to serve*, no matter how radical and altruistic, is inextricably linked to the *desire to save.*

Within the context of Latin America, it is important to remember that liberation theology gave rise to a theological innovation that logically proceeded from the image of Jesus Christ as liberator. The image reflected a christology that endeavored to couple liberation and salvation.[12] Although the imitation of Jesus Christ, the liberator, was a significant revisioning of a more traditional image and imitation of

---

Gabriel Marcel. In short, it is a notion that takes seriously the experience of embodiment. Drawing upon the insights of Marcel, Fischer-Barnicol explains that such embodiment occurs "when thought becomes aware of its own roots in this experience, it returns home, so to speak, into the concreteness of incarnate existence; it becomes concrete, corporeal, and existential."

11. For further discussion of the *imitatio Christi* and its significance in Christian life and practice, see Margaret R. Miles, *Practicing Christianity: Critical Perspectives for an Embodied Christianity* (New York: Crossroad, 1988) 17–42.

12. See Leonardo Boff, *Jesus Cristo, Libertador* (Petrópolis: Vozes, 1971); Juan Luis Segundo, *The Liberation of Theology* (Maryknoll: Orbis, 1976); and Jon Sobrino, *Christology at the Crossroads* (trans. John Drury; Maryknoll: Orbis, 1978). See also efforts on the part of the Vatican Congregation for the Doctrine of the Faith to clarify the proper relationship between liberation and salvation in Congregation for the Doctrine of Faith, *Instruction on Certain Aspects of the "Theology of Liberation," Origins* 14 (1984) 193–204; and idem, *Instruction on Christian Freedom and Liberation, Origins* 15 (1986) 713–28. Pope John Paul II further explains this relationship in his encyclical *Redemptoris Missio, Origins* 20 (1991) 541–68.

Christ, as exemplified in the writings of Thomas à Kempis,[13] this revision was not free of the pervasive theological assumptions that make it difficult for Christians to perceive the difference between an *imitation of Christ* and a *"temptation of the human spirit."* In effect, the temptation is rooted in the conviction that those who follow Christ, seeking in their own lives to imitate his liberating and saving actions, are in a privileged position: it assumes that they know the form that the liberation and salvation of others should take and thus can endeavor to bring it about.[14] The subtlety of the human temptation contributes to the conscious and unconscious use of the imitation of Christ as a license for individuals and groups to control and confine the *missio dei* in accord with their own claims to know God's will for others. It could be argued that one of the most extreme examples of such a distortion is illustrated by the stance taken by church authorities who believe they are acting in accord with the mind of Christ by refusing women admission to the ministerial priesthood not only on the grounds that because of their biology, women are incapable of fully representing the person of Christ,[15] but on the basis of an authoritative interpretation of scripture and tradition.

In reconsidering how the desire to imitate Christ as savior and liberator has influenced Latin American liberation theology and pas-

13. Thomas à Kempis, *The Imitation of Christ* (trans. William C. Creasy; Notre Dame, IN: Ave Maria Press, 1989).

14. In accord with the thought of Paulo Freire (*Pedagogy of the Oppressed*, 27–56, 75–118), pastoral agents acknowledged the fact that the oppressed must become the agents of their own liberation. Nevertheless, for reasons of expediency, urgency, or impatience, many pastoral agents often found themselves bringing their power and influence to bear on situations where the oppressed were at a decided disadvantage against oppressive systems. Although such action was taken with the "best interest" of the poor and oppressed in mind, it was often defined in terms of the values and world view of the pastoral agent.

15. For those unfamiliar with the debates and discussions surrounding the exclusion of women from the ministerial priesthood within the Roman Catholic tradition, the expectation that the priest be *in persona Christi* ("in the person of Christ") serves as a direct reference to the ways in which a restrictive understanding of embodiment continues to constrain the church's understanding of the humanity of Christ. This, however, may prove to be less problematic than magisterial teachings that claim to know the mind of God as mediated through authoritative interpretations of scripture and tradition.

toral practice, it is necessary to underscore the fact that the contemporary impulse to save and liberate is a legacy of Christianity. The desire to imitate Christ as messiah and redeemer is not unique to liberation theology but rather it is inherent in much of the christological thinking that has guided the moral and ecclesial imagination of Western Christianity. Despite the credal formula of Nicea, *"for us* and *for our salvation* Christ came down from heaven," Roman Christianity has managed to eclipse the statement "for us" by the statement "for our salvation." For centuries, a world view centered on sin has predominated in theological circles rather than a world view centered on Christ. In the former view, humanity's need for redemption is posited as the reason for Christ's coming.[16] At worst, this view implies that the Incarnation was predicated on human sinfulness. At best, it lends itself to a one-sided view of the mystery of God's love and action in the world. It contributes to an understanding of an imitation of Christ that finds expression in human efforts to influence God and to control evil through heroic and charismatic acts of expiatory suffering and messianic virtue.

I wish to clarify that the purpose of this critique is not to repudiate or supplant the doctrine of salvation with that of the Incarnation. Rather, my intention is to stress the importance of their interrelatedness[17] and to argue that inasmuch as the doctrine of the Incarnation holds the potential for offering a radically different approach to understanding the imitation of Christ, its value as a theological orientation for ministry merits the attention of practical theologians. My appeal here is that the primary purpose of the Incarnation must be understood in broader theological terms than those identified with the utilitarian end of supplying for humanity's need of redemption. For this reason, I advocate an understanding of the Incarnation that is rooted in the mystery of God's love. To this end, I recommend a retrieval of the subtle and orthodox arguments of the Franciscan theo-

16. A classic example of this position is articulated by Anselm in *Cur Deus Homo?* (translated in Anselm of Canterbury, *Why God Became Man, and The Virgin Conception and Original Sin* [trans. James M. Colleran; Albany, NY: Magi, 1969]).

17. For further discussion of this point see Karl Rahner, "On the Theology of the Incarnation: Nature and Grace," in *Theological Investigations* (23 vols.; Baltimore, MD: Helicon, 1966) 4. 176–77.

logian John Duns Scotus (1266–1308) regarding the primacy of Christ as well as a consideration of the philosophical reflections of the French philosopher Gabriel Marcel (1889–1973) regarding incarnate presence.

According to Scotus's thought, it is important to understand the relationship of the primacy of Christ to the primary purpose of the Incarnation. This primary purpose may be best described in terms of God's *first* intention. The divine will was moved by love for its creation and the desire to be one with that creation, at its beginning and its end.[18] In Scotus's understanding of the Incarnation, God, in an act of gratuitous love, affirms through the first intention that every person, by virtue of his or her creation in the image and likeness of God, is worthy of God's love and presence. In short, God's first intention is to be one with humanity. This is not predicated on humanity's need for salvation, but on the power and desire of the divine will to be "God with us."

Scotus's line of reasoning is significant for theology because it makes possible the conjoining of incarnation and liberation as a complement to the coupling of salvation and liberation. Through the coupling of incarnation and liberation, it is possible to understand freedom not only in terms of freedom *from*, but primarily in terms of freedom *for*. In effect, Scotus engaged the theological imagination in a consideration of what it means for the human person to be free for God and free for good.

As stated earlier, my reason for appealing to the thought of Scotus is grounded in the conviction that the church's understanding of mission cannot be limited to an imitation of Christ that is founded exclusively upon a theology of redemption. Although I am invested in recovering a valuable insight from the Franciscan theological tradition, I am more interested in calling into question the ways in which predominant theological perspectives on such themes as incarnation and redemption serve to limit, constrain, and even undermine the church's ability to realize its expressed desire to be one with the poor.

In an age when increasing numbers of Christian ministers are confronted daily by the magnitude of human need, the extent of human hopelessness, and the pervasiveness of dehumanization, local churches

---

18. See Wolter, "John Duns Scotus on the Primacy and Personality of Christ," 153–82.

throughout the world are compelled to reconsider the adequacy of the theological foundations that undergird their understanding of both the *missio ecclesiae* and, perhaps even more importantly, the *missio Dei*. In light of the challenges that emerge from these realities, there is a growing need for Christian theologians to provide the church with additional ways of understanding and responding to God's intention for humanity.[19] In effect, there is a vocational responsibility to make known the horizon of truth that exists within the tradition with regard to equally correct, yet distinctly diverse, theological opinions and pastoral actions.[20] When this does not take place, preferred opinions often predominate as the *only* opinions, which may lead to a church that is increasingly less capable of engaging creatively a diversity of right opinions and right actions as it realizes its identity and mission.

While it is not surprising to find the world church resistant to recognizing the limitations inherent in its preferred theological orientation, the future of the *missio ecclesiae* may be contingent upon whether or not such resistance is overcome. At issue here is the fact that the world church, whether moved by duress or by desire, must come to terms with the stark reality of limits. The church must acknowledge that it is unable to carry out the work of human liberation in a way that adequately responds to the extent of human need. In a similar fashion, it must recognize that it is unable, for any number of reasons, to make available to a large segment of the world's population the word and sacraments that it claims are essential to the work of salvation.

We must not forget that in an era when the church has gone to great lengths to reaffirm its commitment to the task of evangelization and human liberation,[21] it does so mindful of the fact that the percent-

19. See Congregation for the Doctrine of the Faith, *Instruction on the Ecclesial Vocation of the Theologian*, *Origins* 20 (1990) 120 (§10).

20. To the extent that the Roman Catholic tradition has tended to advance and defend *preferred* opinions and modes of ministerial action to the exclusion of other valid possibilities, it is important to note that the church historically has distinguished correct opinions from incorrect opinions. It also has promoted preferred opinions so as to preclude broad knowledge of other opinions, which, although differing from the preferred, are nonetheless acknowledged to be true.

21. See John Paul II, *Redemptoris Missio*, 557–58 (§§58–59).

age of Christians in the world remains, as it has since the turn of the
century, roughly one-third of the total population.[22] The church is
also mindful of the widespread incidence of human suffering and
oppression caused by disease, natural disaster, famine, and war. Given
these realities, the theological foundations to which the church turns
in its effort to understand its participation in the mission of Christ are
critical and consequential not only to the church's identity, but to its
vitality as well. Is the apparent failure and inability of the church to
realize the *missio ecclesiae*, which it has narrowly defined for itself
in terms of salvation and liberation, a question of theodicy or a question of theology? Could it be that there is something the church has
yet to comprehend fully about the *missio Dei* and the *imitatio Christi*?
Has the church become so taken up with itself that it has lost sight
of the fundamental relationship between the great commission—the
injunction to teach and baptize all nations—and the great command-
ment—the requirement to love God with all one's heart, soul, and
mind, and to love one's neighbor as oneself?[23]

It is undoubtedly true that the church, as an institution, will only
find itself in a position to address such questions as it is brought face
to face with the limits of its own resources, be they spiritual or
material. This awareness, however, need not be an occasion for
ecclesial despair, if the church recognizes in this awareness an ecclesial
opportunity to remember the example of countless missionaries and
ministers, who, throughout the ages, courageously and creatively
embraced an imitation of Christ that was not exclusively defined or
solely measured in terms of their power to save and liberate others.
I especially number among these men and women those who commit-

22. For more detailed information on the growth of Christianity in different regions of the world, see David B. Barrett, "Annual Statistical Table on
Global Mission: 1990," *International Bulletin of Missionary Research* 14 (1990)
26; and idem, *The Encyclopedia of World Christianity* (New York: Oxford
University Press, 1982) 5.

23. See Matt 22:36–40, 28:18–20. This particular question was posed by
Christopher Duraisingh in a lecture entitled "The Nature of the *Missio Dei* in
a World of Competing Identities," paper presented at the Orlando Costas
Consulation on Mission sponsored by the Boston Theological Institute, 24
February 1992, at Newton, MA.

ted themselves to lives of ministry in the underworld of the world church. For the most part, these are not individuals who, in the face of failure and frustration, settled for being "present," primarily because they could not bear to abandon their missions and ministries altogether. Rather, they are individuals, who, from the very beginning, understood incarnate presence not as a means, but as an end in itself. For these individuals, the way of incarnate presence was neither a given nor a last resort. It was chosen. Moved by an imitation of Christ that expressed itself in the desire *to be one with others*, they were aware that participation in the *missio Dei*—understood as God's universal loving will for all humanity—was not without its risks and consequences. Grounded in this knowledge and experience, they dared to come face to face not only with the mystery of God's love, but with the problem of God's love as well, a problem that is particularly acute for a church marked by the vestiges of the teaching that *extra ecclesiae nulla salus* ("outside the church there is no salvation").

Inasmuch as those involved in ministries of presence have understood the *missio ecclesiae* in a radically different way, some ecclesial critics have judged them as unproductive and, at times, as morally or religiously compromising. This is especially true for those who have "pitched their tents" among marginalized women. Few have been left unscathed by severe criticisms and vicious scrutinies.[24] Although, under some circumstances, ministries of presence have been tolerated as one dimension of the *missio ecclesiae*, this usually has been in circumstances where the church approved of such ministries primarily as a means to another end. Rarely has the church been comfortable with the idea that a ministry of presence among those identified as nonbelievers, sinners, or victims could be regarded as an end in itself. Propositions to the contrary are thus often subject to reproach as are those individuals who, in advancing such positions, run the risk of

---

24. For examples of such criticism see Plínio Corrêa de Oliveira, "D. José Maria Pires, corifeu do movimento das CEBs, proclama a prostituição como um verdadeiro serviço de Deus!" in *As CEBs— das quais muito se fala, pouco se conhece—a TFP as descreve como são* (6th ed; São Paulo: Vera Cruz, 1982) 163–67.

being judged as imprudent, indifferent, or unfaithful when it comes to carrying out the mission of the church.

The *Missio Ecclesiae* and Ministerial Approaches to Those in Need of Salvation and Liberation

In looking back over the course of the history of Christian missionary activity, we find a common thread woven through many of the church's efforts to carry out its mission in the world. This thread may best be described as the need to establish ecclesial criteria for evaluating the ministerial effectiveness of individuals and groups. For centuries, the church often has felt a need to prove that it is accomplishing its perceived mission in the world. The drive to fulfill this need accounts, at least in part, for why the church hesitates to acknowledge the value of ministries of presence not only among prostitutes, but among all those identified as being in need of salvation and liberation.   ·

Once the church casts people into categories of nonbelievers, sinners, or victims, it not only reaffirms its fundamental theological orientation toward mission, but it also positions itself in such a way that its objectives are clearly defined. In doing so, the church determines the measure of its effectiveness in terms of its success in bringing about conversions, combatting vice, and caring for the poor and oppressed. It is important to keep in mind, however, that regardless of how individuals are categorized, the church's approach to them is essentially the same. It identifies their problem and sets out to solve it in accord with its own understanding of the divine commission.

In some cases, the church assumes that individuals are able and willing to change their lives in accord with ecclesial expectations. In other cases, it assumes that individuals are not able and therefore are not free to choose on their own behalf. The individuals in such cases are deemed subject to the better judgment of the church. In almost all cases, however, the church defines the problem that it intends to solve in accord with a particular set of anthropological and soteriological assumptions. For the most part these assumptions tend to be in continuity with an ecclesial understanding of the role and function of a given person within a given society. To the extent that it is possible, the church supplies or guarantees the necessary resources for ensuring the realization of solutions that best conform with ecclesial views on how to save nonbelievers, sinners, and victims. In accordance with the chosen plan of action, the church and its ministers become the agents of salvation in the spiritual order and, often times, the agents of liberation in the temporal order as well.

In the case of prostitutes, the church has been and continues to be particularly careful about distinguishing among women capable of changing their lives and those who are neither able nor free to choose another way. It is important to note, however, that regardless of whether the prostitute is cast as a nonbeliever, sinner, or victim, the church recognizes her as a woman and ministers to her in accord with a particular set of ecclesial assumptions regarding the essential nature of woman as well as her role and function within the church and society.[25]

Because of these assumptions, the agency and availability of the church as an instrument of salvation and liberation is not only limited but frequently compromised. The archetypal characterizations of woman as virgin, mother, or whore, while not invented by the ecclesial imagination, often have been appropriated by it. Thus, the church is constrained by a fairly limited repertoire of attitudes that define and determine its ministerial outreach to all women. Idealization, contempt, and pity are the strategies upon which the church often relies in its efforts to distinguish and distance itself from the problems faced by women, problems that it cannot or will not solve. In the effort to account for the reasons why the church often tends to disengage itself from direct contact with marginalized women identified as prostitutes, the previous observations and insights are particularly important. On the one hand, they are a reminder to the church of its real limitations as a human institution. On the other hand, they alert the church to its unwillingness to be associated with prostitutes even though church fathers and church reformers alike used the image of a prostitute as a metaphor for the church itself.

25. Although this study does not lend itself to a thorough examination and analysis of the church's teachings on the essential nature of woman, the traditional position of the church and a contemporary understanding of that position are represented in the thought of John Paul II in *Apostolic Exhortation on the Family*, 437–68; and idem, *On the Dignity and Vocation of Women*, *Origins* 18 (1988) 261–83.

Given the fact that biblical harlots are often found in the ranks of nonbelievers, sinners, and victims, the church that is cast in their image and likeness has many possible faces. Allusions include the whore of Babylon (Revelation 17), Gomer (Hosea 1), or Tamar (Genesis 38). For the sake of argument, however, I would like to consider once again the image of Rahab, a woman of faith and justice, who belongs to the ranks of survivors and protagonists alike. Although as noted in chapter one, Jerome has provided the church with some insights into this biblical analogy, it seems to me that many of the women involved in the Pastoral da Mulher Marginalizada may offer even more.

As survivors and protagonists, prostitutes alert the church to the inadequacy and, at times, irrelevance of its *modus operandi*. They call into question the biases, assumptions, and limitations of its preferred theologies. Above all, they force the church to be honest with itself by never allowing it to forget its hidden secrets and its complicity of silence which they know about from firsthand experience. Prostitutes stand as a constant reminder to the church that it cannot save those whom it does not include. Survivors and protagonists have ways of requiring the church—including missionaries and ministers, known or unknown for their practices of abandonment or abuse of nonbelievers, sinners, and victims alike—to listen to the truth that they speak. With the question, "Do you love me?" (John 21:15–19), they alert the church along with its representatives that one day the church and its ministers will be taken where they would not go, reminding them as Christ did Peter that the imitation of Christ is realized in loving action and incarnate presence.

Toward a Theology of Incarnate Presence for the World Church

Rarely is it the case that the church, as an institution, gives serious reflection to the insights and experiences of prostitutes, particularly to those of survivors and protagonists. During the past three decades, the church in Brazil proved itself to be an exception to the rule. It attended to the voices and visions of marginalized women, and, in doing so, allowed itself to be touched, if not changed, by an experiential understanding of a theology of incarnate presence.

Although I found no explicit or formal articulation of such a theology, it seems to me that its experiential foundations are well in place. To the extent that my own way of theological thinking has been influenced and changed as a consequence of my own personal encounters and documented reflections on the experiences of individuals involved in the Pastoral da Mulher Marginalizada, I believe there is a value in giving further expression to their *thinking in action*.

Just as the thought of Clarice Lispector provides a wedge for prying open the theological imagination of the Christian community, the argument of John Duns Scotus supplies an indispensable theological foundation for augmenting the predominant understanding of God's action in the world. Inasmuch as reflection on the Pastoral da Mulher Marginalizada helps to disclose the practical dimension of a theology of incarnate presence, I now turn to selected ideas from the works of the French philosopher Gabriel Marcel (1889–1973),[26] a proponent of incarnate presence, to assist me in articulating the theoretical dimension of my theological proposal in terms of its conceptual framework.

It has been argued that the notion of incarnate presence was understood by Marcel to be the central datum of metaphysical reflection.[27] In one of his early works, he advanced the position that "we only understand on the basis of what we are."[28] For Marcel, incarnate

26. In making an appeal to selected insights from the works of Gabriel Marcel, I am conscious of the fact that, as with any philosopher, the corpus of his writings, taken as whole, leaves room for numerous questions and concerns. Marcel was embedded in his own time and history. His works and commitments clearly reflect his assumptions, biases, social location, and life trajectory. Nevertheless, to the extent that Marcel's insights into the particular concepts highlighted in this section resonate with the theological proposal at issue in this chapter, I find them to be a compelling and constructive contribution.

27. See Robert Rosthall, "Introduction," in Gabriel Marcel, *Creative Fidelity* (trans. Robert Rosthall; New York: Crossroad, 1982) xiv; this text is a translation of Gabriel Marcel's *Du Refus à L'Invocation*.

28. See Marcel, *Being and Having*, 81. This statement was embedded in an extended reflection in which Marcel distinguished between thinking and understanding, between coexistence and copresence, and, ultimately, between having a body and being a body. Throughout the course of his life, he revisited these distinctions in his work as a philosopher and playwright.

being was not the object of thought but its condition. His philosophy did not proceed from the Cartesian conviction "I think, therefore I am," but rather from a conviction that summarized his fundamental attitude toward being, namely, "I feel, therefore I am."[29] For Marcel, feeling was inextricably linked to mutual participation;[30] this was expressed in what some have called his doctrine of intersubjectivity.[31] The self is constituted by relations with others, presence implies copresence, and "to be is to be together."[32] The starting-point of ontology is not the "I think" but the "we are."[33]

In my effort to elaborate a theology of incarnate presence for the world church, I have found the similarities that exist among the pastoral expectations of marginalized women, the personal testimonies of committed missionaries and ministers, and the convictions of Gabriel Marcel to be quite compelling. Although some might view the recurrence of certain concepts to be nothing more than serendipitous, I would argue to the contrary that the emergence of such commonalities is a logical and predictable outcome of shared convictions about fundamental beliefs and values that find expression in given attitudes, principles, and practices. For the sake of illustration and in the interest of providing a point of departure for further reflection on the ministerial imperatives warranted by a theology of incarnate presence, I shall simply introduce these attitudes, principles, and practices and briefly discuss their significance.

Among the ministerial attitudes warranted by a theology of incarnate presence, three are of particular importance. They include *inqui-*

29. For further discussion of this point, see Gallagher, *The Philosophy of Gabriel Marcel,* 19–21.

30. See Gabriel Marcel, *Metaphysical Journal* (trans. Bernard Wall; Chicago: Henry Regnery Company, 1952) 258.

31. See Edward G. Ballard, "Gabriel Marcel: The Mystery of Being," in George Alfred Schrader, Jr., ed., *Existential Philosophers: Kierkegaard to Merleau-Ponty* (New York: McGraw-Hill, 1967) 245.

32. See Gabriel Marcel, *The Mystery of Being,* vol. 2; *Faith and Reality* (trans. René Hague; Chicago: Henry Regnery, 1951) 9; cited in Gallagher, *The Philosophy of Gabriel Marcel,* 22.

33. See Alfred O. Schmitz, "Marcel's Dialectical Method," in Schlipp and Hahn, *The Philosophy of Gabriel Marcel,* 164.

étude, *disponibilité*, and *esprit*.[34] I believe each of these attitudes is grounded in an experiential understanding of ministry that proceeds from the desire *to be* and *to be with*.

The first of these attitudes, that of *inquiétude*, must be distinguished from anguish and anxiety.[35] Some would suggest that an attitude of *inquiétude* is incompatible with genuine faith; Marcel proposed, however, that it is one of the primary requisites for faith. In effect, *inquiétude* precludes the degeneration of the minister into passive abandon[36] and acquiescence. At the heart of the experience of *inquiétude*, one is given over to the transcendent action of grace and freedom.[37] In a world where ministerial identity is frequently linked to function, to what one does, *inquiétude* is inextricably linked to the aspiration to be, to the experience of incarnate presence.[38] It is to be expected that this attitude will be viewed as potentially problematic by those who are troubled by its potential to disturb and unsettle the status quo of a technocratic sense of mission. Unlike the experience of anguish that pervades the lives of many ministers who are overwhelmed by the needs they cannot meet, *inquiétude* does not lead to paralysis or inertia. Unlike the experience of anxiety that pervades the lives of others who are overcome by frustration and failure, it does not lead to worry or fear. Rather, it is the disposition that allows ministers to detach themselves from the vise in which they are squeezed by daily life, with its hundreds of cares that mask the true realities.[39] In doing so, *inquiétude* leads to the attitude of *disponibilité*.

34. The French word *inquiétude* is difficult to render in English. Some have translated it as "uneasiness" or "dis-ease." There is also no single English word into which the French *disponibilité* translates in a satisfactory fashion. "Availability" is one approximation, inasmuch as it is understood as a complete openness to the other. The French *esprit* is understood to mean openness to the "spirit of truth." The term, however, has a much deeper meaning than the English phrase is able to convey.

35. See Gabriel Marcel, *Problematic Man* (trans. Brian Thompson; New York: Herder & Herder, 1967) 67–71.

36. Ibid., 71.

37. Ibid., 85.

38. Ibid., 139.

39. Ibid., 142.

The attitude of *disponibilité* may best be understood as a state of availability and receptivity.[40] It represents a fundamental openness to others which can be described by the image of the door of one's soul being left ajar. It is the disposition that allows for communion and copresence, in contrast to nonpresence, self-preoccupation,[41] and impermeability. To be more precise, *disponibilité* is contrasted with the experience of ministers who attend to ministerial functions in ways that reinforce their functional self-understanding while insuring that they themselves remain unchanged and unchangeable. In accord with the attitude of *disponibilité*, the minister must be attentive to the "thou-ness" of the other or others[42] and reverence the dynamic of relationality, without which genuine dialogue is impossible. Essentially, the attitude of *disponibilité* reflects an unwavering commitment on the part of the minister to be affected by the reality of the other. Because of this commitment, the minister allows for the possibility of being changed by truths previously unknown and unexperienced. Such a commitment, however, can only be made by one who is attuned to *l'esprit*, the spirit of truth.

Ministers committed to cultivating a spirit of truth must be prepared to recognize within themselves the "desiring self" that perpetuates illusions and sees the world as it wants the world to be. To incorporate the spirit of truth one must have the courage to face the facts of life,[43] and be prepared to challenge the "life-lie" as it is lived by those who exist in a state of non-awareness, not seeing reality, shutting out what they would otherwise know or come to realize.[44]

Although much more could be said about each of these ministerial attitudes, it is also important to explore the relationship between these attitudes and the three ministerial principles that flow from them,

40. For a more detailed discussion of this attitude, see Otto Friedrich Bollnow, "Marcel's Concept of Availability," in Schlipp and Hahn, *The Philosophy of Gabriel Marcel*, 177–99.

41. See Marcel, *Being and Having*, 72–73.

42. See Gabriel Marcel, "Martin Buber's Philosophical Anthropology," in idem, *Searchings* (New York: Newman, 1967) 82.

43. See Schmitz, "Marcel's Dialectical Method," 164–67. See also Marcel, *Metaphysical Journal*, 2, 13, 28–29; and idem, *Mystery of Being*, vol. 1: *Reflection and Mystery* (trans. René Hague; Chicago: Regnery, 1951) 64, 67–68.

44. See Schmitz, "Marcel's Dialectical Method," 167–68.

namely *creative fidelity, hope, and love.* These are the principles that make it possible for ministers to come to grips "with the temptations of denial, introversion, and hard-heartedness."[45]

The principle of *creative fidelity* distinguishes between constancy and fidelity. Not only does it require the differentiation between doing and being, but, ultimately, it is reflective of a commitment to a "thou," rather than to a duty.[46] In effect, this principle serves to remind ministers that "fidelity can only be shown towards a person, never at all to a notion or ideal."[47] Above all, ministers must live and realize creative fidelity *within* human history, not outside of it. This principle of action involves resisting those tendencies "to reduce the thou to an object of interest, having, or instrumentality of various sorts."[48] For ministers, creative fidelity represents an important challenge, for linked to the possibility of fidelity there remains the possibility of betrayal.[49]

As for the principle of *hope,* ministers must learn to distinguish it from optimism.[50] Hope implies a radical refusal to reckon possibilities. It touches a "principle hidden in the heart of things, or rather in the heart of events, which mocks such reckonings;"[51] it is "outside the range of purely objective reason."[52] Hope is a "knowing which outstrips the unknown, but it is a knowing which excludes all presumption, a knowing accorded, granted, a knowing which may be a grace but is in no degree a conquest."[53] In a world marked by despair, "hope is to the soul" of the minister "what breathing is for the living organism."[54] Where hope is lacking, ministry is no more than a func-

45. See Marcel, *Being and Having,* 119.

46. See Marcel, *Creative Fidelity,* 147–74.

47. Marcel, *Being and Having,* 96.

48. Thomas W. Busch, "Introduction," in idem, ed., *The Participant Perspective: A Gabriel Marcel Reader* (Lanham, MD: University of America Press, 1987) 164.

49. Ibid., 165.

50. See Gabriel Marcel, *Homo Viator: Introduction to a Metaphysic of Hope* (trans. Emma Craufurd; Gloucester, MA: Peter Smith, 1978) 33.

51. Marcel, *Being and Having,* 79.

52. Ibid., 80.

53. Marcel, *Homo Viator,* 10.

54. Ibid., 10–11.

tion. Where hope prevails, it becomes "a memory of the future" that aims at "reunion, at recollection, at reconciliation."[55] As a principle of action, hope enables ministers to continue to believe in what cannot yet be seen.

This belief, however, cannot be understood apart from an experience of the principle of *love*, for insofar as the love expressed by a minister "bears on a thou, it rises above the entire order of *things* and of the destruction that preys upon things."[56] In this sense, "love only addresses itself to what is eternal"[57] and in doing so allows the minister to realize that "to love another is to say to that person: 'Thou at least shalt not die.'"[58] In this regard, to love another truly is to love the person in God and to affirm that incarnate presence carries with it the promise of a Presence that will not fail. It is to say, "the more I love you, the surer I am of your eternity: the more I grow in authentic love for you, the deeper becomes my trust and faith in the Being which founds your being."[59]

In reflecting upon the interconnectedness between ministerial principles and ministerial attitudes, it is important to consider the dynamic relationship between these principles and attitudes, as well as the ministerial practices that contribute to the articulation of a theology of incarnate presence. These ministerial practices include *secondary reflection*, *participation*, and *creative testimony*. Although these practices have given rise to the process of thinking theologically about the meaning of incarnate presence and its implications for ministry, particularly in the underworld of the world church, they ultimately flow from such theological thinking as well.

First, it is important to distinguish the process of *secondary reflection* from that of primary reflection. Primary reflection makes it possible to separate knowledge from experience: it distinguishes what one thinks from what one experiences. It assumes the possibility of

---

55. Ibid., 53.
56. See Gallagher, *The Philosophy of Gabriel Marcel*, 80.
57. Marcel, *Metaphysical Journal*, 63.
58. Gallagher, *The Philosophy of Gabriel Marcel*, 80. See Gallagher's comparison of the thought of Marcel with that of Nicolas Berdyaev (p. 168 n. 44).
59. Ibid., 80. For another perspective on this conviction, see Margaret A. Farley, *Personal Commitments* (San Francisco: Harper & Row, 1990) 30, 80.

radical detachment, disinterest, and objectivity; and it reinforces dualism and the absolute validity of abstract knowledge. Secondary reflection, while not denying the possibility of validity, refuses to accept the results of primary reflection as final.[60] In this regard it seeks to achieve the integration of knowledge and experience as it overcomes the separation of theory and practice. Secondary reflection is restorative and recuperative, not divisive and disunifying.[61] Essentially, in terms of ministerial practice, it is a contemplation of experience. The implications of secondary reflection for the church are numerous; a radical reconsideration of the foundations that undergird ecclesial teachings and practices is significant among these implications.

Second, the ministerial practice of *participation* must be understood at three levels of experience: incarnation (understood as a ministry of embodied presence), communion (understood as a ministry that begins in love, proceeds in hope, and persists in fidelity), and transcendence (understood as the ministerial intuition of the Divine Presence). At the heart of every concrete experience of participation is an intersubjective encounter. In this encounter, the minister comes to terms with the essential difference between an experience of ministry that is understood as problem solving and an experience of ministry that is understood as involvement in the mystery of being.[62] In the former, ministry is a matter of function and technique. In the latter, ministry is an experience that is marked by wonder, humility, and reverence for the other. Participation is an experience in which the distinction between the minister and the persons before the minister loses its meaning and initial validity.[63] Ultimately, it is an experience in which the minister is recalled into the presence of the mystery that is the foundation of his or her very being, apart from which the minister is nothing.[64]

Finally, the ministerial practice of *creative testimony* brings together justice and truth.[65] In effect, it is more than a ministerial prac-

---

60. See Ballard, "Gabriel Marcel: The Mystery of Being," 237.
61. Ibid, 237.
62. Marcel, *Being and Having*, 117–18.
63. Ibid., 117.
64. Ibid., 175.
65. See Marcel, *Searchings*, 17.

tice: it is the fundamental vocation. "To fail against justice implies contributing to, or fostering in oneself or others, everything that opposes this appeal, this vocation. But it also means being responsible for concealing or excluding truth, insofar as truth is spirit and light."[66] If our being in the world as ministers has a meaning, it is that "history itself is that very process in which we are personally called upon to give our testimony."[67] The creative testimony of ministers continues to give witness and meaning to the mystery of incarnate presence, and this testimony gives rise to a theology that finds one of its clearest expressions in the invocation: "You alone possess the secret of what we are and what we are capable of becoming."[68]

Conclusion

In the attempt to assess the value that the church as an institution places on an incarnational approach to ministry, recorded history speaks for itself. Still, before questioning the church's inability or unwillingness to act another way, we must first question the church's ability and willingness to think in another way. As I intimated earlier, the church's unwillingness to act differently may be due, at least in part, to the fact that the church has failed to cultivate and promote the very theological orientation that could enhance its understanding of the *missio Dei.*

Throughout the world, it is not only ministers in the underworld of the world church who desperately need a more adequate understanding of incarnational theology: this is a need of the entire church. In short, the recognition of an *imitatio Christi* that acknowledges both the primacy of incarnate presence and the validity of ministries of presence is a theological and pastoral imperative for mission and ministry in the twenty-first century, particularly for those whose imitation of Christ is lived in the midst of persons involved in prostitution.

To the extent that the world church acknowledges that it has something to learn from the lesson that ministers in its underworld have

66. Ibid., 21.
67. Ibid., 17.
68. Marcel, *Problematic Man*, 63.

learned throughout the centuries, it will discover that the way of incarnate presence is the starting point of the *missio Dei*. The way of
incarnate presence is not a means to a greater good; it is in itself the
beginning, the end, and the greatest good. It is not a mere given of
salvation history, but a divine exercise of the power of choice. Although I suspect that some will find this line of thinking unconvinc-
ing and questionable, there are many who will find it persuasive,
primarily for one reason: because it resonates with their experience.

6

Conclusion
Marginalized Women, the Church, and the New Evangelization

Our history, [the history] of the Pastoral da Mulher Marginalizada, is built upon this foundation: to provide the marginalized woman with an incentive to struggle on her own behalf so that one day she will be recognized as WOMAN. Also, [it is founded upon the conviction] that she, as a prostituted woman, may come to discover her personhood, as a creature of God, knowing that the past that marks her can empower her to lead a more authentic life. Finally, we think that the marginalized woman is able to accomplish her lifelong struggle to participate in society and to become an agent of her own liberation as well as that of her *companheiras* ("companions in the struggle").[1]

Monique Laroche

Throughout the course of my research on the church of liberation and the problem of prostitution, I have made use of an integrative method for doing practical theology. This method draws upon various theological disciplines and fields of social science. For specialists in these disciplines and fields, the potential limitations of such a methodology are numerous; as with other studies of a similar genre, it runs the risk of being judged as diffuse or superficial. A more likely concern, however, is that specific sections, each of which could serve as the basis for a book, are limited to the confines of a single chapter. Nonetheless, for generalists in the area of religion and

1. See Monique Laroche, "Serviço à Mulher Marginalizada/Pastoral da Mulher Marginalizada," *Mulher/Libertação* 26 (1991) 17–18.

society, the possibilities of such a methodology are promising and challenging. Not only does the method provide a framework for exploring the interactive dynamics that inform and influence the church and its world view, but it also offers a format for examining the relationship of faith and tradition to history and culture. Above all, the method allows for critical and constructive reflection on the adequacy and appropriateness of Christian mission and ministry. To this end, I set the following conclusions at the service of the church and the academy.

Although many aims and objectives have been accomplished in each of the previous chapters, I would like to conclude by reflecting briefly upon what I believe to be the theoretical and practical consequences of thinking theologically about the problem of prostitution.

The Church and Marginalized Women: Concluding Insights

The Pastoral da Mulher Marginalizada is one example of how the church, although deeply committed to ministries of faith and justice, faced a number of limitations in its efforts to accompany and support marginalized women. At a certain point, the church, as an institution, was required to acknowledge the inconsistencies and contradictions inherent in its own teachings.[2] Nowhere was this made clearer than in the church's efforts to negotiate between its historically conscious social teachings on human rights and its essentialist teachings on the dignity of women.[3] The institutional church had its own understanding about serving and saving women, and this understanding clearly illustrates the interactive dynamic between theological foundations and ministerial practice. Theology, which interprets and safeguards the *missio ecclesiae*, also plays an important role in determining the church's proper relationship to those whom it seeks to save and serve.

I admit that generalizations about the relationships between Christian communities and women in prostitution cannot be sustained on the basis of one particular example. Nevertheless, the analysis of this

2. See Charles E. Curran, "Catholic Social Teaching and Sexual Teaching: A Methodological Comparison," *TToday* 44 (1988) 425–40.

3. See Maria Riley, "Catholic Social Thought Encounters Feminism," *The Way* (1991) 150–62.

Brazilian case study, subjective and contextual as it may be, does alert Christian communities throughout the world that the ecclesial and social questions raised by the problem of prostitution are not unique to Brazil. If nothing else, the study of the evolution of the Pastoral da Mulher Marginalizada provides the church with unsettling evidence about the possibilities and limits that must be faced by Christians who take up ministries among prostitutes. Such evidence is a sobering reminder that for the church and its ministers, there often comes a point beyond which the institution and its representatives are unfree, unable, or unwilling to go. At the same time, the evidence also reminds us of how courageous and creative individuals find ways of moving through the theological and ministerial impasses shored up by beliefs and customs.

The confounding irony is that one thread runs through every piece of historical and contemporary evidence. This thread is none other than the conviction held by the leaders, ministers, and members of Christian communities—however disparate and contradictory their actions may be—that they are acting in accord with the teachings and traditions entrusted to them.

Prostitutes, Women, and Ecclesial Consciousness: Rethinking the Feminine Face of the Church

For centuries, discriminating Christians have perceived the need to distinguish between the church as "she" and the church as "it." By this differentiation, they have attempted to make a clear distinction between the church as a divinely inspired witness to God's action in the world and the church as a human institution. In the former distinction, the church commonly is personified as "she," hearkening back to images of the faithful spouse, the good mother, the undefiled virgin, the teacher of wisdom and compassion. In the latter, the church is often objectified as "it," reminiscent of the process of depersonification to which a woman is subjected if she fails to live up to the theological criteria for feminine idealization. This is particularly true of the so-called public woman.

Although numerous interests have been served in attempts to establish and nuance such distinctions, I make my own appeal to this differentiation as a means of illustrating how the self-identification of the church with preferred feminine images may in itself be one of the critical and unexamined factors involved in the ways certain women and their experiences continue to be marginalized. To the extent that the church denies and defends itself against any and all aspersions involving metaphorical allusions to prostitution, it reinforces the false consciousness that separates good women from bad women and ensures that women continue to be divided among themselves into mutually exclusive categories. Without fully realizing the consequences of its actions, the church reproduces such representations in its own classifications of the good church and the bad church, the true church and the misguided church, the right church and the wrong church, the ultramundane church and the underworld church.

If and when the church commits itself to reflecting upon the problem of prostitution, it could find itself gazing into a mirror. The challenge to reflect upon itself as it reflects upon prostitutes could lead the church to a new way of seeing itself. In this process, the church might come to see how it has divided itself in the same way that it has divided women, and that these divisions are ultimately ways of avoiding the complexities of embodiment, human relationship, power, and knowledge. Such realization could open the church to an understanding of how it has internalized the assumptions of patriarchy so much that it has suppressed within itself the desire and capacity for thinking in action. In doing so, the church punishes itself and others for daring, on the basis of experience, to question its exercise of absolute control, its toleration of abuse, its rationalization of human expendability, and its abdication of moral responsibility for immoral actions carried out in the name of God.

As noted in the previous chapter, critics and commentators, within and outside the ranks of Christianity, have ascribed to the institutional church characteristics commonly associated with women engaged in prostitution: perfidious, sinful, seductive, corrupt, lacking in integrity, gullible, and weak. Metaphorically speaking, the complex trajectory of ecclesial history, especially as seen in the Roman Catholic tradition, illustrates how the church has been moved to prostitute itself, allowed itself to be prostituted by others, has been led into prostitution unknowingly, or has been forced into prostitution against its will. As with women engaged in prostitution for the sake of power and privilege, the church has been moved by unbridled greed and lust. As with other prostitutes, the church has traded its integrity in exchange for the guarantee of relative status and security. As with unsuspecting women lured into prostitution, the church has been unaware of the devastating consequences of initially attractive promises and social compromises. As with women in desperate situations of violence and need, sociopolitical realities and economic necessity have driven the church to prostitute itself; the church has been left with no alternative other than to abandon virtue and sacrifice its reputation in order to ensure its own survival and that of its children.

It is important, however, to extend this powerful metaphor beyond illustrations of the church's sinfulness, compromise, credulity, and powerlessness. In recovering the narrative of Rahab and its allegorical interpretation, we see the church unfolding as a protagonist; it is the church that comes to know God by attending to the signs of the times, the church that makes possible the passage of the people of God into the promised land. This church, cast as a prostitute in the figure of Rahab, is a public woman, a woman of her time, and, above all, a woman whose actions are critical to the realization of the divine plan.

For the purposes of this study, it seems to me that the image of Rahab, while having particular significance for Brazilian prostitutes, is also an important biblical image for affirming the church of liberation and its creative agency. The identification of the church with Rahab in no way excludes its identification as bride, spouse, mother, and teacher. If anything, it highlights the reality in stark terms and challenges the idealizations of woman that have long kept her on pedestals, far removed from the real world.

At a certain point, the questions of how this church can be metaphorically understood as a prostitute are secondary to the question of what the presence of this church has meant for a struggling people in search of a promised land. Like Rahab, the church of liberation has given birth to countless prophets and sages, to political leaders and teachers. Like Rahab, the church of liberation participates in the coming of Christ and serves as a model of faith and justice.

The Challenge of the New Evangelization

In 1990, it was estimated that the world of prostitution included within its ranks more than one hundred million women, children, and men. We can reasonably assume that as the magnitude of the phenomenon increases, Christian communities throughout the world—be they Roman Catholic, Protestant, or Orthodox—will find themselves in the unsettling position of having to come to terms with the stark realities of prostitution in all its forms. We should not assume, however, that increased ecclesial awareness and knowledge about the phenomenon of prostitution is in itself sufficient. The church does not merely need to understand the phenomenon of prostitution intellectually; the more pressing need is for the church to come to terms with its own power of choice and its own willingness to recognize the contingent nature of every ecclesial response it makes, even the response of not responding.

As word of the "New Evangelization"[4] makes it way throughout the world in conjunction with the quincentenary commemoration of Christianity in the Americas, the story of Rahab, while compelling on one level, is a sobering, if not a harrowing reminder that a religious world view constructed solely on God's plan of salvation and liberation for a chosen people has serious theological limitations.[5] If there

---

4. The phrase "new evangelization" was first used by Pope John Paul II during an address to the Latin American Episcopal Conference on 9 March 1983 in Port-au-Prince, Haiti. In the address, the pope called for a decade of commemoration for the half a millenium of evangelization in Latin America. John Paul II stressed that the "new evangelization" was not simply a commitment to re-evangelization, but a commitment to an evangelization that was new in ardor, methods, and expressions. To this end he emphasized the need for more priests, an active laity, and an implementation of the Puebla message in its integrity. See Pope John Paul II, "The Task of the Latin American Bishop," *Origins* 12 (1983) 661–62. Use of this phrase was developed and refined during the next ten years. It became the theme for the Fourth General Conference of Latin American Bishops. See Conferência General del Episcopado Latinoamericano, *Santo Domingo and Beyond: Documents and Commentaries from the Fourth General Conference of Latin American Bishops* (ed., Alfred T. Hennelly; Maryknoll: Orbis, 1993).

5. It should be noted that since 1988, the theme of "New Evangelization" has been a source of disagreement, division, and dissension throughout the

is one fatal flaw in the analogical use of the Exodus, it is the justification of slaughter and conquest in which the Christian tradition
grounds itself and from which none of us associated with the tradition
can extricate ourselves. If there is anything truly "new" about evangelization at the turn of the twenty-first century, perhaps it is that the
church is being called to acknowledge the limits of the Exodus paradigm.

Given the realities of our world, there is an urgent need for the
church to ponder the limits of its preferred biblical and theological
foundations. While some would argue that such foundations should be
abandoned altogether, my own appeal is not to antifoundationalism,
but to what I would call multifoundationalism, understood as the
acknowledgement of a multiplicity of orthodox beliefs that constitute
multiversal expressions of truth. The advancement of such a position,
however, requires more of the church than the exercise of its powers
of intellect and will. The advancement of such a position demands
more than knowledge and agency. Such a stance is dependent on

Roman Catholic church in Latin America. See Clodovis M. Boff, "Para onde
irá a Igreja da América Latina?" *Revista Eclesiástica Brasileira* 50 (1990)
275–86; Francis McDonagh, "Saving Santo Domingo," *The Tablet*, 30 January 1993, 128–29; Ian Linden, "Reflections on Santo Domingo," *The Month*
26 (1993) 17–21; João Batista Libânio, "Introdução," in Antônio Aparecido
da Silva, ed., *América Latiná 500 anos de evangelização: reflexões teológico-
pastorais* (São Paulo: Paulinas, 1990) 1–9; and Leonardo Boff, *New Evangelization: Good News to the Poor* (trans. Robert R. Barr; Maryknoll: Orbis,
1991) 61–92. The Santo Domingo document cited in the previous note is
understood by some to represent a growing current of theological and
ecclesiological neoconservativism within the ranks of the hierarchy, clergy,
religious and lay leaders. Although the document failed to represent fully the
expectations of many identified with the church of liberation, it is important
to note the attention given to women and to the subject of prostitution
(Conferência, *Santo Domingo and Beyond*, §§ 104–10 and 110, 235, respectively). With regard to women, the document may be the strongest position
ever taken by the Latin American bishops. It should be underscored, however,
that the document appeals strongly to the "essential" nature of woman, the
dignity of which the church is obliged to defend. "Prostituted women" are
included at the end of an exhaustive listing of all kinds of women affected by
the processes of dehumanization, exploitation, and victimization. As for prostitution, it is treated along with pornography as one of the many consequences
of sexual permissiveness and promiscuity within Latin American society.

judgment, the practical wisdom born of experience, participation, and presence, the *modus operandi* of the church known by the people of God as the "church with us." In this understanding of the church, the *missio Dei* and the *imitatio Christi* come together, not only in the realm of theological speculation, but also in the realm of experiential confidence in the God who proclaims "know that I am with you always; yes, to the end of time" (Matt 28:20).

To the extent that the church embraces a theology of incarnate presence, it must pray for a heart to understand how to discern between good and evil. Secondary to prayer it must learn to be attentive not only to claims of truth but perhaps more importantly to relationships of truth. In this regard, the church could benefit greatly from reflecting at length on another biblical narrative dealing with prostitutes, namely, the judgment of Solomon (1 Kgs 3:16–28). In this narrative the church is alerted to the pastoral complexities of arbitrating the claims of prostitutes. Any effort to act with wisdom and integrity must be predicated on a recognition of who the prostitute is as a person, as a woman, as a mother, as a worker, and as a believer.[6] From the perspective of the prostitute, it is not enough for the church to dare to know the mind of God; it must dare to be the heart of God.[7]

6. For insightful studies of this narrative see W. A. M. Beukin, "No Wise King Without a Wise Woman (I Kings III 16–28)" and K. A. Deurloo, "The King's Judgment in Wisdom," in A. S. Van der Woude, ed., *New Avenues in the Study of the Old Testament* (Oudtestamentische Studiën d. 25; New York: Brill, 1989) 1–10, 11–21; Carole Fontaine, "The Bearing of Wisdom on the Shape of 2 Samuel 11–12 and 1 Kings 3," *JSOT* 34 (1986) 61–77; and Stuart Lasine, "The Riddle of Solomon's Judgment and the Riddle of Human Nature in the Hebrew Bible," *JSOT* 45 (1989) 61–86.

7. This concluding statement is inspired by the words of Dom Paulo Evaristo Arns: "The modern Job has great poems to write. And these poems will not be read except by the heart of God. Do the churches have the courage to be the heart of God?"

Appendix
A Documentary History of the
Pastoral da Mulher Marginalizada*

As women, who are treated unjustly, we think that the time has come for us to give a cry of denunciation and liberation. We find ourselves drowning in a sea of fear, injustice and exploitation, social discrimination and oppression. We do not want our children to experience the same situation. We have to change this reality. For this reason we do not hesitate to face difficulties and misunderstandings in order that our movement may grow and achieve its most important objective: "the liberation and integration of woman in a just and fraternal society."[1]

Introduction

The movement of the Pastoral da Mulher Marginalizada had its beginnings in the early 1970s. Between July of 1974 and July of 1990, eight national meetings of the Pastoral da Mulher Marginalizada took place in various regions of Brazil.[2] Prior

*In the interest of making the historical record of the Pastoral da Mulher Marginalizada accessible to a wider audience, I have summarized, paraphrased, and/or translated in their entirety the documents presented in this appendix. It is important to note that the substance, literary quality, and method of organization, as recorded in Portuguese, is varied and uneven. I wish to underscore the fact that these translations were completed for informational purposes. With the exception of occasional explanatory comments or notes, the content contained in the following pages is derived from the documents of the P. M. M., appropriately referenced, and is not to be identified as original writing of my own.

1. Taken from the Proceedings of the Eighth National Encounter of the P. M. M., "Open Letter to the Bishops of Brazil, 11 Coronel Fabriciano," 22 July 1990; see *Mulher/Libertação* 22 (1990) 2.

2. In 1974, 1976, 1978, and 1980, the conference was held in Rio de Janeiro; in 1982, in João Pessoa, Paraíba; in 1984, in Salvador, Bahia; in 1987, in Brasília;

to the first meeting in 1974, regional efforts had been underway in northern and northeastern Brazil for nearly a decade.[3]

Over the course of twenty years, the P. M. M. was shaped in different ways through the efforts of bishops, clergy, religious, laity, and, most importantly, women who themselves were engaged in prostitution. The movement accompanied a turbulent time for the church in Brazil and was affected by the dramatic changes and upheavals that occurred within Brazilian society during the same period.[4] Political, economic, cultural, and religious factors all had some bearing on the emergence and evolution of the P. M. M. Organized initially under the aegis of the National Conference of Brazilian Bishops (C. N. B. B.), the first National Encounter of the P. M. M. in 1974 gave visibility to an emergent ecclesial movement with a life and purpose of its own.

In the course of a twenty-year period, the P. M. M. urged church leaders to attend not only to the problem of prostitution in the social arena, but to recognize the ramifications of the problem within the ecclesial arena as well. From the beginning, the movement challenged the church to deal with its own complicity in exacerbating the phenomenon of prostitution. Inasmuch as the P. M. M. posed serious challenges to the church from within the ecclesial arena, it called into question the silence and hypocrisy of one of the most powerful and influential institutions within Brazilian society.

First National Encounter: Rio de Janeiro, 1–3 July 1974

The preliminary findings of the First National Encounter of the P. M. M. were included in the 1976 C. N. B. B. publication of *Prostituição: desafio à sociedade e à Igréja* ("Prostitution: A Challenge to Society and to the Church").[5] The conclu-

---

and in 1990, in Coronel Fabriciano, Minas Gerais. For additional documentation on the eight national meetings see "Pastoral da Mulher Marginalizada: evolução de uma caminhada," *Serviço de Documentação*, 17 (1985) 771–869; *Mulher/ Libertação* 10 (1987); and *Mulher/Libertação* 22 (1990).

3. Regional efforts took place in Ceará (1966), Pernambuco (1967), Bahia (1968), Sergipe (1967), Alagoas (1969), Paraíba (1960), and other states such as Rio Grande do Norte, Piauí, Pará, and Maranhão. Many of these efforts were under the auspices of the Movimento de Promoção da Mulher ("Movement for the Advancement of Women") and Ninho, a Brazilian counterpart to NID, a French pastoral initiative on behalf of prostitutes, founded by Père André Talvas in 1943; see p. 81.

4. For a detailed discussion of the Roman Catholic church and its relationship to the sociopolitical order of Brazil during this period, see Bruneau, *The Church in Brazil: The Politics of Religion*; and Mainwaring, *The Catholic Church and Politics in Brazil*.

5. Conferência Nacional dos Bispos do Brasil, *Prostituição* (São Paulo: Paulinas, 1976) 36–44

sions and resolutions of the meeting provided a perspective on the issues and concerns that were brought to the fore at the First National Encounter.

At the end of the First National Encounter of the P. M. M. , the following objectives were set:[6]

(1) To consider prostitution a collective sin, thereby requiring that pastoral agents engaged in this ministry—like the church that is servant of the poor—to search out ways to liberate human beings from this depressing situation.

(2) In addition to simply withdrawing the prostitute from the business, to seek out ways of giving distinct value to the human person, so as to create in her an awareness of her dignity as a child of God.

(3) Given the physically, psychologically, and morally degrading situation that weighs upon the prostitute, to provide her the opportunity for an adequate and liberating education, so that she will be in a position to decide for herself whether or not to abandon prostitution.

(4) To make the prostitute aware of her human rights; mindful of the fact that the provision of services (such as medical assistance, child care, and education), although indispensable, are only one means to this end.

(5) The ministry should envision the advancement of the prostitute in global and collective terms, so as not to reinforce the idea that her situation of marginalization can be understood in local and individual terms alone.

(6) At the same time, the ministry, in its efforts to further the cause of the prostitute, should denounce and disturb a society that prostitutes a woman and then rejects her.

In addition to general objectives, the assembly set for itself specific short-term and long-term goals.

The short-term goals are as follows:[7]

(1) To raise the consciousness of society and make the people of God aware of the serious problem of prostitution by

• *making use of the means of social communication, and avoiding sensationalism;*

• *seeking out interaction and dialogue with people living in close proximity to the zona, so as to explain to them the work that the volunteers propose to undertake in the hope of encouraging community-based support and collaboration;*

• *informing the public of important information and statistics relative to the problem: namely, that there are one and a half million prostitutes in the country; that abject poverty causes prostitution; and that disease and social marginalization are consequences of prostitution;*

• *cooperating with associations of domestic workers and social service networks, using consciousness raising and education in order to prevent harm to vulnerable women and girls;*

---

6. *Serviço de Documentação* 17 (1985) 775–76.

7. Ibid., 776–77.

• *starting support groups, such as "Friends of the Movement" in the north-eastern region;*

• *offering specialized input to bishops and parish priests who would like to bring new energy to this area of ministry in their respective dioceses or parishes.*

(2) To awaken and give rise to a vocational call among pastoral agents for this area of ministry by

• *making contact with movements of lay people (such as Cursilhistas, the Catholic Family Movement, and youth groups) in order to create a climate of interest and engagement;*

• *contacting the pastors of parishes where the problem of prostitution exists;*

• *taking advantage of special holidays, such as Children's Day, Mother's Day, and Father's Day, in order to address the subject.*

(3) To organize strong working groups that include:

• *professionals, especially doctors, nurses, psychologists, sociologists;*

• *young people, who can be witnesses of a normal life given for the common good;*

• *married couples, who can be witnesses of true love and well-adjusted marriages;*

• *priests, who can be witnesses of the church's concern for the rejected and marginalized.*

(4) To provide pastoral agents with adequate preparation by:

• *accompanying persons interested in this type of ministry in specific field work experiences;*

• *organizing adequate field work experiences in areas where the work has been going on for some time;*

• *raising the consciousness of those preparing themselves for this ministry—which in general is treated as a pioneering work and viewed negatively by the society that gives rise to it—regarding the need for a great deal of personal stability, deep love of neighbor, sincere loyalty, and sufficient persistence.*

(5) To create a coordinating committee at the national level to facilitate communication among the various working groups throughout the country and to facilitate contact with the C. N. B. B.

(6) To present to the C. N. B. B. the names of Dona Maria do Carmo Neves, Dona Loila Barbosa, and Frei Barruel de Lagenest, who are recommended by the participants of the encounter as a coordinating committee for this pastoral area.

In specifying long-term goals, the group cited the following:[8]

(1) To give effective support to the activities that are developed for single mothers by providing a necessary introduction to the services that are available and by drawing from the experience and expertise of those already working with single mothers.

(2) Whenever possible, to contact the family of the forsaken woman by means of visits and various types of correspondence.

8. Ibid., 777–78.

(3) To create a "Center of Information" as a service for interested dioceses and parishes, making use of the expertise of the National Coordinating Committee and requesting assistance from the C. N. B. B.

(4) To make contact and to raise the awareness of representative organizations (such as the Council of Laity and Parent and Teacher Associations), however problematic this may be, by means of seminars, talks, and encounters.

(5) To become involved with other areas of ministry, such as prison ministry, ministry to migrants, ministry to travellers, so as to unite forces for a truly valid work, principally in reference to the prevention of prostitution by

• setting up information booths at bus and railroad stations in order to prevent young and naive girls, arriving from the interior and searching for work in the large cities, from being allured into prostitution;

• alerting parishes and social service centers in the interior of the country so as to discourage them from facilitating the travel of young girls to urban centers without knowing who will receive the girls when they arrive at their destinations;

• entering into ecumenical dialogue with persons of other faiths and traditions in order to achieve works that have a common purpose;

• organizing periodic encounters, such as this one, for the purpose of evaluating and improving the apostolic activities of this pastoral area.

At the conclusion of the encounter, the participants affirmed the following resolutions and motions:[9]

(1) given that current statistics and socioeconomic data on prostitution in Brazil are necessary for the future planning and development of pastoral programs, it is recommended that a request be made to the Centro de Estatistica Religiosa e Investigações Sociais ("Center of Religious Statistics and Social Investigations")[10] to undertake a national study of the problem of prostitution;

(2) given that the Empressa Brasileira de Turismo ("Brazilian Tourism Company"), in order to promote tourism, supports and provides financial incentives for the construction of moteis ("hotels for prostitution") and goes against the laws that combat the exploitation of sex trade and prostitution throughout the country,[11] it is recommended that the Commission of Peace and Justice should be asked to verify and prove this reality with sufficient documentation in order to present this fact to the legal authorities;

(3) with regard to the flagrant existence of organizations which promote prostitution, including that of children, the silence that prevails in our midst signifies complacency and consent. For this reason the Commission of Peace and Justice

9. See Conferência Nacional dos Bispos do Brasil, *Prostituição*, 42–44.

10. This center is under the auspices of the National Conference of Brazilian Bishops.

11. This is in conformity with article 43 of decree 60.224 of February 1967, as stated in chapter 5 of the Brazilian Penal Code. For a more detailed discussion of this legal issue, see Conferência Nacional dos Bispos do Brasil, *Prostituição*, 161.

should be asked to denounce Brazil's failure to comply with the existing treaty[12]
between Brazil and other countries concerning the prohibition of the trafficking of
women and the promotion of prostitution;

(4) given that the expression paternidade responsável ("responsible fatherhood")
can be interpreted only as the responsibility of the man and not of the woman as
well, the C. N. B. B. should be asked to change the pastoral usage of the expression
"responsible fatherhood" to "responsible parenthood";

(5) given that the expression "marginalized woman" is demeaning for a group
of persons already marked by society, the C. N. B. B. should be asked to change the
designated title of this pastoral initiative from Mulher Marginalizada to Mulher,
só e desamparada ("woman, alone and forsaken");

(6) given that some priests still do not understand the work that is being done by
pastoral teams among prostitutes, or, when they do become involved, these priests
act in ways that are paternalistic and overprotective, the C. N. B. B. should be asked
to suggest that the pastoral curriculum for seminaries include classes and confer-
ences by specialists in this particular ministry.

Second National Encounter: Rio, 26–28 March 1976[13]

At the Second National Encounter, held under the auspices of the C. N. B. B., the
Pastoral Junto à Mulher Só e Desamparada ("Pastoral United to the Alone and
Forsaken Woman")[14] articulated its identity, purpose, and objectives with greater
clarity and authority. In the concluding statement, participants delineated their observations regarding the confinement of victims of prostitution and proposed directions for pastoral engagement.[15]

Calling to mind the purpose for which the group was gathered and reiterating
the grim statistics of the increasing numbers of prostitutes in every region of Brazil, the document set out to identify and analyze the various positions taken toward

---

12. This is a reference to the Eighth International Abolitionist Convention,
signed by Brazil on 5 October 1950. See Conferência Nacional dos Bispos do
Brasil, *Prostituição*, 105–18.

13. See ibid., 79–86; *Serviço de Documentação* 17 (1985) 778–80.

14. Note that the name of the pastoral was altered in accord with the 1974
recommendation. In subsequent years the movement was again named the Pastoral da Mulher Marginalizada. The sensitivity of the pastoral agents to language
and its meaning should be underscored. Return to the nomenclature of "marginalized
woman" occurred at the initiative of the prostitutes themselves. They asserted the
importance of naming the social truth, rather than accommodating the best intentions of the pastoral agents to diminish the harshness of the reality by describing
it in other terms.

15. See *Serviço de Documentação* 17 (1985) 778–80.

prostitution throughout the world. The document highlighted the three most common positions:[16]

(1) regulation, a position that both sets boundaries for the confinement of prostitutes to specific areas and, through legislation, institutionalizes the exercise of prostitution;

(2) prohibition, which prohibits prostitution and punishes prostitutes;

(3) abolition, a position that struggles to combat sex trade and trafficking.[17]

The document concluded that the third position, that of abolitionism, was to be preferred, inasmuch as it provided the greatest number of possibilities for combatting sexual exploitation.[18] The group underscored that this position coincided with existing legislation as outlined in the Brazilian Penal Code (1958) and the

16. For a more detailed discussion of these three positions, see Maria do Carmo R. Neves, "Abolicionismo, Regulamentarismo, Proibicionismo," in Conferência Nacional dos Bispos do Brasil, *Prostituição*, 47–78.

17. This is the position advanced by the International Abolitionist Federation, a nongovernmental organization in consultative status with the Economic and Social Council of the United Nations. It was founded in England in 1875 and on the continent of Europe in 1879 by Josephine Butler (1828–1906), an eminent Victorian. The aim of the federation was to abolish traffic in women and children and to prevent their sexual exploitation. Butler's primary goal was to fight against the social evils induced by the stationing of "military bases" in India and in the port cities of England. In the mid-1980s, the federation identified its primary goal as an effort to inform the international community that "prostitution is now more than a moral problem. It is highly organized and linked with other social crimes such as drug-pushing, torture, fraud and murder. It has become a dangerous and hazardous profession. Besides this, it is a profession where women are utterly dependent on their procurers and clients, who are men. Perhaps no other profession or means of livelihood makes women so totally dependent on men when, at this point of history, women are looking for economic and individual independence from male domination. To accept prostitution (willingly or under duress) is a totally retrograde step depriving women of their independence, privacy and, above all, human dignity, and reducing them to the level of servitude. The gradual decline in the world economic situation, especially in Third World countries, provides a major incentive towards an increase in the exploitation and prostitution of others" ("Forward," in *Prostitution: Survival of Slavery*, Record of the Twenty-eighth International Congress of the International Abolitionist Federation, Vienna, Austria, 3–6 September 1984).

18. It is important to note that this position is not usually the choice of the Roman Catholic church. In fact, it has often been opposed by church authorities. See Mary Gibson, *Prostitution and the State of Italy: 1860–1915* (New Brunswick: Rutgers University Press, 1986); and Rina Macrelli, *L'indegna schiavitu: Anna Maria Mozzoni e a lotta contro la prostituzione di Stato* (Roma: Reuniti, 1981).

International Treaty to Repress the Trafficking of Persons and Sex Trade.[19] In accord with this law, Brazilian authorities were obliged to take legal action against any efforts to regulate prostitution (for example, the registration, inspection, or documentation of prostitutes) and any individuals who made financial gains by means of organized prostitution (such as brothel keepers and pimps). The document asserted that the more recent Brazilian Penal Code (1969),[20] which was approved although not yet fully in effect at the time, included the same dispositions.[21]

The document went on to argue that the reality of the *baixo meretrício* ("low level prostitution") was in complete contradiction with the principles outlined in the International Treaty to Repress the Trafficking of Persons and Sex Trade and that no regard whatsoever was given to enforcing the Brazilian law. In every city of the country, from the largest to the smallest, prostitutes were confined and restricted to houses of prostitution or to designated districts. In these places there was clear evidence of the detestable enslavement of women.[22]

Participants at the encounter concluded that, under the threat of infidelity to the gospel, they had to speak out against the violation of human rights that prevailed in the *zona*, where women were robbed of their rights; were placed under the discretionary power of bosses, pimps, and police; were exploited as commercial objects, victims of abuse and violence; were denied basic necessities or forced to have abortions, with no means of legal or social recourse. Once they were registered by the police, it was virtually impossible for any of them to free themselves from the situation.[23]

The participants emphasized that the confinement of prostitutes in a *zona* resulted in the degradation of the women as well as those in charge of them. The financial gain of this enterprise was dependent upon the permanent seduction of the young girls and women, who were coerced through the power of intermediaries who used all forms of persuasion and force, including false promises, blackmail, abduction, and violent abuse.[24]

The internal trafficking of women was unquestionably on the rise due to the growing number of new highways, factories, mills, and other enterprises that led to high concentrations of male workers in given areas. Such workers provided a market for procurers intent upon exploiting the situation to their own ends and avid to

---

19. See *Anexo 5* in *Serviço de Documentação*, 17 (1985) 880–87. This appendix provides documentation on the legislative decree approved by the Brazilian National Congress in 1958 along with the complete documentation of the International Treaty.

20. See reference to *Código Penal*, decreto Lei, n. 1.004, 21 October 1969 as cited in *Serviço de Documentação* 17 (1985) 778–79.

21. Ibid.

22. Ibid., 779.

23. Ibid., 780.

24. Ibid.

extend the net of sex trade. Noting that the consequences of such trafficking were as serious, if not more serious, than those commonly associated with the international sex trade industry, the effort to combat sex trafficking, especially that of minors, required severe and urgent legislation on the part of authorities.[25]

The report reminded the C. N. B. B. of the public debates that had taken place six months earlier over a bill that was introduced to the Brazilian Congress and that recommended the regulation of prostitution and the registration of prostitutes by the state. The proposal flew in the face of the actual Brazilian law as well as Brazil's commitment to the international treaty.[26] Public debates and discussion of the bill were fueled by the mass media. In the end, the bill failed, in part on account of the lobbying efforts of several organizations, including the *Grupo de Estudos sobre a Mulher na Sociedade e na Igreja*, a group of researchers focused on the role of woman in society and in the church.[27] In their refutation of the proposed legislation, this group's researchers addressed the inconsistencies and incoherencies of the bill. For example, the bill would provide prostitutes with health care, when the prostitutes, as Brazilian citizens, already were entitled by law to the benefits provided by Instituto Nacional de Previdência Social, the national institute for social services, set up to provide health care for the general population. Overall, the *Grupo de Estudos* case was built on the failure of Brazilian authorities to enforce the existing laws, infractions of which presented a far greater threat to Brazilian society. It asserted that in the end the bill would accomplish nothing more than the further humiliation, degradation, and marginalization of women in prostitution, without addressing the social, cultural, economic, and psychological realities that contributed to its exacerbation in Brazilian society. The bill would not make prostitution any less of a police problem, as its advocates argued. It would not make prostitution a broader social concern. Rather, it would make prostitution even more lucrative for the underworld of organized vice and corruption. Citing the recommendations of the World Health Organization that were in total opposition to the regulation of prostitution, the *Grupo de Estudos sobre a Mulher na Sociedade e na Igreja* reasserted the rationality of abolition and the conformity of existing Brazilian laws with that position.[28] In accord with the Brazilian Penal Code and the aims of the

25. Ibid.

26. This bill (Projcto n. 1.312) was introduced to Congress in September 1975, by Representative Roberto de Carvalho of São Paulo. Carvalho was a member of the Movimento Democrático Brasileiro, the nominal opposition party to Aliança Renovadora Nacional, the official government party of the military dictatorship. Essentially the bill sought to introduce legislation that would "establish measures to bring about the confinement of prostitution, control of hygiene, social welfare and rehabilitation of prostitutes, and supply other provisions." For the complete text, see Conferência Nacional dos Bispos do Brasil, *Prostituição*, 89–104.

27. For a complete version of the group's refutation of the Carvalho bill, see ibid., 99–104.

28. Ibid.

Twenty-sixth Congress of the International Abolitionist Federation, which met in October 1975, the *Grupo de Estudos* emphasized the need to enforce existing laws not to repeal them.

In turning its attention from law to ministry, the report of the Second National Encounter reiterated that no local church could afford to be uninterested in the lives of victims of prostitution.[29] As individuals and groups actively involved in pastoral outreach to women in prostitution, the representatives asserted that the major problem was an exploitation that reduces a woman to a commodity. This form of exploitation manifests itself in the total dependence of the woman upon those who exploit her, namely, those who control her money, her body, and her will.[30] The list of exploiters included *madrinhas* ("madams"), pimps, brothel keepers, seducers, procurers, clients, drug dealers, and police. They argued that the world of sexual exploitation relies on the passivity and disengagement of the society that excuses itself, the church that remains silent, and public authorities that support a de facto system of confinement.[31]

Conscious of the powerlessness that pastoral agents experience and aware of the magnitude of sexual exploitation, the participants discussed viable strategies for helping victims to escape from the situation in which growing numbers of women found themselves. The participants made specific recommendations to the bishops for immediate action, urging them to give concrete signs that they had not rejected victims of prostitution, for whom, as their pastors, the bishops were responsible. Whenever the bishops assumed such responsibility, they would be required to denounce the exploitation of prostitutes and to educate the Christian community about its duties and responsibilities in this regard. Because engagement with reality is often the best laboratory for learning, the report suggested that the following measures for prevention and social reintegration be taken up by pastoral agents involved in every area of ministry. In the area of prevention, these included pastoral outreach to domestic workers, former prostitutes, and migrant women; assistance to single mothers; the active presence of the church among juvenile offenders; and the use of mass media to spread information about the reality of the problem of prostitution.

In the area of social reintegration, representatives proposed to make the Christian community aware of its duty to facilitate the reintegration of prostitutes; to make priests and religious aware of the need to help in these efforts; to support and encourage pastoral agents to pursue this type of ministry; to orient the evangelization of prostitutes in ways that would help them become aware of their own dignity; to support and encourage pastoral agents who have committed themselves to this apostolate, by providing them with opportunities to reflect on their ministry within the church.

29. See *Serviço de Documentação* 17 (1985) 780–81.
30. Ibid.
31. Ibid., 781.

In light of the final report and suggestions of the Second National Encounter of the P. M. M., the National Conference of Brazilian Bishops took up the challenge to set forth some specific reflections and recommendations for the church in Brazil. From March 1976 to September 1976, the C. N. B. B. responded to the requests of pastoral agents involved in ministry to women who were "alone and forsaken" with the publication of *Prostituição: desafio à sociedade e à Igreja* (*Prostitution: A Challenge to Society and to the Church*).[32]

Third National Encounter: Rio, 16–18 March 1978[33]

The Third National Encounter of the Pastoral da Mulher Só e Desamparada met for three days during March 1978. In the course of this meeting, new observations and concerns arose. The proceedings of the meeting reveal that the critique of the *realidade brasileira* ("Brazilian reality") was derived from more than the impressionistic evidence of pastoral agents. Socioeconomic factors, although still considered to be among the major causes of prostitution, were no longer viewed as the only causes meriting the attention of the group. In particular, the subject of culture emerged as a relevant category of analysis.

After several years of pastoral work among prostitutes, members of the assembly concluded that the cultural factors influencing a woman's entry into a life of prostitution required serious reflection and discussion. Citing the words of Elena G. Bellotti, the group focused its concern:

"The culture to which we belong, like any other culture, takes advantage of all the means at its disposal to obtain from individuals of both sexes the behavior that most conforms to the values that the culture wishes to preserve and pass on."[34]

The group report observed that within the Brazilian cultural context

"there exists a value that advances the superiority of the man over the woman that leads to the establishment of roles and functions (said to be traditional) ascribed to men and to women. Beginning with the myth of the weakness and inferiority of the woman, the culture inculcates absolute respect for the man, the head of the family, attributing to him every type of privilege and attention. Independent of whether or not these beliefs are real, such myths establish habits, customs, and activities that set the feminine sex apart, thus determining its behavior. The masculine sex, inasmuch as it is dominant in all the social spheres of life, advances this domination as legitimate, thereby creating moral norms to perpetuate it. The power of the masculine sex is arbitrary and its will is without restrictions: 'women' and 'objects' are goods over which, in similar ways, one exercises unlimited power."[35]

---

32. See Conferência Nacional dos Bispos do Brasil, *Prostituição*.
33. See *Serviço de Documentação* 17 (1985) 782–96.
34. Ibid., 782.
35. Ibid., 783.

Turning to the subject of prostitution, the report explained how the prostitute is "*a woman who experiences in a more intense and marked way this set of values, taboos and prejudices that contribute to the 'feminine way of being'.*"[36] The report pointed to the fact that women rarely "choose" prostitution as a life option: "*The entrance of a woman into a life of prostitution is based upon a series of motives that are woven together in the structure of her personality so as to influence the development of her sociosexual self-understanding.*"[37] Realities, such as the loss of virginity and expulsion from the home, are fundamental to the increasing destruction of the prostitute's concept of self and as such contribute to the woman's own sense of being a person who has no place in society. Thus, it should come as no surprise that such a woman accepts any way of life that justifies her existence. Carried away by a life of prostitution, she appears to adapt herself to the situation. The group report stated that many pastoral agents note that "*within the prostitute there exists an instability that is always present. In reality, that which torments her and makes her appear unaffected is a great dissatisfaction with her life and an unconscious awareness of her powerlessness to find herself.*"[38] Through prostitution, the woman seeks a method of camouflaging the pain and unhappiness that wound her as a person.

The report asserted that prostitution does not exist as an isolated fact. Rather, it is described as a hypertrophy of the social situation of women in general. In effect, prostitution synthesizes and accentuates the problematic of sexual discrimination in Brazilian culture. The report emphasized that the roots of discrimination are present from birth, when the masculine and feminine roles are determined, often in ways that are detrimental to common human characteristics. The woman is raised within a schema of activity that requires of her a denial of self. She is raised to marry—to join herself to a man, not in a mutual union of the two, but rather as someone who is "taken" in order to serve. In short, the entire myth can be summarized in terms of the relation between greater and lesser degrees of power. The group concluded that only through the questioning of such values can society realize an alternative means of relating among persons that is not predicated on domination.

Moving the focus from culture to psychology, the group report affirmed that while there is much discussion about the psychological factors that lead women into lives of prostitution, these psychological factors do not arise by accident. Women are not born to be prostitutes. The prostitution of women within Brazilian society is only one indication of a widespread prostitution that is greater in scope and magnitude, namely, the prostitution of Brazilian cultural values.

The exclusion of young girls from their homes when there is proof or suspicion that they are no longer virgins is an example of the ways in which the sexual taboo

36. Ibid., 784.
37. Ibid., 783.
38. Ibid., 783. The implications of observations such as these are discussed more completely in chapters three and four of this book.

influences morality. Citing this example, the report underscored the way in which this taboo continues to function at another level by ensuring that women lack the formal training necessary for survival outside of the home. Feeling alone, the young woman becomes an easy catch for those who suggest to her that she make use of her body, a suggestion that translates into what she has been taught all along: to put herself at the service of men.

The report acknowledged that, as a result of the crisis in values through which the entire society was passing, changes were taking place in relation to taboos and prejudices. Nevertheless, due to the lack of information available to those in the lowest socioeconomic bracket, such people suffered even more because their cultural and moral principles were deeply ingrained and their perspectives were often limited by social conditioning.[39]

The long-term psychological effects of exploitation are not easily overcome. How does a woman forget that she was sold or offered to a man by her own father? The report confirmed that many prostitutes often spoke of the great anguish that they endured because of their families, principally their fathers. The actual relationship that they maintain with men is deemed to be representative of continued aggression toward the paternal figure. The pastoral agents reported that the prostitutes often said that "man is worthless," that they "are getting even," that "if a man wants pleasure, he is going to have to pay for it."[40] On the other hand, the majority of these women continued to try to connect with one steady man, as they sought protection and affection from someone with whom they maintained a relationship of dependency in exchange for the guarantees of personal survival. Even though such protection and affection came at a high price, this did not seem to disturb them, for women have been trained to pay a high price to obtain the minimum of satisfactions for their existence.

The report contended that discrimination between the sexes, the assignment of roles, and the expectations placed on women and men are all part of the same culture. Everyone in Brazilian society is subject to it. To question these values, to overcome oneself, and to find one's place in society is a function of personal growth. In effect, prostitution is only one facet of life where the distortions of Brazilian culture are most accentuated. To the extent that there is no collective critical reflection on these values, they go unquestioned. The interaction between persons becomes camouflaged in such a way that interests and advantages are given priority

39. In this regard, it is important to point out the degree to which education and cross-cultural experience make exercises in probabalism, casuistry, and relativistic thinking an escape hatch for the privileged, who have the resources to free themselves at will from the cultural and moral ties that bind. Those, however, who are not the beneficiaries of such privileges are often caught in the simple dualism of black or white, right or wrong, either/or. Such views do not necessarily alter behaviors, but they do influence the ways in which people interpret those behaviors and regard themselves as good or bad.

40. *Serviço de Documentação* 17 (1985) 784.

over basic human needs such as love, acceptance, and personal growth.

The working paper concluded that small steps could be taken at the personal level. At this point, equality among persons moves out of the realm of philosophy and into everyday reality. In order to examine this situation with a view to change, a united effort is necessary for those who confront the situation that results from sexism day after day. Several suggestions were set forth, including a reformulation of the image of woman in educational materials (such as textbooks, magazines, and advertising); the inclusion of sex education in the educational curriculum (beginning in the primary grades), using a balanced approach that does not reinforce double standards; increased opportunities for women to receive professional training; and the redress of injustices such as discriminatory wages and lack of child care that affect the lives of women who work outside of the home.

In the final document of the Third National Encounter, the participants articulated what they considered to be the root of the evils at issue, namely, the inversion of values.[41] The basic and fundamental value is not that one is important because one is human, but rather that one is important only when one is a man, with all the prerogatives that accompany this condition. As for the woman, all of the dependencies and devaluations that accompany the feminine condition are imputed to her. By virtue of this inversion of values, the prostitute continues to judge herself to be no one, an object that is marginal and without value; and the prostitute herself, like the majority of women, does not consider herself to be equal with the "partner" that seeks her out. Members of the church cannot avoid responsibility for the widespread complacency that allows this fundamental evil to be obscured and camouflaged. The document advanced the insights of the group by summarizing its perspectives on the Brazilian reality and providing suggestions for future action.

In the first section of the final report,[42] the participants noted that in past analyses of prostitution it had been common practice to emphasize economic and psychological factors as determinative in the life of the prostitute. In the Third National Encounter, however, greater attention was given to the fact that the root causes were much broader.

Without disregarding the complex interconnectedness of motives involved in this problem, the discrimination between men and women in Brazilian culture was a factor that in its own right contributed to inequalities in the development of human beings and society in general. The following examples set forth the consequences of this discrimination:

(1) the relationship between man and woman is transformed into an object relation; the woman is an object that can be used, especially if she is a prostitute;

(2) there is a distinction and difference between the rights of men and the rights of women;

(3) social discrimination and devaluation exist with regard to the work undertaken by women (lower wages, differentiations in responsibilities, and the lack of professional training opportunities for women);

41. See *Serviço de Documentação* 17 (1985) 793–96.
42. Ibid., 794–95.

(4) in general, society accepts the uncontrollable sexual desires on the part of men (to whom everything is permitted) and insists on the absolute chastity on the part of women, imposing virginity as a moral value.
As such, prostitution as a social institution serves as a hypertrophy of the general situation that exists between women and men. In light of this observation, the interconnectedness of socioeconomic, psychological, political, and cultural factors must be called into question.

The report underscored that in the documentation received from grass roots groups throughout the country, cultural manifestations were repeatedly mentioned in terms of the specific and particular forms that they took in various regions of Brazil. The report also included facts about the serious causal agents of seduction as well as the means used to keep women in lives of prostitution. On the one hand, it was noted that the influence of certain cultural values varied from region to region. The reports presented by the grass roots highlighted numerous particularities. On the other hand, these values contributed to some form of discrimination between persons, particularly in the relation of power based on the division of masculine and feminine roles to the detriment of human values.

In accord with this line of thought and in light of the ongoing study of the complex nature of prostitution, the participants of the encounter concluded that attention must be directed to men. The group also suggested some ideas for action among men and women in general. The second part of the final document dealt with these recommendations.[43]

The participants believed that one principle was central for bringing about change with regard to the equality between human beings: *to make individuals aware of their value as persons.* In order to bring about such cultural change, greater activity would be required from women, as they discovered themselves by coming to terms with their personal identities. In this regard, a major step would be taken; from that point on, each woman would pass from being an accomplice and contributor to her own objectification to becoming, in contrast, an agent of change.

In accord with this line of thinking, the group highlighted the fundamental need to raise consciousness about human values, developmental characteristics, and respect among persons. Such consciousness raising could be the responsibility of the church or other organizations and would occur by means of neighborhood meetings that would focus on the following:

(1) presenting insights about sexuality without double standards, without mysteries or faults, and highlighting an awareness of sexuality as a natural dynamic. Sex education in the schools (from primary schools through the university) would emphasize the existence of one single human nature that is independent of sexual differences. The meetings would emphasize the basic equality that exists between men and women, including the search for sexual satisfaction. Such work is important because it is the best hope for breaking down and overcoming certain folkloric notions and popular beliefs about sex and sexual desires;

43. Ibid., 795–96.

(2) explaining to women the way in which they themselves can improve and strengthen their situations, thereby entrusting them with the primary responsibility of education, which is to transmit and perpetuate values;

(3) promoting groups that can work together to raise consciousness about the whole context of relationships between men and women, so as to bring about critical and personal reflection on the social implications of such relationships.

The group also recommended that a broader effort of consciousness raising should occur over the course of time. In this regard, the group urged various representative groups to engage in educational campaigns to inform and influence the broader society. Such campaigns would include

(1) changing the image of woman as portrayed in magazines, soap operas, textbooks, trash literature, and advertising;

(2) pressuring political leaders and business managers to ensure that protective laws governing the rights of working women are upheld, particularly with regard to women who are pregnant and those who are affected by various forms of discrimination;

(3) creating day care and preschool centers in neighborhoods, since the majority of urban workers live on the periphery of large cities, at a considerable distance from their place of employment, and are dependent on forms of transportation that are undependable. This results in worry and danger for women who must work and who wish to be assured that their children are cared for in a safe environment;

(4) providing more professional opportunities for women, particularly in areas that have been limited to men;

(5) developing public education campaigns to address the situation of the domestic worker, in order to bring about a change in attitude on the part of employers with regard to her status and rights, especially with regard to daily work schedule, days off, and other assured provisions;

(6) reviewing once again the suggestions and recommendations of previous encounters, so as to give priority to the ongoing questioning and analysis of cultural and religious values. Such a review would occur under the direction of regional and diocesan councils that are in touch with grass roots efforts and concerns, and the national coordination of this pastoral effort would be maintained and biennial meetings would be continued.

During the course of the Third National Encounter, a radical shift in consciousness took place among the participants. Even as they identified and articulated that cultural values were a major factor in the exacerbation of prostitution in Brazilian society, they also emphasized the fact that the reality of women in prostitution was essentially the same reality as that of all women, although a more exaggerated version of that reality.

In addition to collaborating on the working paper on cultural values, the group as a whole was exposed to the reflections of Úrsula de Nielander Ribeiro on "the daily life of women."[44] Ribeiro spoke with candor about the oppression of women

44. See Úrsula de Nielander Ribeiro, "Cotidiano das mulheres," *Serviço de Documentação* 17 (1985) 785–93.

in Brazilian society. Leaving no stone unturned, she drew on the statistics and research of economists, sociologists, demographers, media specialists, and others, underscoring the fact that the oppression of women is not an imaginary preoccupation of an elite, privileged sorority. Rather, it is the everyday reality of all women who experience oppression as persons and as workers, but who have internalized the belief that this is right and natural. Ribeiro alerted her audience to the fact that her presentation was not a feminist tirade, but rather a position of advocacy for human rights and the rights of workers everywhere, regardless of sex, race, age, or nationality.[45]

The combination of input, experiences, and reflection set a new agenda for the P. M. M. By virtue of its preoccupation with prostitutes, the P. M. M. was required to face the challenge of addressing the issues facing all women in Brazilian society. The intensification of its scrutiny of economy and culture, its critique of society, and its recommendations for change were based on a conviction that public education could inform and influence social relationships as well as transform social structures.

Fourth National Encounter: Rio de Janeiro, 31 July–2 August 1980[46]

The Fourth National Encounter of the Pastoral da Mulher Só e Desamparada included forty participants, representing sixteen pastoral teams from nine states. These participants were actively involved in ministry to prostitutes from the *baixo meretrício*. In light of the issues and concerns addressed by the three previous encounters, the participants selected three topics for reflection and discussion. These included addressing the realities of Brazil, in contrast to the ideals set forth by Brazilian legislation and the International Abolitionist Treaty; evaluating the work that had been accomplished by pastoral teams during the past two years; and developing a clear definition of the group's aim and objectives. Employing a methodology reminiscent of that of Catholic Action, the group developed its program in accord with the process of "see, judge, and act."[47]

In reviewing the Brazilian reality, the group made the following listing of observations and concerns:[48]

(1) Houses of prostitution are in existence throughout Brazil. They support and sustain an immense and complex network of human exploitation: the sex trade industry.

(2) Sex trade as a process of exploitation of third parties is the springboard of seductive schemes that result in the inducement of women and young girls into

45. Ibid., 789.
46. Ibid., 797–804. As in previous accounts, the following overview of the Fourth National Encounter is a paraphrased translation of the final report. Ongoing footnotes will be provided to aid the reader in locating respective sections of the proceedings.
47. *Serviço de Documentação* 17 (1985) 797.
48. See ibid., 797–98.

prostitution in order that they may become sources of lucrative income. These women and girls are persuaded by means of promises and fantasies and are thereby involved in closed circles that prevent them from pursuing any other life options.

(3) The existence of a house of prostitution, or of persons interested in obtaining financial gain from the prostitution of others, intensifies the following conditions: the seduction of women (including minors); their registration in pseudolegal listings; the organization of schemes that shape their wills and place them in situations of complete dependency; annulment of their rights to freedom; and all other methods that contribute to the objective of profit from the prostitution of women.

(4) The alleged freedom (for third parties to profit from organized prostitution) contradicts the foundations of Brazilian legislation, which is clear and exact about providing sufficient legal means for combatting sex trade, while respecting the figure of the prostitute.[49]

(5) In addition to establishing the Penal Code, Brazil signed the International Abolitionist Treaty, which expresses respect for the prostitute, while at the same time combatting all forms of sex trade and exploitation of women in prostitution.

In accord with these findings, the group cited various observations and concerns that merited the assembly's consideration. The preoccupations of the group included:

(1) the ways in which a lack of understanding and naïveté make possible every type of exploitation;

(2) the conditions that serve as an impetus into prostitution for domestic workers who are forced to accept unjust salaries and abusive human relationships;

(3) the lack of any sort of professional training for women;

(4) the registration of prostitutes by "legal" authorities and the illicit actions of some elected governmental representatives who have taken it upon themselves to improve or move houses of prostitution;

(5) the growing need to raise the consciousness of society with regard to the facts about prostitution, in all their magnitude;

(6) ongoing efforts to urge greater involvement on the part of society;

(7) the failure of society to recognize that not prostitution but rather sex trade constitutes a crime;

(8) the need to include the cause of prostitutes within the cause of women in general;

(9) the right to demand from competent powers and authorities the enforcement of laws;

(10) the need to raise consciousness among the prostitutes themselves with regard to their situation;

(11) the importance of placing prostitution in a sphere of misery that is broader than the economic order and that addresses the social and cultural orders as well.

49. See Brazilian Penal Code, chap. 5, article 227–31, Código Penal (4th ed.; São Paulo: Saraiva, 1964).

During the plenary session, an effort was made to delineate the types of work being done at the grass roots level by pastoral teams.[50] The vast majority of involvements were connected in some way to the church. All of them were unified in their underlying commitment to the principles of the Christian faith and human dignity. In general, a component of direct service was present. Such service responded to the immediate needs of the women with regard to health care, education, and ongoing concern for the personal growth of each person in search of liberation.[51]

In some areas, houses were set up in order to facilitate a change of life for individuals desiring to make a move out of prostitution. Women could stay within these houses until they acquired new beliefs about themselves and confidence in their human worth. Through this work of Christian evangelization, it was hoped that women would be able to begin their lives anew. The stigma of their past, however, remained only one of the barriers that prevented prostitutes from breaking out of the circle to which they are consigned by society.

As one might expect, this consciousness led to a series of questions regarding the relationship between prostitutes and society in general. Among the points most discussed were those related to the causes and maintenance of women's involvement in prostitution. Efforts to face prostitution as a social fact, in terms of its broadest dimensions, resulted in debates about the intrinsic relationship between the (Brazilian) model of a capitalist and essentially *machista* society and the contribution that both capitalism and machismo make to the maintenance of prostitution as a "necessary evil."

Based on the reports and discussions that had taken place throughout the encounter, the group addressed itself to a final reflection on questions of identity, future direction, and specific courses of action.[52] Initially, small groups discussed the various areas that needed to be considered in terms of plans for action. The group's position against the expanding sex trade industry was clearly articulated. Conscious of the ways in which the industry exacerbated the process of dehumanization, the group identified and agreed to direct its attention to four specific fields of action, namely, involvement with society, involvement with the *meninas* ("girls"),[53] involvement with authorities, and involvement with the church. With regard to these fields of action, members of the group arrived at the following conclusions regarding the form and content of their involvement.

In terms of involvement with society, the group decided the following:

50. *Serviço de Documentação* 17 (1985) 798–99.
51. Ibid., 799.
52. Ibid., 799–804.
53. The word *menina* is multivalent. It can be a term of endearment or familiarity. It also carries with it paternalistic overtones that reveal the pastoral worker's attitude or perception of the woman prostitute as less than an adult. When used as street language, it has a negative connotation referring to a woman or girl of the streets.

*(1) by means of public denouncements, the group proposed to use the press
(standard, alternative, and religious) and systems of broadcasting to articulate
through debates and documentaries its position regarding the following points:*

• *the failure of society to comply with Brazilian legislation and to uphold its
commitment to the International Abolitionist Treaty;*

• *the reality of prostitution in Brazilian society, highlighting in particular the
illegal confinement of women to prostitution districts, the practices and activities
of procurers, and the ongoing exploitation of these women by means of a false
morality that separates women into two categories—young women from respect-
able families and worthless women;*

• *the transmission in families and in schools of a double standard of morality
for boys and for girls;*

• *the failure to encourage and support the education and training of women for
trades and professions;*

• *the use of explicit sex as a consumer incentive for systems of mass communication;*

• *overt and discreet methods of advertising and promoting prostitution in the
press;*

• *condemnation of the use and abuse of domestic workers as sexual objects by
male employers and their sons;*

• *political lobbying to include the category of domestic worker in the labor laws
governing the rights of workers;*

*(2) to develop networks with other sectors of the population, such as the Asso-
ciation of Domestic Workers, Mothers' Clubs, Association of Housewives, Neighborhood Associations, labor unions, and other public education initiatives; and*

*(3) to form local support groups for urgent and serious cases, such as disap-
pearances, unpunished crimes, and torture.*

In terms of involvement with the *"meninas,"* the group decided the following:[54]

*(1) In an endeavor to promote the search for personal liberation, individual
and group reflections are encouraged. Throughout this process, it is recommended
that the following points be addressed:*

• *the two realities in which prostitutes live—the zona and society in general;*

• *the discrimination against women in society, principally discrimination against
women involved in prostitution;*

• *the overt or hidden exploitation to which women involved in prostitution submit themselves; this investigation would cultivate a critical conscience about such
exploitation;*

• *questioning other life options, to the extent that there is space for this, mindful
that fixed solutions not be handed out but rather that they be arrived at through a
process of reflection and deliberation;*

• *reflections on Brazilian legislation regarding prostitution that do not lose sight
of the value and human dignity of each person;*

54. *Serviço de Documentação* 17 (1985) 800–801.

• *the participation of meninas on pastoral teams and at encounters, in order that they may be engaged in the process and may be motivated toward involvement.*

(2) In addition, the group raised questions related to the fundamental conditions for entrance into this type of pastoral work, namely:

• *that one must be adequately prepared, having both a basic understanding of prostitution and the capacity to be a significant presence in offering assistance;*

• *that one possess a Christian attitude of love and respect without being paternalistic or imposing ideas, behaviors, or ideologies.*

The involvement of the church should take into account the three levels of "church" that every pastoral agent must consider:

(1) Those organizing the national encounters would issue invitations to bishops from every diocese where work in this area already exists, and additional invitations would be sent to representatives of Caritas.[55]

(2) Regional encounters would be initiated following a model resembling the format of the national encounter.

(3) The Pastoral would be mobilized:

• *to present this ministry as a pastoral work of liberating evangelization;*

• *to insist that the responsibility for covering this area of pastoral ministry be taken seriously as a ministerial possibility in every diocese;*

• *to send copies of the final reports of national and regional encounters to local bishops and regional secretaries of the C. N. B. B.;*

• *to attend to the formation of pastoral agents for work in this ministry with prostitutes, requesting the collaboration of religious congregations that work in this area (for example, in the region of São Paulo, the Good Shepherd sisters);*

• *to be ready to accompany the struggles that arise in moments of crisis;*

• *to take advantage of every type of pastoral encounter to make the Christian community aware of the problem of prostitution;*

• *to promote the inclusion of one member of this pastoral ministry on every diocesan council.*

The members of the group cited as a major concern the need to inform authorities about Brazilian legislation regarding prostitution.[56] They observed that:

(1) The entities that struggle with this problem should be recognized as a society, an association, or by some other title, since it is much easier to make claims under a juridical name than under that of an individual.

(2) In times of peace, these entities ought to inform authorities of their existence, by means of legal documents that explain in detail their objectives. One such objective is to ensure compliance with current legislation.

(3) These entities ought to make contact with authorities that are in solidarity

55. Caritas Internationalis is a Catholic organization based in Rome that coordinates and represents national member organizations in more than a hundred countries. In Brazil, the organization operates in the fields of development, emergency aid, and social action.

56. *Serviço de Documentação* 17 (1985) 802.

with those who seek to remedy the problem and who have the means to provide fitting solutions to the cases that arise.

At the end of the Fourth National Encounter, it was clear to the participants that they had arrived at a new point of unity and that the organization and self-understanding of the group had developed in terms of structure and purpose. As a consequence, future plans were articulated and set in motion.[57] Some of these included a change in the name of the group from Pastoral da Mulher Só e Desamparada to Pastoral da Mulher Marginalizada.[58] Given the importance and necessity of ongoing contact, it was proposed that biennial national encounters and annual regional encounters take place.[59] It was also recommended that the team from Rio de Janeiro accept the nomination to serve as a clearing house for information from the various regions of Brazil. Every three months, a newsletter would be put together and sent out to groups throughout the country. At the end of the encounter, there was a general sense of satisfaction and gratitude for the opportunity to gather together, to share experiences, to acquire new insights, and to strengthen a common commitment to the valorization and liberation of each human person as a child of God.[60]

As the issues of identity and purpose were negotiated in a more deliberate and self-conscious fashion, the P. M. M. entered into a new chapter of its history that was marked by public documentation and broad communication. It moved beyond

57. Ibid., 802–3.

58. The debates surrounding the issue of nomenclature are noteworthy. Pastoral da Mulher Marginalizada was the original name of the group. The name, however, was changed at the Second National Encounter on the basis of recommendations made by pastoral agents who felt the title *Mulher Marginalizada* was pejorative and counterproductive. Essentially, an effort was made on the part of pastoral agents to "soften" the stigma and its contagion by employing the phrase *mulher só e desamparada* ("woman alone and forsaken"). In effect, the pastoral agents determined the name by which the women they served would be called. At subsequent meetings, the inclusion of prostitutes in this discussion surrounding nomenclature resulted in a new awareness that required the pastoral agents to recognize the importance of naming the truth. The softened title served as another means to camouflage the reality. It was ambiguous. Was the woman who was "alone and forsaken" a prostitute or not? Were the pastoral agents themselves splitting hairs, afraid that a woman who was not a prostitute (such as an unwed mother or domestic worker) might be labeled as such? Was not the larger truth that all women were marginalized and that some, such as prostitutes, were marginalized to a greater extent than others? The title Pastoral da Mulher Marginalizada was fixed.

59. The next national encounter was scheduled for 1982. The designated location was the city of João Pessoa in the state of Paraíba. Two regional encounters were set for 1981 in Belém, Pará, and São Paulo. As in the past, the costs of transportation and housing would be assumed by the participants themselves.

60. *Serviço de Documentação* 17 (1985) 802–3.

its previous confinement to a limited sphere of action. Although the group continued to consist largely of pastoral agents, the inclusion of a few prostitutes as participant-observers in the Fourth National Encounter set the agenda for broader representation and participation in the future.

Fifth National Encounter: João Pessoa, 23–25 July 1982

The Fifth National Encounter of the P. M. M. was held in João Pessoa, the capital of the northeastern state of Paraíba. The participants numbered fifty-three.[61] Bishops, priests, men and women religious, and lay people came from ten states throughout Brazil. A French member of Ninho and a representative of the C. N. B. B. also attended.

This encounter followed a schema similar to those used at previous national meetings. Once again, the group took up the challenge of setting its future direction. As in the past, those in attendance attempted to respond to the question: "What involvement should we have with the church, society, prostitutes and government authorities?"[62]

After three days of meetings, the following conclusions were reached:[63]

(1) Over the course of ten years, courses of action are perceived with greater clarity, but the work itself moves very slowly. In effect, liberation will not be achieved until the "least one" believes in the "least one" and the system that oppresses and enslaves is brought down.

(2) As a result of the testimonies given by prostitutes themselves, it is clear that society is remiss and that its very structure allows misery and slavery to occur. The church should not limit itself to redressing injustices, but rather, it should find ways of providing opportunities to women who are overwhelmed by the realities of their lives. Under the federal constitution, they possess the same rights as every other citizen and are entitled to equal protection under the law.

(3) In accord with the Puebla document, the Pastoral da Mulher Marginalizada is a "preferential option for the poor."[64]

Unlike previous encounters, the final document of this national gathering was relatively short. Although an extensive evaluation of the movement's progress since the 1980 encounter took place during the course of three days, the process was not

61. Ibid., 803. Documentation on attendance is not consistent with the report given in d'Ans, *O grito de milhões de escravas*, which listed forty-six participants. This may be due to the fact that in the latter, only registered participants were included, whereas in the former, committee members and staff were also listed.

62. D'Ans, *O grito de milhões de escravas*, 195. It is important to note how the order of interest shifts. At the previous encounter in 1980, the list began with society, followed by prostitutes, government authorities, and, ultimately, the church.

63. Ibid., 195–96.

64. Ibid.

designed to result in the elaboration of another document. Rather, the focus was on examining from within the movement whether it accomplished its objectives. The reordering of "fields of action," coupled with direct references to the responsibility of the church and the identification of the P. M. M. within the Puebla document's "preferential option for the poor," served to highlight the movement's heightened awareness of the need to address the problem of prostitution within the ecclesial arena.

Sixth National Encounter: Salvador, 19–22 July 1984[65]

The Sixth National Encounter of the P. M. M. was held in Salvador, Bahia. A total of one hundred and eight persons were in attendance, including one participant from Germany and two from Uruguay. There were representatives from thirteen states and the federal district. Presentations were made to the assembly by Leonardo Boff and Dom José Rodrigues de Souza, bishop of Juazeiro. Other bishops included Dom Antônio Fragoso of Cratéus and Dom Afonso Gregory. Four representatives of the Women's Liberation Movement, including one prostitute, were present as well.

The meeting began with the reading of a message of welcome from Dom Brandão Vilela, the archbishop of Salvador. This was followed by introductions and an overview of the schedule. The goals and expectations set for the national encounter included taking from the experiences recounted by the *meninas* those points that demonstrate how the process of liberation unfolds; evaluating the progress that was made since the last gathering in 1982; and assessing the work of pastoral agents and the participation of the *meninas* by questioning whether the P. M. M. was with them, for them, or by them.

The work of the assembly commenced with listening to the testimonies of several *meninas*.[66] Excerpts from fourteen of their testimonies were noted in the final document.

• *"I began the work [of escaping prostitution] alone. The movement was unknown to me. I was pushed along by my maternal instinct, the desire to be with my children. But when I began to look for work, it was very difficult. For this reason, I was involved in various courses in order to acquire some professional training. I left to find work in São Paulo. I worked in a factory. I returned to prostitution in order to take out of the hands of the 'lawyer' the house that I had built. After all of this, a young man helped me find another job. I work during the day and study at night."*

• *"It has been five years since I left the* zona *and two years since I became familiar with the movement through the invitation of a married couple who urged me to participate."*

• *"I have been active [in the movement] for a short time. In Ceará, the* meninas

65. *Serviço de Documentação* 17 (1985) 857–71.
66. Ibid., 858–61. All of the following citations are taken from these pages.

do not like to participate. Personally, I grew up. There is a great deal of aggression that exists among the meninas. *We are overused. The life of a prostitute is awful. The* meninas *begin at twelve or thirteen years of age. I would like to see more attention given to reflection and the search for ways out. Social services exist, but they do not address the deeper issues. The work has to be done, regardless of the number [of prostitutes]. We are more sought after near Encostas. The* meninas *like to stay in the* zona *but they are worn out in the periphery."*

• *"When I arrived in Sorocaba, the movement was already in existence. A few persons had started it up, but a certain malaise set in. They thought that the work of escaping prostitution was going against their lifestyle, that ultimately it would invade their personal life. More or less, there are four of us who are active participants in the group. We have a place to meet and the costs are covered with funds received from manual labor."*

• *"I was deceived into going to the* zona. *I became pregnant. I decided to leave the* zona. *I found help and support from the [pastoral] team. I spent one month in the sisters' house, and after that, I began to work in a day care center. The decision [to start] a day care center [came] from a group of* meninas, *during a three day encounter. I began to participate in the 'Stations of the Cross.' The majority of* meninas, *when they realized that they had to figure out ways to organize themselves, left [the group]."*

• *"I began to participate in the meetings because of the sisters. I went to the* zona *at a young age, with the hope of leaving by the time I was thirty. I didn't want it to be a life choice. At twenty-two years of age, I was able to free myself. I didn't know how to read or write. Now that I am away from it, I forget the others that are there. When one is in the midst of it, she is afraid of society. She is afraid to speak, thinking that she is not going to amount to anything."*

• *"I left home at thirteen. I was very reluctant to accept the invitations [of the pastoral team]. Today, I stand up to the police. I know how to demand my rights."*

• *"I entered prostitution at fourteen. I didn't want to stay in it for my entire life. Everyone wants to get out, but the difficulties outside are even greater. I began to participate in training programs, but I never thought I would be given a job. At the present time I work in food service for a school. I earn a gratuity for this work."*

• *"When I began to feel all alone, wanting to do something to help my companions, I began to take part in* reuniões populares *('grass roots gatherings'). At first, I went by myself, unsure of how I would be received. Afterwards, I took my colleagues along. We gained a space alongside the women of P.T. [Partido Trabalhista, the Workers' Party of Brazil], the neighborhood associations (I am director of the association in my own neighborhood), the Black Unity Movement, all this without knowing that the Pastoral even existed. Today, when we arrive at the meetings, we are already recognized. The people say, 'the group of prostitutes has arrived.' At a meeting of the secretary of health with the neighborhood associations, I asked that the secretary would inspect the houses [in my area], so as to improve hygiene by putting in sewers and water pipes. Along with my colleagues, we were invited to* make visits to women imprisoned at Talavera Bruce. There are many prostitutes who are jailed, not for being prostitutes, but for other reasons, such as robbery. I came to this meeting to learn and to come to know [something about] the Pastoral. I came to see if it might make me change my mind about some radical positions that I have about prostitution."

• "When I came to the encounter I had many reservations regarding [this type of] pastoral work. But soon after I arrived and made contact with [the group presenting] the report on violence in Maciel, I began to realize that my reservations were more specifically directed toward the Banco de Providência [a social service agency run by the state] in Rio de Janeiro. Overall, it does very good work, that has a great deal of value, only that essentially it is assistencialista.[67] It does not resolve [problems] in terms of liberation from oppression; rather, instead of bringing about liberation through a restructuring of everything in the process of oppression, it reaffirms the domination and, consequently, the dependency of women."

• "I was raised by the Banco da Providência through an agency called "Vida" ('life'), an organization that had as one of its purposes the denunciation of various types of violence committed against women from the zona of Rio de Janeiro, except it never really functioned as such.

"I think it would be good if as a result of this encounter, women could reorganize themselves in order to be able to make use of 'Vida.' Women that leave prostitution in order to work as agentes [intermediaries between prostitutes and social service agencies] continue to live in a state of dependency. That is to say, there is a change in the oppressor from the madame to the agentes. They become part of movements, assume responsibilities, receive small stipends, but without any stability or job security.

"Another question that must continue to be raised regards the way in which women are called meninas; a menina is a child, and as such she has no responsibility, nor is her sexuality defined."

• "In Ceará, our lives have changed along with work. We participate in many things: pray the rosary, have meetings during Lent, commemorations with other workers on May Day. In the church, we are well received. We are able to make a poster such as this because of these meetings.[68] The hospitals of the city do not accept prostitutes. I have completed three courses in midwifery. I am a midwife for many women in the zona. When I am not able to do a delivery, we go to the hospital. The men there no longer hit women. If they try it, they will be beat up by all the others [the other women]. We struggle a great deal to find work, but we find nothing. The result was to get a piece of land and plant cotton, rice, and beans. The owner of the land is given one-fourth of the cotton crop. We don't think this is right.

---

67. *Assistencialismo* refers to that form of social service that perpetuates dependency on the part of the recipient without ever addressing the systemic causes of social problems.

68. Creative art work, such as making posters, was often a part of the gatherings of marginalized women.

We are organizing ourselves not to pay next year. The products of the land— rice and beans— are not sold; they are for people to eat and to give away to those who have nothing."

• *"Some friends from the* zona *are working on dealing effectively with* madames. *It is not possible to have a meeting with* madames *and police officers together, because it always ends in an argument. The* madames *have deals going with the police."*

"If the pastoral team is paternalistic, it helps the madames, *but it does nothing to help the women liberate themselves."*

• *"Before coming to know the pastoral team, I was a dead person. After I became familiar [with the group], my life changed a great deal and I found liberation. Today, I am part of the team. At the moment, I am studying nursing and I have hope of achieving complete liberation."*

The second part of the meeting addressed itself to evaluating the accomplishments that had taken place over a period of two years.[69] It was noted that the pastoral work with prostitutes began to take its lead from the needs of prostitutes themselves. The women began to take up a great deal of the work on their own and some even became the coordinators. In some cases, this gave rise to becoming independent from the P. M. M. In some places, the number of representatives who were prostitutes or ex-prostitutes exceeded that of pastoral agents. Many more pastoral teams had surfaced, and there also had been an increase in the number of pastoral agents committing themselves to this ministry. Such action occurred through participation in regional and national encounters, talks, debates, and workshops, and led to the integration of the movement of marginalized women with other popular movements, such as the neighborhood organizations. It was important that the women came to feel that the movement was their movement.

At the time of the Sixth National Encounter some dioceses had started to include the P. M. M. in their overall pastoral planning, with the women themselves securing the P. M. M.'s place in such diocesan activities. The C. N. B. B. and Dom Avelar Brandão had supported the P. M. M. as one among many *trabalhos de base* ("grass roots efforts"). At that time attention was being given to informing the broader society about problems such as prostitution and the exploitation of women.

After reflection upon the national encounter itself, it was noted that broad participation existed among various pastoral teams. Greater unity among the women themselves had forced authorities to attend to some of the central concerns of women in prostitution. Although much had been accomplished in comparison to the past, there was still a great deal to be done.

At the Sixth National Encounter, a new vision for the activities of pastoral agents and of the women was articulated. "The work ought to be done *with them* [the women] and on occasion it may be done *for them*, that is in specific cases of human solidarity."[70]

69. *Serviço de Documentação* 17 (1985) 861–62.
70. Ibid., 862.

The P. M. M.'s methodology and its anticipated results were also set forth. These were as follows: to visit the houses of prostitution, night clubs, and bars; to arrange meetings with the women to promote greater *conscientização* ("social awareness"); to provide some essential services, such as courses, medical treatment, and legal aid; to respect the expectations of the women; to encourage the participation of women in all kinds of movements in order to create a space for group and community organizations; to become acquainted with the reactions of women to a number of situations, such as exploitation, violence, and lack of respect; and to encourage the women to take informed actions of solidarity through self-initiated group meetings.

Finally, representatives agreed that paternalistic activities and *assistencialist*[71] practices create and sustain dependency relationships that impede the liberation of women. In effect, "a *menina* who is dependent on the pastoral team rarely frees herself from the *madames*."[72]

At the conclusion of the first three sessions of the encounter, Dom José Rodrigues summarized the goals developed during the Sixth National Encounter.[73] Participants in the conference upheld integral liberation for themselves and for prostitutes. In particular, they sought to be free from social and structural sin as well as socioeconomic structures and political and cultural injustices. With regard to the activities of pastoral agents and the participation of prostitutes, representatives agreed that the method of work should uphold the following principles: it should not be *for* the prostitutes, giving assistance and creating dependency; it should not be *through* them; as trying to represent them gives rise to dependency and childishness. It should rather be *with* them. Pastoral agents should live with the prostitutes, visit the houses where they live and work, reflect with them, and transmit to them information about political, economic, and social questions. Prostitutes must be subjects of their own liberation, just as other participants seek their own liberation alongside of the prostitutes. This work, moreover, should be recognized as one among many works representative of the struggles of oppressed peoples. Finally, participants agreed that they should create a new society where having, controlling, and knowing are not restricted to a few, but accessible to the broader society.

One session at the Sixth National Encounter explored the attitudes of Jesus.[74] Facilitated by Leonardo Boff, O.F.M., this reflection was divided into four sections. The first of these identified the attitudes of Jesus. Small working groups stated that Jesus embodied justice, obedience to God, trust, love, goodness, respect, happiness, openness, self-acceptance, forgiveness, and a nonjudgmental attitude.

The session also explored how such attitudes were reflected in the practice of participants, acknowledging that these attitudes challenged participants' everyday

71. See n. 67.
72. *Serviço de Documentação* 17 (1985) 862.
73. Ibid., 862–63.
74. Ibid., 863–67. See also Leonardo Boff's reflection, "Deixar-nos questionar pelas atitudes de Jesus," *Serviço de Documentação* 17 (1985) 871–74.

lives, while reflecting on their distance from these attitudes. Women, for example, were still outside of the reflection and pastoral practice of the church. While isolated efforts to incorporate women were taking place, these efforts were not articulated in any public way. Moreover, the hope of leaving prostitution was often sustained by prostitutes alone; their goals were not supported by pastoral efforts. Participants also recognized the danger of limiting themselves to comparing their practices with the attitudes of Jesus: it was necessary to take action to bring about effective change in a society that generated the causes of prostitution.

The session acknowledged that the church as an institution does not always live out Jesus' attitudes. When grass roots efforts accomodated the status quo, the church hierarchy did not improve; laity, moreover, were often dependent on priests and bishops for their progress. The church itself supported a sinful situation by means of religious attitudes and practices that did not promote justice or human rights. God is with the poor, and while a church that serves the poor might suffer persecution, it is stronger because of such a commitment.

The attitudes with which Jesus faced social and structural sin cause Christians to review their ways of living. The session acknowledged that participants themselves were guilty of sin; by their silence they contributed to making others poor. While Catholics go to Mass and pray, they also judge the marginalized. Sin exists when life is destroyed and a human being is denied his or her rights.

Participants determined that there was a lack of coherence among the diverse types of pastoral agents. Some agents were concerned with liberation; others perpetuated paternalism. Sometimes, those who worked with prostitutes were like the older son in the story of the prodigal son; they grieved for themselves and would not accept the growth of another. Many times, Christians—and the church as a whole—maintained relationships of dependency and continued to grasp the power to exploit others.

Participants also allowed themselves to be questioned about their own practices. They wondered whether they were hypocrites, only giving lip service to the idea of a preferential option for the poor. They questioned whether pastoral agents truly united with the poor or merely associated with the poor, and whether pastoral agents sided with prostitutes or with society in general. Was information about the Pastoral da Mulher Marginalizada dispersed through other church organizations? The ecclesial perspective concerning the prostitute was questioned. How did the church live out Jesus' attitudes? Who constitutes the church? Participants wondered whether they themselves questioned their practices as they examined their consciences, and were distressed that while they proclaimed life for everyone, countless children of God were engaged in prostitution and were not able to have a full life.

Finally, participants in the session on the attitudes of Jesus articulated their hopes for the future of the Pastoral da Mulher Marginalizada. Common action must exist between *meninas*, pastoral teams, and the working class. These groups should walk together, serving as witnesses to each other; they should inspire each other to move quickly toward liberation by practicing self-examination, a readiness to change, and personal commitment. Pastoral teams should cohere and should be humble, respecting all persons; and all Christians should live without pretense. Moreover, pastoral teams should be open to evaluation; more experienced pastoral agents should not become ultimate authorities and thus prevent strong contributions from less experienced pastoral agents. Pastoral agents should advise and support the *meninas*, while the *meninas* should be responsible for organizing themselves and for struggling to bring about liberation. In this manner, pastoral agents should guard against making *meninas* dependent upon the agents.

The group work of the entire encounter was synthesized as responses to five questions.[75] The first question was what the pedagogy of Jesus would be today, given the social reality that gives rise to oppressor and oppressed. The group answered that the pedagogy of Jesus would be the same as that which he used in his own time. First, he would go to the people to listen to them. Jesus would not condemn the people, but rather the system that people had created to denigrate the dignity of human persons. Jesus would take his lead from concrete facts, from life, from daily reality, and he would raise questions about the causes of prostitution by means of a friendly dialogue with the prostitute. The prostitute herself would thus recognize the causes of her oppression. Jesus would value the oppressed person, placing that person before all of Jesus' other organized endeavors. Jesus would confront the critics representing various groups within the church. Whoever takes up the defense of the oppressed is thus following the pedagogy that Jesus taught and put into practice.

Second, the group asked how they could recover and apply this pedagogy of Jesus today. They deduced that conscientization alone, in isolation, is not effective; action is needed. People must discover injustice and then search for those who suffer injustice and those who are enslaved.

People, moreover, must search for interior change, perhaps transforming our ideologies. People must not encourage the practices of assistance, protection, and sympathy, but rather commit to practices that are genuinely liberating.

Third, the group questioned what they hoped to gain from their work, determining that they hoped both to attend to various types of people and to bring about not only economic and political changes, but also affective changes as well. In order to bring about these changes in society, they acknowledged that they must first understand the causes of oppression. In particular, they needed to demonstrate the relationship between economic oppression within the family and its effect on the prostitute. They hoped to restore to the person the right to be human. They hoped both to transform society, freeing it from the system of oppression, and to build a society based on the proposal of Christ.

Fourth, the group explored the following question: As the church, to whom have we committed ourselves? In theory, the church is committed to the poor, as demonstrated by the documents of Medellín and Puebla, the group determined. In

75. *Serviço de Documentação* 17 (1985) 865–67.

practice, however, there was a great range of responses to taking up the cause of the poor. A vital commitment to the poor was difficult because of varying interpretations of this task. The group wondered whether the church was committed to changing structures through pastoral organization and to favoring the most poor by means of a practice that tries an integrative approach to organizing, reclaiming, and struggling for change in the political, ideological, and economic system.

The group determined that those involved in the Pastoral da Mulher Marginalizada were committed to an integral liberation. To accomplish this end, all those involved must integrate themselves into other movements, such as the Movimento Negro Unificado ("Black Unity Movement"), the Movimento de Empregadas Domésticas ("Domestic Workers Movement"), and the Movimento de Mulheres ("Women's Movement"). The Pastoral da Mulher Marginalizada must awaken in a woman's consciousness that she is the agent of her own liberation. The organization must be committed to letting go of practices that are individualistic. In order to bring about total liberation, all members must walk together.

The marginalized woman, moreover, must develop her own sense of social consciousness. In this manner she can help her companions, since only they understand fully the inferiority of their being and the problematic reality of their world. The marginalized woman will liberate herself completely only when she sets herself free from all her dependent ties to pastoral agents. Only by cutting through the ties of dependency will pastoral agents and prostitutes together bring about a total liberation.

Finally, the group asked how a base community could be formed among the *meninas*. They determined that it was important to gather knowledge about relations that exist among the *meninas* and to encourage bonds of friendship among pastoral agents and among the women themselves. It was agreed that the Pastoral da Mulher Marginalizada should initiate a process of shared struggle whenever possible, together with other popular movements, so as to bring about a communitarian practice.

Taking their lead from the resolutions of the previous national encounter in João Pessoa, the groups discussed regional statements and national statements. In the east/south region (including Rio de Janeiro, São Paulo, Minas Gerais, Paraná, Mato Grosso du Sul), it was decided that each team would elect a representative who would be in direct contact with the region so as to improve communication. This communication would allow groups to receive materials sent by the teams about ongoing efforts, to send such materials on to other regional coordinators, to organize a documentation center, and to arrange for and coordinate visits. The pastoral team would elect another person in the event that the representative could not complete these tasks.

The group observed that in 1984, there was not a regional encounter, but rather state encounters. The next regional encounter would take place in Teófilo Otoni, Minas Gerais. The greater northeast region would be divided into a northern region, including Amazonas, Pará, Goiás and Mato Grosso do Norte, and a northeastern region, including Bahia, Alagoas, Pernambuco, Paraíba, Ceará, Rio Grande do Norte and Piauí. The state of Maranhão would decide, in accord with its membership, the region to which it belonged.

Discussing further administrative details, participants concluded that a lack of communication had existed between regions, but that the interaction between both local and regional groups and the group that planned the national encounter was effective. It was also decided that the National Committee would receive information from various groups and send it to the pastoral team in Lins, São Paulo, which was responsible for the publication and circulation of the *Boletim*. In addition to news items, the bulletin would provide a brief but meaningful article about prostitution. Among various names that were suggested for the bulletin, *Mulher Liberataçāo* was chosen. In order to cover expenses such as mail and travel, each diocese would send to the National Committee fifteen thousand cruzeiros every three months. Maria Geralda and Elizabeth Santos Chagas would comprise the National Communication Committee and would perhaps be aided by a priest or bishop consultant who would serve as a national advisor.

It was announced that the next national encounter would take place in Brasília in 1987; the time of year would be determined at a later date. Participants would include pastoral agents and regional delegates. The criteria for participation would be examined in depth at regional meetings and forwarded to the National Committee. Pastoral teams, moreover, would send committee members suggestions so as to better define the aims and objectives of the national encounter.

The Sixth National Encounter concluded with the formulation and signing of two important letters. The first was sent to Rome in support of Leonardo Boff, O.F.M.

Testimony on Behalf of Friar Leonardo Boff

From 22–24 July 1984, at the training center for the Archdiocese of Salvador on the Isle of Itaparica, the Sixth National Encounter of the Pastoral da Mulher Marginalizada took place, with the participation of two bishops, eighteen priests, twelve religious women, pastoral agents, and marginalized women.

During this encounter, Friar Leonardo Boff replenished our faith, hope, and love. He highlighted for us the words and practice of Jesus as presented in the gospels and explained how they apply to women. He later showed us how the Pastoral da Mulher Marginalizada is a part of the "preferential option for the poor" made by the church of Latin America during the Puebla Conference in 1979.

In order to be with us, Friar Leonardo Boff had to cancel other important meetings. He thought it was important for him to participate in the meeting of the Pastoral da Mulher Marginalizada, a movement that concerns itself with the life and the destiny of the three million prostitutes in Brazil. Friar Leonardo Boff reminded us of the words that Pope John Paul II spoke at the opening of the Puebla Conference saying that the dehumanizing and generalized poverty in Latin America is produced by social, economic and political structures that generate the rich who are getting richer at the expense of the poor who are becoming poorer.[76]

At the end of this encounter, which provided a great deal to all of us and to our pastoral efforts, we would like to give witness to the valuable assistance that Friar Leonardo Boff has given to the dioceses of Brazil, especially to those who are among the poorest. For this reason, we do not agree with the criticisms that are being made about the books and work of our dear brother, Friar Leonardo Boff. To understand the work of Friar Leonardo Boff is, after all, to understand the journey of our church.

In light of this, freely and spontaneously, we give this testimony and our solidarity to Friar Leonardo Boff, O.F.M.

Salvador, Isle of Itaparíca, 22 July 1984

The second letter was sent to the church in Brazil and was addressed to the people of God.

An Open Letter to the People of God

What women prostitutes need most is the right to be part of society and to be equal to other persons. We hope that their experience of marginalization and inferiority comes to end and that they no longer fear society or the church.

We hope that the Pastoral da Mulher Marginalizada continues to improve, that it becomes stronger; that other companions will become enthusiastic and join us.

We have a very strong hope that some day we will set ourselves free. We hope that one day we will be able to reach all our companions, so that together we will gain our liberation. We hope that all of our colleagues understand that this is good for us and also good for society.

We want to work for our liberation and to have more help from pastoral teams. We need to unite ourselves with other persons, because together we can make this journey toward liberation so that one day we will be able to be truly who we are.

We desire greater unity with our colleagues, so that together we might grow, become ever more animated and never become discouraged, because even though we struggle, we will make it; it will take time, but we will make it.

We wish that our colleagues had the courage to participate in encounters and meetings so that we could know people at different levels and struggle together.

We hope that at the next national encounter there will be more companions.

What we want is our right to be persons. We want the church to baptize our children as it baptizes others. We want the church to share our struggle so that we are not marginalized by society, so that society looks upon us with more respect

76. Pope John Paul II, "Opening Address at Puebla," *Puebla and Beyond* (John Eagleson and Philip Scharper, eds.; Maryknoll: Orbis, 1979) 67–68.

and does not deny us work.
May all our companions encounter the power of liberation.

The Marginalized Women
Participants of the Sixth National Encounter

Seventh National Encounter: Brasília, 26–29 August 1987

The Seventh National Encounter of the Pastoral da Mulher Marginalizada took place in Brasília.[77] Unlike previous meetings, the proceedings of this encounter received little attention in major ecclesial publications such as *Serviço de Documentação* and *Revista Ecclesiástica Brasileira*. The major questions and themes of the encounter addressed the socioeconomic realities of prostitution in Brazilian society; analyzed the liberating action of the P. M. M., given its objectives, activities, and accomplishments; and discussed the advantages and disadvantages of professionalization.[78] Participants also wondered what factors led to the increase or diminishment of the causes of prostitution in the actual situation of Brazilian society, how the church should look at the problem of prostitution, and how the P. M. M. could be integrated into the overall pastoral project of the church in Brazil.

The encounter began with an introduction of the coordinating committee, which included various representatives from the three regions. Consultants for the encounter included Lourdes Carvalho, Dom José Rodrigues de Souza (Bishop of Juazeiro, Bahia), Dom José Maria Pires (Archbishop of Paraíba), and Father Hugues d'Ans. The committee director of the *Pastoral Social* ("Pastoral for Social Concerns") of the National Conference of Brazilian Bishops, Bishop Gregory, addressed the group and guaranteed that representatives would have an opportunity to speak

77. The documentation for this section is translated and paraphrased from the secretarial report of the proceedings found in the archival files of the P. M. M. See "Relatório do *VII Encontro Nacional da Pastoral da Mulher Marginalizada*" (Brasília, D.F., 1987) 1–14 (photocopied).

78. The issue of professionalization became particularly volatile in various regions of Brazil in the late 1980s. Following the lead of prostitutes from other countries, activist prostitutes in Brazil sought the recognition of prostitution as a profession. This would mean that prostitutes had a right under law to a *carteira de trabalho* ("worker's card"). Such a card would guarantee them certain privileges, such as eligibility for national health insurance. This move was seen as upsetting the social order significantly. Since most domestic workers were unorganized and left without recourse in claiming their rights as workers, the possibility of organized prostitutes securing such rights would place domestic workers below prostitutes in the social hierarchy of labor. Whether or not the church would support the workers' rights of prostitutes was not the only issue. If the prostitutes were successful in making their case, the church would be forced to enter the social arena and demand that all domestic workers be guaranteed their rights as workers—or admit to the fact that the plight of domestic workers was in effect worse than that of prostitutes. How could the church stand in judgment of

directly to members of the committee as it was simultaneously convened in Brasília. After responding to numerous questions, Bishop Gregory informed the group of the financial contribution made by the C. N. B. B. to assist in covering the costs of the encounter.

The activities of the first full day of meetings began with a group process designed to elicit from participants their observations regarding specific factors contributing to the growth and diminishment of prostitution in Brazilian society. The first group stated:

"We are not prostitutes, but rather we are prostituted. We find ourselves at the margins of a social situation that requires us each day to prostitute ourselves. Prostitution is on the rise because of lack of employment and housing, poverty, lack of support from families and from a society that does nothing to improve the condition of women, but rather finds way of exploiting them even more. What is diminishing is the income from prostitution. Because of the threat of AIDS, customers are staying away from the zona. Every day, the violence against women increases within the zona, as does the exploitation by pimps and madames. Prostitution is not diminishing. For every one woman whose consciousness is raised and who manages to leave prostitution, ten other women fall into it."

They also observed:

"We experience a great deal of support from our pastoral agent. But we would appreciate it if he gave us more opportunity to express our own opinions. Also, when he speaks with us, he should speak in such a way that everyone can understand him. Women with limited educational backgrounds find it difficult to follow his ideas and vocabulary."[79]

The second group determined that the enslavement of domestic workers was on the rise, particularly with regard to working hours. Society in general, moreover, was ignorant about the reasons why young women become prostitutes. There was a growing belief that a prostitute was incapable of study or academic achievement, and that society for the most part humiliated and ignored women. Racism was on the rise, as was a breakdown in familial, social, and economic structures. Violence was continually escalating.

On the positive side, certain factors could contribute to the diminishment of prostitution, such as the presence of friends to provide moral support in the good times and the bad. To be treated with love, care, concern, and sincerity could make an important difference. The intervention of individuals who counsel and advise young women who are newcomers to prostitution could influence the choices these women make regarding entry into a life of prostitution. Expressions of unity and recovery among prostitutes themselves could contribute to the diminishment of prostitution.

---

women whose futures would be more secure as prostitutes than as domestic laborers? This single issue required the church to recognize that it had a part to play in the systematic oppression of women in Brazilian society.

79 "Relatório do *VII Encontro*," 9–11. See section entitled *Conteúdo dos Grupos de Trabalho.*

The third group named several factors contributing to the rise of prostitution. Economic factors included capitalism, low salaries, unemployment, exodus from rural areas, exploitation of domestic workers, economic structures, and housing. Social factors consisted of breakdown in family structures, irresponsible paternity, lack of dialogue between parents and children, juvenile prostitution, lack of preparation for marriage, and the bankruptcy of marriage as an institution. Cultural factors included *machismo*, the myth of virginity, ideas about women such as the idea that one woman is pure and to be preserved while another woman is not and can be used and thrown away, dissolution of culture and customs, inversion and confusion of values, consumerism, illiteracy, mass communication, commercialization of sex, pornography, eroticism, discrimination, and racism. Finally, religious factors included lack of Christian living, a lack of religious understanding, and moralism.

According to this group, factors contributing to the diminishment of prostitution included AIDS, *planos cruzados*,[80] the work of liberation, and competition with male homosexual prostitutes. Factors that could contribute to the diminishment of prostitution included a refusal to participate in *machismo*, instead acknowledging the work and value of women. This would be enhanced if the church would change its position regarding the baptism of prostitutes' children and encourage the participation of prostitutes in the life of the Christian community. Such transformation also would be facilitated if the church would use the methodology of Jesus and address prostitution as a problem that is social and ideological, rather than individual. Finally, the church should be less moralistic and legalistic and more human, participating in the liberation of women by recognizing them as partners in reflection and sojourners in faith.

The fourth group stated that factors contributing to the increase in prostitution included unemployment, lack of personal formation within the family, exploitation by employers, lack of proper orientation in the school, unjust distribution of land, rural exodus, migration, lack of support from public services, *machismo*, drugs, alienation, negative influence of friends, poverty, misery, mass communication, advertising, luxury motels, moralism, and illiteracy. Factors that could contribute to the diminishment of prostitution, in contrast, included liberating forms of education, just salaries, changes in social systems and structures, agrarian reform, conscientization of families through Christian base communities, greater openness on the part of the church, greater participation of prostitutes on pastoral teams, and unity with other movements.

The fifth group felt that factors contributing to the increase in prostitution included the lack of acceptance by families, rejection by society, starvation wages, deceit, and the false love of men. Factors contributing to the decrease in prostitution include more job opportunities, better education, child care centers, just salaries, greater societal concern and support for women, more unity among the prosti-

80. *Planos cruzados* was an economic austerity plan designed to combat inflation through wage and price controls. It was introduced during the administration of President Sarney.

tutes themselves, decline in the oppressive tactics of police, and the ongoing development of the work of the P. M. M. with greater participation on the part of prostitutes. This group also hoped to address further concerns, such as discrimination within Brazilian society, sexual freedom, inability of families to comprehend the social reality, equal rights, reciprocity, and economic justice.

At the conclusion of the group reports, Dom José Rodrigues provided the assembly with an overview of the grave economic, social, political, and ethical crises affecting Brazilian society in general and prostitution in particular. He identified two factors as contributing to the diminishment of prostitution. The first was a heightened consciousness about the causes of prostitution. The second was a greater openness on the part of the church to deal with the problem of prostitution. Following the presentation of Dom José Rodrigues, Dom José Maria Pires went on to examine prostitution as a moral and social problem that exists within a world filled with growing numbers of *putos* and *putas* —men and women engaged in prostitution—and communication networks that erode all common decency. In such a society, the idea of sin, fear of God, and respect for the other disappears; prostitution becomes a means for survival. According to Dom José, any effort to end prostitution would require that a sense of unity be established among all who are engaged in the defense of human rights: in the effort to love one's neighbor, society at large must discover Jesus Christ in the other.

During the third session, five groups were formed to deal with selected questions related to the aims, activities, and achievements of the P. M. M. Four of these groups were made up of the *mulheres*.[81] One group was made up of pastoral agents. The first group gave its report through a brief dramatization, demonstrating the activities of the Movimento de Promoção da Mulher ("Movement for the Advancement of Women"). It served as a testimony to the ways in which the lives of the women had changed since they first became involved in the movement.

The second group gave detailed consideration to the importance of continuing the work of the P. M. M., emphasizing the importance of the presence of *mulheres* at all P. M. M. encounters as fundamental to a broader process of conscientization. They affirmed that by working together prostitutes would gain sufficient courage and faith in God to continue the struggle for their rights in order that society come to treat them as human beings.

The third group expressed their satisfaction with the encounter inasmuch as it involved all the participants in a collaborative process and affirmed the value of continuing the journey to the end. It highlighted what it believed to be the most critical and immediate challenges to the P. M. M. These included the need for the P. M. M. to preoccupy itself with *meninos e meninas da rua* ("street children") whose numbers increased daily; ongoing efforts to establish fixed locations where the meetings and work of the P. M. M. could be accomplished, particularly where par-

81. It is important to note that the word *mulheres* ("women") replaced the word *meninas* ("girls") in the discourse of the P. M. M.

ticipants were few; the importance of encouraging participants to continue in the struggle and to work to achieve what was still lacking in terms of opportunities and resources. The group also affirmed the need to foster creativity and availability, so as to encourage the *meninas* to recover the will to live, assuring them of the existence of individuals working on their behalf; and, finally, participants supported greater collaboration among the *meninas* and improved relations with pastoral agents in terms of attention and respect.

The fourth group affirmed that the work of the P. M. M. was valuable, because it was one of the first steps that a prostitute could take in her struggle for liberation. The existence of the P. M. M. was thus essential, for it provided one of the few places in which prostitutes could express what they experience. The principal cause for the struggle was noted in a sense of *companheirismo* ("comradeship and solidarity") among prostitutes and pastoral agents.

The fifth group, which was made up largely of pastoral agents, took up the issue of the value of existing activities such as literacy and job training. The significance of these activities was important in varying degrees for all women, they determined, and these activities were particularly vital for those seeking to leave prostitution. The pastoral agents affirmed that they had seen evidence of the evolution of a transformation of consciousness; such evidence was found in friendship, unity, organization, meetings, recognition of personal worth, insight into experiences of exploitation, and discoveries about the reality of dependency experienced by *donas de casa* ("housewives"). Literacy, moreover, was a clear sign of liberation. Bonds of friendship between agents and prostitutes fostered a sense of solidarity which provided victims with the strength they needed to leave prostitution by taking hold of their personal worth and searching for their independence.

After the process of reporting was complete, a document was prepared for presentation to the National Conference of Brazilian Bishops. Three representatives of the group were elected to bring the letter to the Bishops' Committee.

Open Letter to the National Conference of Brazilian Bishops

The participating delegates of the Seventh National Encounter of the Pastoral da Mulher Marginalizada, meeting in Brasilia from 26–29 August 1987, at the Assumption Retreat House, expressing the will of the groups they represent and grounding themselves in the gospel of Jesus Christ—"I come so that all may have life and that they may have it to the fullest" (John 10:10)—make the following claims to the C. N. B. B.

(1) that the church of Brazil consider the woman to be equal to and to have the same rights as man, and that it recognize the contribution that she makes to the journey of the church;

(2) that the woman prostitute be considered not as sinner, but as a victim of an unjust social and economic structure;

(3) that the Pastoral da Mulher Marginalizada become an integral part of the Pastoral Conjunto ("Joint Pastoral") and be considered as one of its priorities;

(4) that the Pastoral da Mulher Marginalizada have an advisor to the C. N. B. B., to be elected by the grass roots membership during the Seventh National Encounter;

(5) that the sacraments not be denied to mulheres prostituídas *("women who are prostituted") and their families, because they too are part of the body of Christ;*

(6) that mulheres prostituídas *be accepted as godmothers;*

(7) that WOMAN be the theme for the Campanha da Fraternidade in 1990.

Considering that the church of Latin America made a preferential option for the poor, the delegates of the Seventh National Encounter of the Pastoral da Mulher Marginalizada hope that the C. N. B. B. will receive these claims and transform them into reality.

Brasilia, 27 August 1987

The next session of the encounter brought to the floor a discussion about the professionalization of prostitutes. It was reported that the professionalization of prostitution in Brazil would not move forward, but that state associations of prostitutes would be created. Gabriela Silva Leite, the coordinator for the First National Encounter of Prostitutes,[82] affirmed the report and emphasized the need for doctors, lawyers, and the press to take up the issues surrounding violence against women, especially prostitutes.[83]

Dom José Maria Pires concluded the activities of the first day with a review of the important points and tensions highlighted in the various discussions and presentations. Citing the prophet Samuel and the parable of the prodigal son as biblical points of reference, he noted the presence of a certain anxiety on the part of some women in their efforts to take up their own journeys.

The second full day of the encounter was devoted to an analysis of the means by which the church should address the problem of prostitution. The working groups reconvened to discuss the issue at length. The first group recommended that the church should look at prostitution not as a crime, but rather look at the prostitutes as human beings, treating them with love and concern; the church also should recognize that humans are more victims than sinners. Opening itself to women, and addressing the problem of prostitution in the same way that it does other problems,

82. The first encounter took place in July 1987, one month prior to the Seventh National Encounter of the P. M. M. At that time, Brazil was in the process of working through its new federal constitution. Efforts to keep constitutional issues related to women's rights and human sexuality in the public arena met with varying degrees of resistance and support.

83. Throughout Brazil, reports of increasing violence against women were documented through various organizations such as the Delegacias da Mulher, which were special police stations set up to deal with violence against women in major urban areas. Physical abuse, torture, rape, and murder continued to escalate as did impunity for offenders.

the church could truly provide prostitutes with support, since few prostitutes have families. The church should provide prostitutes with more support, especially at the time of baptism; moreover, the church should work against the great prejudice that some parishes maintained against baptizing the children of prostitutes. The children of prostitutes are Christians and children of God, the first group asserted, even though they are not the children of married couples.

The second group determined that the church should view the prostitute not as a problem individual—for she also is a Christian—but as a victim. The church must respond to those who knock at its door asking for religious support and assistance. This group recommended that the church should ask its bishops to increase the number of pastoral agents devoted to the Pastoral da Mulher Marginalizada. Priests and sisters served as a manifestation of the Christian spirit of solidarity, especially to the many prostitutes who are daughters of God.

The third group maintained that the church should not seek to address the problem of prostitution as the individual problem of the prostitute, but as a social and ideological problem. The church should break with the *machismo* of its structures, acknowledging the worth of women as partners in the processes of analysis and decision making. The church should wage a battle against prostitution, not against prostitutes, coming to a deeper understanding of the way Jesus engaged with women in general and prostitutes in particular, so as to cultivate relationships that are more humane, just, and equal. Along with the Christian base communities, the church should foster conscientization regarding the problem of prostitution, in order that the prostitutes themselves can be integrated into the struggle for liberation. The church also should assume responsibility for the formation of pastoral teams for marginalized women and provide them with support and encouragement.

The fourth group stated that the church should view prostitutes with human kindness, not looking at prostitution as an incurable disease, since such an action represents a lack of justice and respect for the human person. The church should follow the example of Jesus with the Samaritan woman; without making demands, Jesus recognized her worth, was a liberating presence, and gave her space for her journey. Supporting the person engaged in prostitution, but condemning prostitution, the church should work to raise the consciousness of people in order to get to the root of the problem of prostitution. Making more concrete its preferential option for the poor, the church should address prostitution as a social sin, not only an individual one. Finally, the church should consider women not as something to be formed and molded, but as persons who have their own minds and are capable of making their own decisions.

The fifth group asserted that the church should recognize that prostitutes are daughters of God who face society because they are prostitutes and products of society. The church, moreover, should recognize that prostitutes are part of the church and that the church belongs to everyone, whether they are prostitutes or not, because the church is the house of God, and everyone is the work of the Creator. Members of the church, as Christians and descendants of Adam and Eve, must support prostitutes.

In light of the prior discussion on the critical concerns at issue with regard to the church and the problem of prostitution, the working groups considered strategies for promoting the integration of the P. M. M. into the broader pastoral planning process of the National Conference of Brazilian Bishops. In an effort to outline procedures for facilitating the desired integration, the following suggestions were presented:

• *In order to bring about greater unity among diverse pastoral initiatives, it is imperative that the pastoral teams work in a more unified fashion.*

• *It is necessary to begin seeking the support of other pastoral initiatives so as to ensure that the P. M. M. becomes an interest of theirs.*

• *It is important for the P. M. M. to unite with other social movements.*

• *It is critical for members of the P. M. M. to participate in various sorts of diocesan meetings for the purpose of fostering mutual understanding and support.*

• *It is necessary to question why prostitutes are not invited to diocesan meetings and other types of pastoral encounters.*

• *A prominent church figure who is also an advisor and advocate of the P. M. M. may have to facilitate the entrance of prostitutes into dialogue with other pastoral projects.*

• *A poster, through the image of a bouquet of flowers, could depict the inclusion of various pastoral initiatives such as factory workers, land reform, and health care into an "organic" pastoral plan. The poster would be used to highlight the hope that, through its persistent desire, its capacity to struggle and survive, and its faith and understanding, the P. M. M. would one day become part of the organic pastoral plan as well.*

• *It is important that the P. M. M. itself promote greater interaction with other pastoral initiatives, creating a space whereby all concerned would be made aware of the efforts and needs of others.*

• *It is critical for pastoral agents to struggle in the effort to foster a greater openness on the part of local churches so as to bring about the conversion of the church itself and a process of evangelization that takes its lead from those who are marginalized.*

• *It is necessary to make bishops and clergy aware of the P. M. M. and sensitive to the needs of prostitutes so as to provide adequate pastoral care and support.*

• *It is important to ensure that there be an official liaison between the C. N. B. B. and the P. M. M. who can bring the needs and concerns of the P. M. M. to the bishops.*

In response to the suggestions made during the plenary session, Maria de Lourdes Carvalho, an advisor to the P. M. M. and a liaison with the C. N. B. B., began by saying, "No one is given a space; a space must be taken."[84] She underscored the idea that a pastoral initiative focused on women must take place within the parish, among the grass roots.

84. "Relatório do *VII Encontro*," 5.

Dom José Maria Pires continued by emphasizing that to become involved in the pastoral initiative is to bear the good news, and such involvement requires participation in every effort committed to seeking a just and fraternal society that bears witness to the reign of God. In order to bring this about, every group must be responsible. He concluded by noting that the integration of the P. M. M. into the "organic" pastoral project would occur by upholding the goals formulated during this national encounter, and by identifying the interests and concerns of other movements, discovering what the P. M. M. could accomplish together with those organizations.

Preparation for the liturgy extended throughout the day. At different intervals, the liturgy of the word and the offering of representative gifts from various regions took place. At the conclusion of the plenary session the assembly moved in procession to the chapel where the eucharist was celebrated.

The assembly decided to retain the name Pastoral da Mulher Marginalizada as the official name of the pastoral project until the 1990 national encounter. The P. M. M. of São Sebastião in the state of São Paulo, under the direction of Maria Geralda Rezende, assumed responsibility for the ongoing publication of the national P. M. M. bulletin. It was decided that the next encounter would be held in Belo Horizonte in July 1990. The National Committee of the P. M. M. would be comprised of one advisor, three coordinators from the state of São Paulo, and one from each of the four regions. All participants agreed to promote local initiatives to ensure that 1990 *Campanha da Fraternidade* would deal with the issue of women in the church and society. Maria de Lourdes de Carvalho was elected advisor to the C. N. B. B. and Monique Laroche was elected as an alternate. Bishops Dom José Maria Pires, Dom José Rodrigues, and Dom Antônio Fragoso were recommended to the C. N. B. B. as candidates for the episcopal liaison to the P. M. M. It was recommended that the Eighth National Encounter of the P. M. M. extend invitations to similar pastoral teams in other countries of Latin America.

Evaluations of the Seventh National Encounter included positive and negative elements. The financial support of Caritas;[85] the openness of the C. N. B. B.; the balance in representation between pastoral agents and women; the location of Brasília; the accommodations of the Assumption Retreat Center; the prevailing atmosphere of respect, freedom, and friendship; the clarity of presentations; and the broad participation and purposefulness of the encounter were affirmed. Constraints of time and energy, the establishment of set working groups throughout the encounter, the lack of participation of more women, the failure of pastoral teams to prepare women representatives more effectively, the use of language that was beyond the grasp of some participants, and inadequate press coverage surfaced as noteworthy concerns. It was suggested that participation at regional levels be encouraged, that more prostitutes need to be included, that the press should take account of the opinions of various representatives, and, finally, that the process and dynamics of the encounter should be given further consideration.

85. Caritas, which is based in Rome, is an international funding agency for religious and human development activities, particularly in Latin America.

During the concluding prayer of the Seventh National Encounter of the P. M. M., representatives from each state shared with the group an articulation of their renewed commitment to the P. M. M. Their promises included the following: to transmit the good news; to plant the good seed and help it to grow; to continue disclosing the hidden realities and the interconnectedness of all human struggles; to commit themselves to greater involvement; to get more groups to become involved in the work; to maintain a more united and in-depth correspondence. Other goals were also stated: to be connected with other pastoral initiatives that concern themselves with suffering people, to raise the awareness of more people who journey within the church, to invite *meninas* to learn about the encounter, to assume this work once again and to move forward.

Eighth National Encounter: Coronel Fabriciano, 19–22 July 1990

The Eighth National Encounter of the Pastoral da Mulher Marginalizada occurred in Coronel Fabriciano in the state of Minas Gerais. The proceedings of the encounter were published in the *Boletim* of the P. M. M.[86] Outside of short announcements and brief reports, the encounter received little mention in ecclesial or secular publications.

On 19 July 1990 the meetings took place at the retreat house Recanto das Mangueiras. Edilene Eufrásia Costa, spokesperson for the southeastern region, opened the conference. She welcomed the participants and presented the facilitators for the meeting, including Maria Soares de Camargo[87] and Herilda Balduino de Souza;[88] she also introduced Inácio Neutzling, S.J., the representative facilitator from the C. N. B. B. Neutzling reviewed other pastoral initiatives, in addition to the P. M. M., that comprise the sector of ecclesial activities directly related to social concerns.[89] Underscoring his support of the movement and struggles of the P. M. M., he emphasized that it is necessary to continue to challenge the whole church—

86. See *Mulher Libertação* 22 (1990) 9–19. The following report is a paraphrased translation of the proceedings as recorded by the secretaries of the Eight National Encounter of the Pastoral da Mulher Marginalizada.

87. Camargo is the Secretary of Social Welfare for the city of Campinas, São Paulo. She is also a social worker and a professor of theological anthropology at the Pontifical Catholic University at Campinas in São Paulo.

88. Balduino de Souza is a lawyer for the Commission of Justice and Peace in Brasília.

89. The C. N. B. B. has outlined six general dimensions for pastoral action. These include a communitarian and participative dimension, a missionary dimension, a catechetical dimension, a liturgical dimension, an ecumenical dimension and interreligious dialogue, and, finally, a prophetic and transformative dimension. The P. M. M., along with other pastoral initiatives, is located as a part of the prophetic and transformative dimension. See Conferência Nacional dos Bispos do Brasil, *Diretrizes Gerais da Ação Pastoral da Igreja no Brasil* (no. 28; São Paulo: Paulinas, 1984) 72–81.

hierarchy, religious and communities of laity—so as to move the P. M. M. forward, giving voice and opportunity to the true subject of liberation—the marginalized woman.

Representatives of various regions performed in creative presentations, setting the mood for the encounter. These included a musical dramatization entitled "The Spilt Milk" prepared by the group from Teófilo Otoni, a deposition by Lourdes Barreto of Belém about the life of women who harvest Brazil nuts, and a litany followed by a report about the project Menina-Mulher ("Young Girl-Woman"), which focused on juvenile prostitution. The final presentation took the form of a game entitled the "string that unravels itself," showing how the interrelatedness of persons is like a spider web and demonstrating the ways in which the difficulties of work can be overcome by unity and organization. This portion of the opening activities concluded with the singing of "Somos do Nordeste" ("We are from the Northeast").

The presence of Eloisa Valdes Baesa, a social worker working with women in Chile, was noted with appreciation. Zoé da Cunha Menezes of Teófilo Otoni reported on the invitations that were sent to all of the countries of Central and South America. Two Jesuit theologians, Kiko and Paulo Sérgio, were introduced to the group, with an expression of gratitude for their willingness to videotape the encounter.

The presence of Fr. Ernesto of Ipatinga, representative of Dom Lellis Lara, the bishop of Itabira, was acknowledged, along with that of Fr. Camillo Didoné, the coordinator of the retreat house. The presence of pastoral agents from other movements concerned with workers, street children, prisoners, Afro-Brazilians, and indigenous peoples was noted with appreciation.

The work of the first full day began with a morning prayer coordinated by the liturgy committee under the direction of Sr. Carmen Rodrigues. It included the recitation of the psalm of the Latin American woman, a reading from scripture, and the song "Our Father of the Martyrs." A message from Dom Lellis Lara, auxiliary bishop of Itabira, was read by Fr. Miranda of Ipatinga, who, in the bishop's name, offered a welcome to all of the participants of the encounter and gave a brief review of the P. M. M.'s work in the city of Ipatinga under the direction of Edilene Eufrásia Costa.

Maria Soares de Camargo assumed responsibility for the coordination of the morning session focusing on women and violence. She began with a brief presentation on the violence that women suffer on the streets, within the family, in health care, and in other areas. She explored the theme from the perspective of its implications for human relationships. She proposed that five working groups made up of pastoral agents and five made up of women from the grass roots be formed.[90] The groups were presented with several questions for discussion.

90. A distinction is made in Portuguese between *agentes* and *pessoas de base*. The former includes priests, religious, and lay leaders; the latter includes those individuals who are the subject of the movement, namely, marginalized women themselves.

In relation to the violence that a woman suffers on the street, in the family, in health care, what kind of personal relationships are involved? What gives rise to these relationships? What is our desire for how these relationships should be?

The groups met and a synthesis of the major points of discussion was presented to the assembly at large.

The groups concluded that relationships based on violence are hostile, aggressive, threatening, and, at times, fatal. Relationships of this nature arise from the economic and financial problems of Brazil and are a consequence of *machismo*, which is perpetuated through the discriminatory education that both men and women give to their sons. Violent relationships also stem from the fact that the state concerns itself with the privileged classes, thereby relegating the poor to the condition of a noncitizen. The training of physicians focuses on providing services to the wealthy. Those who support a just and fraternal society where persons can relate to one another with respect and dignity should ensure housing, education, and health care for everyone, without discrimination of any sort, as well as promote a greater awareness of the rights of all people.

Camargo concluded the morning's work by speaking about the fundamental characteristic of the human person—difference. She noted that instead of being respected, this characteristic of difference among persons is translated into relationships of inequality.

In the end, relationships based on inequality result in domination, which require the oppressed person—in the case of this discussion, a woman—to be dependent, without autonomy, without identity, existing to serve the will and desires of man— in effect, one who is completely alienated. The greatest violence that is committed against a woman is to reduce her effectively to an object. The more a woman tries to fulfill the expectations that are placed upon her, the more the unjust system of domination and annihilation of oneself is maintained. It is thereby easy for the woman to fall into *victimismo* ("victimization") that does not lead to revolt, but rather to the reversal of roles in such a way that the oppressed themselves become oppressors, and those who are treated as objects become subjects of domination.

Various reports, along with the personal testimonies of women and pastoral agents, served to corroborate the insights of Camargo. Following these presentations, Camargo explained the vicious circle of violence, whereby the reproduction of violent relationships leads to the perpetuation of those same relationships as the basic rule of social interaction. In order to promote a society that is nonviolent, Camargo insisted, it is necessary to create a society without inequalities, one that is based on relationships of love and not of domination.

In the evening of the first day of the encounter, *Ato Show Mulher* ("The Woman's Show") was presented at the municipal hall of Ipatinga. The show was coordinated by Márcia Alaíde Ribeiro, a P. M. M. pastoral agent from Belo Horizonte. The audience received an introductory explanation of the objectives of *Ato Show Mulher*. The performance was intended to be a moment in time and space for denouncing the situation of violence against the rights of women; to be an encounter of solidarity and fraternity for the struggles encountered by those involved in pastoral activities and other movements concerned with the oppressed and marginalized in Brazilian society; and to recall the theme of the *Campanha da Fraternidade* of 1990 — "Woman and Man: the Image of God."

A few grass roots representatives of the P. M. M. addressed the assembly with a message of resistance and hope put forth by marginalized women confronting situations of violence in their daily lives. These experiences were contextualized as part of a larger set of attitudes of social violence that are forced upon women in general. Presentations were given by Lourdes Barreto (from Belém, Pará), Elizabeth Barbosa (from Teófilo Otôni, Minas Gerais), Maria José Alves Marcelino (from Juazeiro, Bahia), and Lucimar da Penha de Jesus (from Ipatinga, Minas Gerais).

The presence and support of Dom Lellis Lara, the auxiliary bishop of the diocese of Itabira, attested to the relevance of the *Ato Show Mulher*. The poem "Meretriz" was read by the author, Roberto de Cássia. The mayor of the city, Chico Ferramenta, offered words of support for the struggles of the marginalized. The "Journey of the Marginalized," an event scheduled for December of 1991, in the hope of bringing together representatives of all marginalized groups for a national demonstration in the city of São Paulo, was also mentioned.[91] Representatives of numerous pastoral movements were present at the Eighth National Encounter of the P. M. M., highlighting the growing efforts toward networking and collaboration among the marginalized.

Expressions of gratitude were given to the ecclesial and civic leaders and representatives that contributed in numerous ways to the realization and success of the national encounter.[92] The *Ato Show Mulher* concluded with musical and artistic performances by Ildeu Francisco, Conan Fernandes, and Haroldo Cigano.

The second day began with a morning prayer which included readings from Luke 2 and the book of Exodus. A sung litany served as background for a procession marking the journey of women with Mary, as they struggled for their liberation. At the end of the procession, a brief dramatization was presented, depicting the liberation of woman from the limitations put on her eyes (that she may see), on her ears (that she may hear), on her hands (that she may act), on her legs (that she may walk). Everyone joined in a circle of unity and sang, "enter into the circle with me."

Before beginning the work of the morning with Herilda Balduino de Souza, a brief presentation was made regarding the elections of a National Coordinating

91. In 1991, the second week of December was set aside in many regions of the country as the Semana dos Marginalizados ("week for the marginalized"). The theme of the campaign was "discrimination is a crime." Those involved in the events of the week included pastoral agents and grass roots communities committed to the rights of children, marginalized women, prisoners, Afro-Brazilians, street people, and persons with disabilities and illnesses such as AIDS. See *Mulher Libertação* 27 (1991) 15.

92. Those mentioned include the national and regional leadership of the P. M. M., bishops, priests, mayors, and congresswoman Irma Passoni of São Paulo.

Committee for the P. M. M. The purpose of the presentation was to explain the functions of the committee, which included the dissemination of information about the
P. M. M.; facilitation of communication with the P. M. M. and between the P. M. M.,
other pastoral movements, and society in general; writing and recording the history
of the struggle of women; and the strengthening of the P. M. M.

Herilda Balduino de Souza's presentation regarding the law and violence against
women is best synthesized in the following remarks.

*"The first mistake is to believe that prostitution is a crime. There is no
paragraph anywhere in the code of law that affirms this. What is a crime is
sex trade, the exploitation of women by pimps and madams who take money
from them. There are not laws for prostitutes, but for all persons. Men and
women are equal and it is an organized society that demands its rights from
authorities. The function of the state is to protect life; it is the primary right
that everyone has. But what is life? Why do women prostitute themselves?
Inequalities have every reason to exist in a world of exploitation. The very
essence of the life of a prostitute is diminished. . . .*

*"The woman prostitute is the one who most suffers the consequences of a
lack of sexual freedom: she does not choose her partners and she has to
serve the man. Everyone has the right to intimacy. To strip a woman in
prison is a crime; however, it is not treated as such, given the arbitrary
nature of the system. . . .*

*"The right to freedom has to be respected. It is not through individualistic
solutions that the problems of violence and the oppression of women are
going to be resolved. However, by organizing themselves in groups that
demand both due process and human rights, women can achieve the claims
made by associations, networking, and unions. . . .*

*"Family is understood as a community of parents (father and/or mother)
with children. This is in the new Constitution and it carries with it a profound modification that will require society to adapt itself to new moral
rules. This change in the Constitution was a hard won struggle for and by
women. [We must remember, however, that] if no regard is given to the new
rules, protests will have to be made to those who promote justice, those who
have the duty and obligation to uphold the juridical order of a democratic
regime and the interests of society. . . .*

*"Torture is a degrading and indefensible crime. It is an abuse of power.
Anyone convicted of torture cannot be allowed to exercise any public function. It is important that those [who are victims of torture] seek out legal
means to make their accusations public."*

After the presentation, cases of degrading tortures against many of the women
in attendance at the encounter were discussed.[93] Following the presentation and the
testimonies, several questions were distributed to the working groups. Groups were

93. Copies of these testimonies were recorded on tapes and are held in the
archive of the National Secretariate of the P. M. M. in São Paulo.

asked to consider why inequalities exist in Brazilian society, to reflect on the statement so frequently heard as women told their stories—"No one gave me any support"—and to identify cases of violence and difficulties encountered in asserting rights.

Herilda took up the work of the individual groups during the plenary session. Groups concluded that inequalities existed in Brazilian society occurred because of a difference in social levels among persons. There was a lack of understanding, information, and cultural awareness. Other qualities present in Brazilian society included selfishness, unnecessary accumulation of goods, disunity, economic power that produces political power, lack of critical consciousness, laws made for the poor to obey.[94]

Having reflected on the statement "No one gave me any support," groups felt that "this signifies that people need more organization; the struggle of women will take form if it has the support of all the oppressed, because one does not free oneself alone" and that "families, instead of helping and supporting young daughters with problems, throw them out of the house and abandon them."[95]

Groups, in identifying cases of violence and difficulties encountered in asserting rights, pointed to the lack of health care and housing education for women. With regard to the difficulties of gaining rights, the group discovered a lack of support for the struggle of women and a lack of awareness regarding the rights of women. With regard to successes, the group acknowledged a growing organization of women and an increasing number of associations, connected or unconnected with the Roman Catholic church, committed to the defense of women.

At the conclusion of the plenary session, Herilda remarked that only through organization can the cause of women be advanced. It is of the utmost importance that actions be taken to ensure the defense of women's rights through legal means that thus obligate the state.

It was decided that the Eighth National Encounter of the P. M. M. would write a letter to the bishops of Brazil and reiterate the points made in the letter written at the conclusion of the encounter in Brasilia in 1987.

Open Letter to the Bishops of Brazil

To our pastors and our brothers in faith and in the hope of liberation

As we participated in the Eighth National Encounter of the Pastoral for Marginalized Women in Coronel Fabriciano, Minas Gerais, from 19–22 July, we decided to send you a letter that has come to signify our commitment of faith and of struggle for the liberation of women and of all the oppressed of our society.

With a great deal of sacrifice, representatives of prostitutes and various pastoral agents travelled from the north, the northeast, the east, and the south so that during these four days we might reflect on the theme "violence against women and women's rights."

94. *Mulher Libertação* 22 (1990) 16–17.
95. Ibid., 17–18.

As women, who are treated unjustly, we think that the time has come for us to give a cry of denunciation and liberation. We find ourselves drowning in a sea of fear injustice, exploitation, social discrimination and oppression. We do not want our children to experience the same situation. For this reason we do not hesitate to face difficulties and misunderstandings in order that our movement may grow and achieve its most important objective, "the liberation and integration of woman in a just and fraternal society."

During the Eighth National Encounter in Brasilia, in August of 1987, a document expressing our concerns was delivered to the C. N. B. B. We are grateful for the support that the church is giving, especially for the Campanha da Fraternidade, devoted to the theme of woman. We hope that this support of our pastors and of all Christians never fails us, so that we do not despair and that we may have the courage to see our struggle through to the end. With grateful hearts we invoke the blessing of God and of our Lady of Aparecida for all of the marginalized and impoverished.

Coronel Fabriciano, 22 July 1990

At this time a copy of a letter from the assembly to the mayor of Ipatinga was read. The mayor was asked to take into consideration the dignity of life that needs to be maintained for the poor and needy of the region, especially marginalized women. The letter was signed by all of the participants of the encounter.

The work of the afternoon continued with an evaluation of the P. M. M. and of its quarterly publication *Mulher Libertação*. The discussion began in regional groups. Several questions were made. Had the P. M. M. fulfilled its major objective—the liberation and integration of the woman victim of prostitution, and the construction of a just and fraternal society? What were the positive and negative features of the publication *Mulher Libertação*? Participants responded that the P. M. M. had fulfilled its major objectives despite some difficulties. The P. M. M. , while effective in its organization and advancement of women's associations, had found liberation to be slow and difficult. In promoting connections with other pastoral initiatives, through friendships among the women, and friendships with the pastoral agents, the P. M. M. had managed to secure for itself a space to work in the society. As a consequence, society slowly had become a little more just and fraternal.

Many aspects of the publication *Mulher Libertação* were deemed positive, especially its ability to acquire subsidies for ongoing research and study; to promote unity within the P. M. M. , principally among pastoral agents; and to promote the dissemination of information about the P. M. M. at the national and international levels. Negative features included its availability to a limited number of readers, articles that were too dense and extended, few illustrations, and high cost. Suggestions for improving *Mulher Libertação* included ensuring a fixed location for its design and publication, more frequent editions, and a format, such as comic book style, that would be more accessible to all people.

Further discussion ensued regarding the ways in which the P. M. M. might be modified in order to improve its organization and effectiveness. At that time, the

P. M. M. was made up of four regions (north, northeast, southeast, and central west) with a regional spokesperson and a national board of representatives that assumed the functions of coordinator, secretary, treasurer, and liaison with the C. N. B. B. It was decided by consensual agreement that some modifications would be introduced. The regions would be expanded from four to six (two north regions, as well as northeast, east, south, and central west regions); one coordinator would be elected for each region. A national secretariat composed of four persons would be designated to carry out administrative functions and executive responsibilities as determined by the national coordinating committee and to facilitate communication within and outside of the P. M. M. This committee, composed of the six regional coordinators and the four persons of the national secretariat, would be responsible for all decisions of the P. M. M. The central offices would be located at the national secretariat in São Paulo, where the management of *Mulher Libertação* by the national secretariat would also take place.

The day concluded with a eucharistic liturgy prepared with a great deal of affection, creativity, and enthusiasm by the women of the grass roots. The Feast of St. Mary Magdalene served as an important occasion for celebrating the struggle of marginalized women and of the P. M. M. In the opinion of many, this was the high point of the national encounter.

On the third day, after the morning prayer, Monique Laroche, from Salvador, Bahia, facilitated the process of decision making and elections for the P. M. M. The proposed modifications for the new restructuring of the P. M. M. were approved unanimously, and the coordinators of the new regions were determined by consensual agreement in their respective regions. The members of the national secretariat were elected by the assembly at large.

Following the decisions and elections, Eloisa Valdés Baesa, a visiting participant from Chile, shared with the assembly her experience of pastoral initiatives among marginalized women in her own country.

"During the time of the dictatorship in Chile (1973–1989), many popular movements sprang up, primarily organizations of women in working cooperative groups as an alternative means for earning a livelihood. Where I live, similar popular organizations arose in a very poor rural area. The communities organized soup kitchens so that people could be fed, given the great misery that so many experienced. There were also other community organizations for bread and vegetables. There was an urgent need to inform the people about hygiene, education, and health care. This information was given specifically to women, so that they might come to better understand their role in society and accept themselves as women and as persons. Courses in human sexuality opened up discussions about machismo and feminism within the popular classes. . . . Practically speaking, there is almost no work with prostitutes even though there is widespread criticism about prostitution. There are persons who work individually with prostitutes, but there are no organizations like the P. M. M. Where I live prostitution exists, including the prostitution of married women who are exploited by their own husbands. . . . In the parishes there are huge dining areas set up to serve food to children and to do various kinds

of educational work as well. Throughout the diocese, there are approximately one hundred and six dining areas supported and maintained by Catholic and Protestant organizations. There is not so much a problem of land being taken from poor farmers, but there is a problem with regard to means for farming itself, such as seeds, equipment and tools. . . . I came to this meeting because of my responsibilities for working with single mothers, the great majority of whom are prostitutes. I am pleased to be here and to have the opportunity to speak with so many of you; I understand more and I return to my country full of energy for the work ahead.”[96]

At the conclusion of the encounter some general announcements were made to the assembly. Hugues d'Ans reported that in October 1990 a meeting sponsored by the Comitê Católico da Infância (“Catholic Committee on Children”) would be held in Uruguay. Along with other topics, the issue of juvenile prostitution would be addressed. Given geographic proximity, it was suggested that a P. M. M. regional representative from the south might be able to participate. D'Ans also announced the publication of the book *Mulher: da escravidão à libertação* and recommended its use among young people and women.[97]

The assembly determined that the Ninth National Encounter of the P. M. M. would be held in Fortaleza, Ceará, during the second weekend of July 1993. The financial report was then presented by Maria de Lourdes Vicari. In a climate of great joy, enthusiasm, unity, and hope, the Eighth National Encounter of the Pastoral da Mulher Marginalizada was brought to a close.

96. Ibid., 17–19.
97. See Hugues d'Ans, *Mulher: da escravidão à libertação.*

Index